PICK OF PUNCH

PICK OF PUNCH

Edited by William Davis

HUTCHINSON OF LONDON

A Punch book, published by
Hutchinson & Co. (*Publishers*) Ltd.
3 Fitzroy Square, London, W.1

London   Melbourne   Sydney
Auckland   Wellington   Johannesburg
and agencies throughout the world

Printed in Great Britain by
George Pulman & Sons Ltd.
ISBN 0 09 125250 4

Contents

*"That's that, I'm afraid. It's incurable.
Have a nice death."*

CONTINUED OVERLEAF

Contents continued

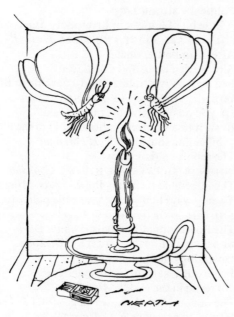

"The moths next door have a light bulb!"

"Take your pick . . . weeping and wailing on the left, moaning and groaning in the middle and sobbing and sighing on the right!"

INTRODUCTION

IT is, you will agree, a sign of the times that Punch is frequently criticised for being too cheerful. "Life," a distinguished politician announced at a Punch lunch during the year, "is too serious for laughter." One can see how he managed to get that impression (he should try reading fewer newspapers) or why he should want to discourage people from laughing at him and his kind. But, of course, he is talking nonsense. Laughter is an antidote to stress, a safety valve. And there is nothing wrong with trying to cheer people up; the world is not exactly short of publications busy doing the opposite. "Journalism," said Chesterton, "largely consists of saying Lord Jones is dead to people who never even knew he was alive." Not at Punch, it doesn't.

The problem with each "Pick" is to provide a reasonably accurate reflection of all the effort which goes into producing a weekly magazine. Punch has become more topical in recent years and, inevitably, much of our comment on politics and current affairs dates very quickly and does not really belong in an anthology which is read all over the world. The task has been even harder than usual in this eventful year. I felt, in the circumstances, that the chief aim of this volume should be to entertain and, as far as possible, to help you to put social as well as political change in perspective.

"The world," Malcolm Muggeridge used to say, "is so overflowing with absurdity that it is difficult for a humorist to compete." I agree about the overflow, and it has certainly been hard to compete with the antics of people like Amin. But one doesn't even have to try: some of our most widely praised features, in recent years, have simply reported what is going on. The "Oil Rush" article by Alan Coren and cartoonist Hewison is a good example, and I have included it in the hope and belief that it will give you as much pleasure as it did me.

Punch has campaigned vigorously on behalf of the individual this year, and will continue to do so. We see no reason to applaud the relentless push towards boring collectivism, or to support the Whitehall planners with their passion for standardisation and slide-rule approach to everything from architecture and design to publishing and travel. We have also tried to be more outward looking: the "Fortress Britain" approach is not for us.

There are people who are always blowing out the candle to see how dark it is. Given a choice of two calamities, they chose both. I'm sure you won't mind if we don't join them.

WILLIAM DAVIS

"All I got was a hard luck tale about inflation and his mortgage repayments."

How can I stretch my pound abroad?

PUNCH offers invaluable advice
to holidaymakers...

COFFEE: The price of coffee in France is about 30p a cup, but at Rio de Janeiro airport coffee is absolutely free—as much as you can drink!

FOOD: If you choose your season, you will find the highways of France covered with entire crops of peaches, beetroots and artichokes. Not long ago a motorway was impassable because of fish.

AUTOMATS: The sandwiches in those little glass boxes are sometimes sold off cheap after a few days. Stick around.

WINE: If you hang about the *mairie* in any French town you should be able to infiltrate a *vin d'honneur*, masquerading if necessary as a Finnish travel agent or a Spanish dermatologist. In the countryside the sign "*Dégustation*" means a free swig of anything going.

YOUR TWIN TOWN: Probably your home town is twinned with a town in Europe. This means that the people of, say, Coulommiers will be unusually well disposed towards folk from Leighton Buzzard. Present yourself with your family at a likely-looking house and say politely, "*Nous sommes vos jumeaux de Leighton Buzzard—oui, Leighton Buzzard, Ses Eglises, Ses Usines, Ses Rues Fleuries.*" If town-twinning means anything, they will welcome you in with delighted cries, urging you to be their guests for a week or two. At the very least, they will probably let you use the toilet.

PEN PALS: Try the same technique on your children's pen pals and on the parents of your au pairs.

SQUATTING: Seek out an empty house near the *plage*, prise open a window and take possession. If the owner remonstrates, explain that, under English law, you cannot be evicted without a court order and he must not use force against you. Say that you understand Mr James Callaghan personally arranged for the incorporation of these provisions into Article 424 of the Treaty of Rome, when the terms of British entry were renegotiated. Then give the owner a cup of English tea to show you have no hard feelings.

REST CURE: Get a friend to break your leg. Then claim free hospitalisation under reciprocal arrangements, assuming that they exist. It's time you had a couple of weeks in bed, with kindly nuns to look after you, to make up for all those foreigners who abuse the British Health Service. See if you can get a smart Italian wig while you're at it.

BUSSING: Buy an old double-decker bus, cover it with Union Jacks and posters of guardsmen, and compete for fares in Paris or Munich, calling everybody darling. If challenged, explain that it is British Week.

SOLIDARITY: Be sure to take your union card, whether you are a worker or a student. This will assist you, as a fraternal delegate, to take part in jolly sit-ins in motor factories or seats of learning. The food, though rough and ready, is often surprisingly good and there is non-stop music.

NIGHT DUTY: For single men only. Wearing an armlet with the letters SVPIBPUW, approach any good-looking young woman not wearing a wedding ring and say that you represent the St Vincent de Paul International Brotherhood for the Protection of Unmarried Women, the members of which have dedicated themselves to sleeping in girls' lodgings to protect them against rapists and such. If this does not earn you a comfortable free fortnight with *un peu de tout droit*, the fault is your own.

FOOTSORE?: Anyone can slumber in a hotel TV lounge for as long as the set is on. In easy-going hotels "guests" in TV lounges are often overlooked for days.

CHILLY?: Buy two war surplus electrically-heated flying suits (unfortunately these are not available for children). Late at night enter a block of flats and plug yourself and your wife into the light sockets on one of the landings. Your plug should have an adaptor so that you can connect up your portable frankfurter grill and toaster. If residents object, explain that you are demonstrating Britain's latent capacity for self-help in difficult times.

FREE PETROL: If your car runs out of petrol, visit the nearest town hall and remind them of their duty to provide the indigent homeless with bed-and-breakfast accommodation. If they hesitate, point silently to your wife's abdomen, grossly distended by a cushion. At worst, they will give you enough petrol to reach the next town.

BICYCLE BLUFF: Cover yourself and your bicycle with foreign stickers (available at any souvenir shop) and slogans like TOKYO OR BUST. Then call on the local newspaper in each town and try to sell them a colourful story of how you cycled across the Matto Grosso, swimming rivers stiff with piranha fish. If all they offer you is an opened packet of Gauloises, take it.

FLOWERS: Train your children to plant these on tourists. The rule is that if the victim accepts the gift, or allows it to be attached to him, he must pay for it. If he does not accept it, he must be jeered at as a "cheap Charlie".

"OUT OF ORDER" SIGNS: Keep a stock of these, in different languages, for hanging on the doors of confessionals, tailors' fitting-rooms, meter cupboards, lifts and telephone boxes in which you are spending the night.

SWEATSHIRTS: If you fancy a short, cheap, cosseted holiday at Ostend or Boulogne, wear a Manchester United shirt. From the moment of landing you will receive individual attention from the authorities, who will provide you with free transport and overnight accommodation and look after your valuables for you; when it is time to leave you will be escorted free to your ship.

"There was an Old Man with a beard,
Who said 'It is just as I feared!
Two Owls and a Hen,
Four Larks and a Wren,
Have all built their nests in my beard!'" *EDWARD LEAR.*

10

A
LITTLE
BIT OF
KUWAIT
IN LIVERPOOL?

STANLEY REYNOLDS urges the Sheikh to buy more British property

DEAR SHEIKH,

This is no begging letter. This is a sound proposition. Or as sound as you'll get these days. As my bank manager says, 'If you can't trust Rolls-Royce who can you trust? You never know these days,' he says, 'what with the damned Arabs owning all the money in the world.'

He's only kidding, Sheikh. He loves the Arabs; he's seen *Lawrence of Arabia* ten times. So you don't have to buy up his bank just to sack him, okay? Ha ha.

The point is Sheikh, it's a funny old world. Only the day before yesterday I wasn't quite sure where this Kuwait of yours was or what it was and then, what do you know, Your Majesty, I happen to be in the laundromat, which is quite handy, but more about that later, and I see what I thought was the Sporting Pink but it is, instead, the *Financial Times* and it is there, Your Highness, that I see how you've just bought a business property in London for £109 million and it says in this newspaper that if Your Holiness wanted to, say for a joke I suppose, you could buy up all the 30 top companies in the U.K. if you just pulled in your belt and saved up all your earnings for six months. It didn't say in this newspaper, Highness, what you could buy if you saved all your wage packets for a whole year but you know and I know it must be something big. All 60 top companies or something like that, eh, Your Excellency?

Well, it came as a big surprise to me, what with me never really having heard of you before. Of course, I knew that Kuwait was what you people like to call a Shiekhdom so there must be a sheikh there, but as I say, I didn't know you from Turin Bey; no offence meant, sir. Yvonne De Carlo is one of my all time great favourite stars and I think it's a crime they don't make shows like *The Desert Song* anymore and my own mother used to have a thing about Rudolph Valentino, so you can see, sire, the Arabs and me go back a long way.

But, as I say, this is no shakedown or sheikhdown, ha ha, Sheikh, this is business. And so, well, I was sitting, as I said, in the laundromat watching the shirts go around just as if the damned thing was the telly, you know how it is, or rather, I suppose you don't, I suppose you got a laundromat all of your own out there in Kuwait. Or maybe you just wear a shirt once and toss it away. But just the same, I'm sitting there and I am thinking, Wow, here is a fellow, Your Majesty, who can buy the top 30 companies in Britain with just six months wages and winning the pools is just not in it when you come to money like that. And I start trying to figure out just how long it would take you to buy my place. Well, sir, it is taking me 25 years on a 90 per cent mortgage but I reckon – and, of course, I don't have the figures on this – I reckon it would take about two or three seconds of your hourly rate to buy a place like mine which is only a semi-detached but highly desirable if it wasn't for that Alsatian next door who is so bad the postman won't deliver to anyone any more and just leaves all our mail at Mrs. Greenwood's at No. 27.

I read somewhere that if Henry Ford, the old one who started it all, dropped a five dollar bill it wasn't worth his time and trouble to bother to stoop over and pick it up. Now I guess you are pretty much in the same fix. Still, you got to do something to occupy your time now that they've got the thing so animated the oil practically drills itself and so if buying up countries like Britain has become your sort of hobby, Sheikh, might I not inform

you that London isn't the whole of the U.K., not by a long shot, your All Highness. Although the Londoners like to think so I would take what they have to say with a pinch of salt. There is an awful lot of the country, the U.K. to you, up here north of Watford Junction and we're not snotty up here in the North, O Prince of the Desert (I've just remembered how the folks talk to you sheikhs out there and so if I was just calling you Majesty and sire and what not, please forgive my ignorance O Star of the East.)

Well, I see I have been a bit previous and before myself like, but I'll come right out with it any road because we people up here in the North don't beat around the bush and run all over the place like some do down there in London, but we come right out and say a thing when it needs saying and we've a mind too. And so here's the deal, O Wisest of the Wise, and this is it. I'm willing to flog you my piece of property at 21 Mossley Hill Gardens South (just off Dudlow Road on the right) Liverpool 18, for what I paid for it, no more, no less, which is fifteen three, as the estate agents like to say, or £15,300 which I figure you could produce cash down in a twinkling of an eye, O Hawk of Araby.

Now, as I said, Mossley Hill Gardens South is handy for the laundromat although you probably got a washer and tumbler-dryer of your own but if it's anything like ours it is always breaking down and trying to get the thing serviced is nobody's business. But, of course, that is the way the country has gone, what with nothing working any more and all these outsiders coming in and just taking over just because they've got the money and we're not what we once was, O Great White Stallion of the Shifting Sands.

O Jewel of the Oasis, this property has four bedrooms and separate bathroom and w.c. plus, although this may seem old-fashioned to you, an outside lavvy which is handy if you happen to be doing the roses or a bit of gardening like and you get caught up short, which is liable to happen at any time given the state of the so-called draught bitter they are selling these days. Take a tip from someone who knows, Prince of all the World, and do not put any money in these so-called British Breweries.

Now we've got a lovely front parlour with double glazing which cuts down most of the traffic noise but as the traffic has become something fierce lately I cannot guarantee it all. Being as we were built in 1912 you can appreciate this house was put together proper as the rot which has set in, in my opinion since 1914-18, had not as yet set in then and a workman knew his job in those days and you could get a fellow for 6 pence an hour. Of course there is a touch of damp, that's only to be expected, but the walls are thick and cuts out all the loudest pop music from their Cynthia, the teenager, next door at the Parkinsons. Nice fellow, Norman. Norman Parkinson, at 23 Mossley Hill Gardens South, Liverpool 18. But he's from Manchester and they eat funny things there, cow heel and thick seamed tripe. Get's a bit much that thick seamed tripe in the summer when Norman Parkinson's in the kitchen and the window is opened. But being as you're from the part of the world you are, O Prince of my Heart, what with sheeps' eyeballs and all that lark, well, I figure you'll be right at home.

Now about the sewage treatment plant, Councillor Taylor, old Jeff Taylor's lad, he assures me it'll never happen, not at least until 1979 although he cannot make any such assurances about the fly-over for the new motorway. But, what the hell, O Just One, you don't get any sun in that part of the garden anyway. I've had a word with the sergeant down at the Dudlow Lane police station and he promises me he'll have a man on duty watching out for those kids from the secondary modern who keep tossing their greasy chip papers over the fence.

A word about Mrs. Barlow at 17. Well, you know what they say about redheaded widows, O Mighty One. But then, maybe you don't. Take if from me, you move into ours and you'll learn soon enough about Marjorie Barlow. In fact, a spell in one of your harem efforts like might be just what Marj Barlow is in need of. Ha ha. If she calls around for a cup of sugar, hide the Tia Maria, is my warning lad. And, naturally, the 68 and 72 stop right outside as we're on the main bus route.

The electrics are, if I do say so myself, immaculate as I did all the re-wiring myself, with a little help from the wife's brother, Bill, but watch out for the switch in the hallway as it tends to get overheated in winter with all the bar fires on. Did I mention we haven't got central heating installed as yet? If you are going to get a builder in, shop around as they tend to be over-pessimistic about the roof. If it's stood through what it's stood through for 60 years without collapsing it's good enough for me. That's what I always say. I should warn you about the third step coming down the stairs of a night when you've forgot to let the cat out and can prove nasty in the dark like.

Listen, O Fair Wind that blows from the East, seeing it's you, I'll let it go for a flat 15, okay, £14,700, my last offer. This, O Fiery Pillar of Wisdom, is a great chance to invest in a piece of real England instead of all that business carry on in London which might get nationalised at any moment. Listen, O Prince of all the World, you can get all this, Norman and Norma Parkinson, their Cynthia, and Marj Barlow, the redheaded widow fron No. 17, for no more than what's tantamount to two seconds work flogging all that oil whilst it'll take me and the good lady wife 25 years to pay off all of that. That's if we're lucky, and with you buggers mucking about with the money, who can tell these days. No offence meant, O Ship of the Desert. Any offers considered.

Yours humbly, Stanley.

Follies are Alive and Well

and living in Thelwellshire

"I'm afraid the squatters have moved in, my Lord."

"Two weeks after I finished it—we got indoor sanitation."

". . . coupled directly to the spin-drier."

"He's a very lucky goldfish."

". . . and this one was built by the ninth Earl for his holiday pictures."

"I preferred the gnomes."

"At the last minute he decided to be cremated."

"When do you think you can fix this shelf over the sink?"

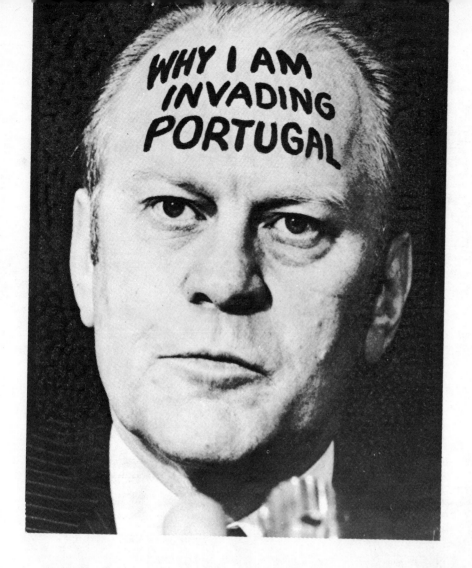

WHY I AM INVADING PORTUGAL

after Cambodia, what?

FELLOW AMERICANS, CITIZENS OF the world, and Henry, wherever you are. As I speak to you, the first wave of American troops are landing on the shores of Portugal and the initial sortie of American planes is bombarding the capital of Portugal. I refer, of course, to Lisbon, a city of 800,000 inhabitants and an annual rainfall of 29.5 inches. These figures are based on the 1960 American Children's Encyclopaedia and may have to be adjusted in later bulletins, though the rainfall is very probably much what it was then. No doubt the population figure I gave you is also accurate again after today's action. I will let you know the truth. This is what I mean by open government.

'Which brings me to the question many of you must be asking yourselves: why has the US invaded Portugal? As this is a question which can be more easily answered by me than by yourselves, let me tell you that I have taken this action to preserve world peace. I think you will agree that I am in a better position to preserve world peace than most of those who I am addressing— I mean no disrespect, but if any of you decided to invade Russia or shell Israel to preserve peace, it would have less effect than if I did it. This is just an example, of course. I have absolutely no intention of bombing Israel in the immediate future. If you're listening, Henry, will you come back at once please?

'As you all know, Portugal has just been taken over by a leftist coup and the communists and their allies are now in charge of a strategically vital country. If you look at your daughter's Girl's Gazetteer of the World, as I did, you cannot help noticing that Portugal lies next to Spain, Spain lies next to France and France lies next to at least six countries and, I think, Liechtenstein, which is not in the Girl's Gazetteer of the World, or rather, I should say, the Youngperson's Gazetteer of the World.

'Why is this important? Let me tell you. Thank you. This is important because if Portugal infects Spain with its new leftist ideas, if Portuguese guerrillas take over areas of Spain, if the Port Cong, in short, infiltrate Spain, it is but a step to France, with its large Communist party, being the next target. It has happened in South East Asia (page 63, Youngperson's Gazetteer) and it could happen in Europe. It is called the domino effect, so called because the guerrillas sneak in at night wearing black masks for camouflage. In ten years Europe could be an entirely communist-controlled continent, except Liechtenstein, which may go undetected.

'Now turn to page 49, the map of the Atlantic. Do you see the country to the west of Portugal? Not counting the Canary Islands, of course. It is indeed the United States, and they are straight across the Atlantic from Portugal, although I notice that to get here a Portuguese guerrilla would have to come through Newfoundland which I believe is something to do with the way the earth curves. In other words, the Port Cong would have no difficulty in directly attacking the US. Or Canada, anyway. Well, the Canaries to begin with, probably. And it is at the behest of the Canary Isles Government that I am taking this action in Portugal to preserve world peace, to remove the cancer of communism before it spreads.

'In practical terms this will alter your lives in no way, except perhaps if you live in Portugal. If you do, may I ask you to make the task of our peace-bringing troops easier by telling them slowly and clearly, in English, where they will find the local Port Cong hide-out? Do not be alarmed if bombs fall nearby. They are falling on your enemies. If they fall on you, this suggests very strongly that you are an enemy of world peace.

'Meanwhile, I shall be in phone contact throughout with the rulers of Soviet Russia and the People's Republic of China, our two great allies, to whom I have explained clearly that this is in no way a hostile gesture aimed at them, but merely a necessary action to eradicate the awful threat of world communism, on which I believe they agree with me.

'Finally, may I ask all of you, whoever you are, wherever you be, if you should happen to know where Henry Kissinger is, to ask him to give me a call. He knows the number.

'Thank you.'

"*. . . after Barry Goldwater told Nixon that he had no longer any support in Congress the President resigned . . . yes, Pat and the girls **were** very upset . . . President Ford was sworn in . . . did I tell you that Gerald Ford became V.P. when Spiro Agnew had to resign? . . . President Ford has chosen Nelson Rockefeller as his Vice-President and says that they will run in '76 . . . no, Spiro didn't go to jail and Ford has given Nixon an absolute pardon . . . NOW WHAT DO YOU THINK?*"

A PROVERB A WEEK . . .

He who laughs first is SPIKE MILLIGAN.

ABSENCE MAKES THE HEART GROW FONDER: This is a mistake; it was misquoted by a drunken Frenchman. What he should have said was, "Absinthe makes the heart grow fonder", or "absent kidneys make the heart grow larger." (This can be verified on any railway timetable).

ACTIONS SPEAK LOUDER THAN WORDS: Yes, this is perfectly true—take the action of the Royal Artillery at Tel el Kibir. During this action nobody heard a word being spoken because of the noise of the action.

ALL'S FAIR IN LOVE AND WAR: A lie—both Cleopatra and Adolf Hitler were dark. (This can be verified on any Southern Railway Poster.)

ALL'S WELL THAT ENDS WELL: Perfectly true—for instance, Dr. Crippen.

ALL ROADS LEAD TO ROME: Nonsense, how do you think I get home to Finchley?

ALL WORK AND NO PLAY MAKES JACK A

DULL BOY: True, as any Jack Jones record will prove.

THE APPLES ON THE OTHER SIDE OF THE WALL ARE SWEETEST: Wrong: apples do not grow on the sides of walls.

BEGGARS MUST NOT BE CHOOSERS: Then why did we choose the Labour Government?

BETTER BE AN OLD MAN'S DARLING THAN A YOUNG MAN'S SLAVE: Why have either of them? Try someone in the middle who won't give you a hard time. This means somebody partially bald with about £17 in the Post Office and one leg in the grave.

BETTER LATE THAN NEVER: Rubbish. If you never show up, you'll never be late.

BETTER THE DEVIL YOU KNOW THAN THE DEVIL YOU DON'T: Next question please.

A BIRD IN THE HAND IS WORTH TWO IN THE BUSH: This is another misquote, which should read "A bird in the Strand is better value than two birds in Shepherds Bush".

BLOOD IS THICKER THAN WATER: Only if you add cornflour and Bovril.

CHERCHEZ LA FEMME: Which, as far as I know, means "Search that woman before it's too late. Lighting up time 7.25 p.m."

CLEANLINESS IS NEXT TO GODLINESS: Oh yeah? Ask any Irish priest where the laundrette is. I've never seen a laundrette next to a church.

DEAD MEN TELL NO TALES: Perfectly true, i.e. Dr. Crippen.

DON'T CHANGE HORSES IN MID STREAM: Supposing the one you are on can't swim?

DON'T HAVE TOO MANY IRONS IN THE FIRE: Some people can't help it. Take Mr. J. Fernanigan Flick, blacksmith whose forge burnt down.

DON'T PUT ALL YOUR EGGS IN ONE BASKET: Sound advice—never wear jockey pants.

IT IS USELESS TO FLOG A DEAD HORSE: Rubbish, take all the money you can get for it.

DON'T WASH YOUR DIRTY LINEN IN PUBLIC: Ask an Irish priest where the laundrette is.

DOG DOES NOT EAT DOG: Nonsense, mine has just eaten his PAL.

THE EARLY BIRD CATCHES THE WORM: Yes, all the birds in my garden have got worms, they shouldn't get up so early.

THE END JUSTIFIES THE MEANS: I don't understand what this means.

FAINT HEART NE'ER WON FAIR LADY: Nor a faint gall-bladder, in fact. No faint organs have ever won a fair lady.

HE WHO HESITATES IS LOST: Very difficult to believe. I have hesitated in the following towns, Acton, Edgware, Kilburn East and never been lost.

FIRST CATCH YOUR HARE: I've just been out and caught one—now what?

DON'T COUNT YOUR CHICKENS BEFORE THEY'RE HATCHED: As I have told you before, wear jockey pants but allow for movement.

A FOOL AND HIS MONEY ARE SOON PARTED: "Ladbroke's Annual Report."

FOR WANT OF A NAIL: The finger was bandaged.

FORBIDDEN FRUIT IS SWEETEST: I've

18

never been forbidden to eat fruit so I wouldn't know.

THE GODS SEND NUTS TO THOSE WHO HAVE NO TEETH: They also send teeth to those who have no nuts.

DON'T TAKE YOUR HARP TO A PARTY: Nonesense—drink all you can.

DISCRETION IS THE BETTER PART OF VALOUR: The other parts are called: "Run for it", "Help", "I surrender", and "Christ! Here they come again".

HE THAT HATH NOT SILVER IN HIS PURSE SHOULD HAVE SILK IN HIS TONGUE: Answer—Edward Heath.

ROME WAS NOT BUILT IN A DAY: No, it actually took three weeks—the bricks were late arriving.

IF THE MOUNTAIN WILL NOT COME TO MAHOMET, THEN MAHOMET MUST GO TO THE MOUNTAIN: A 137a Bus will take him right there.

ILL NEWS COMES A PACE: Ill news—you mean sick humour.

IMITATION IS THE SINCEREST FORM OF FLATTERY: My next impression will be of Spike Milligan.

'TIS BETTER TO GIVE THAN TO TAKE: Like a thud on a jaw.

JACK OF ALL TRADES IS MASTER OF NONE: David Frost.

LAUGH AND THE WORLD LAUGHS WITH YOU: Ha ha ha ha ha ha . . . where's everybody gone?

THE LEOPARD CAN'T CHANGE HIS SPOTS: Not at the present rate of exchange.

MONEY IS THE ROOT OF ALL EVIL: That is why Catholic priests use Barclaycards.

MUCK AND MONEY GO TOGETHER: Go where?

TWO HEADS ARE BETTER THAN ONE: True, but who's going to marry you?

YOU CANNOT BURN THE CANDLE AT BOTH ENDS: Yes, you can, provided you hold it in the middle.

YOU CANNOT HAVE YOUR CAKE AND EAT IT: Rubbish—how can you eat it if you haven't got it?

So much for the proverbs, they just don't stand up under scrutiny, folks. Next week, the Elgin Marbles, guilty or insane?

19

FED UP WITH AUSTRALIA? BUILD

An Australian family who emigrated
to Britain say 'Australia
is a real rat race . . . there
are no worthwhile arts there
. . . money goes much further in Britain
. . . the people are so friendly,
unlike Australia
. . . we love it here . . .'

AN ANNOUNCEMENT

BY THE

COME-TO-BRITAIN BOARD

Why Britain?
There is enormous room for development and investment in Britain. Less than one tenth of the size of
Australia, Britain is already among the top industrial
nations of the world. But there is still plenty of scope for
expansion. The flora and fauna are exotic—there are
birds, trees and flowers you'd never see Down Under.
And no desert.

What about the climate?
Terrific. Tremendously varied, it can be baking hot,
pleasantly cool, deliciously rainy or clear and blue. All
on the same morning. No need to take refuge on the
beach on Christmas Day, either; an old-style frosty, log
fire December 25th is guaranteed.

Will I feel at home?
The moment you arrive, you will never be at a loss for
someone to talk to. Customs officals, immigration
officers, social security officials, plainclothes police—
they will all want to talk to you at length and help you to
fill in forms, then fill them in again, then go to another
office to talk to someone else.

What is the housing situation?
There has never been more property on the market than
there is now—and prices are still dropping.

And jobs?
There are many thousands of jobs open to people
prepared to work hard, get on with it and collaborate
keenly with management.

What are the people like?
Unlike Australia, Britain is a hotch-potch of nationalities.
All those immigrants who have arrived over the years
eager to build Britain up—Angles, Scots, Jews, Irish,
Pakistanis, West Indians—have made the country a
cosmopolitan mixture full of contrast and local colour.
You will find no difficulty in settling in a country used
to change and innovation.

A SHORT HISTORY
For many years a natural paradise, Britain was first
inhabited by colonists from Europe. It's said, for
instance, that the Romans used to send their ex-
convicts and more disreputable citizens here! But that's
all in the past; in the few centuries since then Britain
has rapidly become one of the leading nations of the
world, with links to Africa, Asia and Europe, though
lines to America are engaged—please try later.

Despite the demands of modern technology, Britain
still has a distinctive life style. Nowhere else will you
find the ordinary working man so prepared to interrupt
his work in order to join in a discussion on any subject
in the *Sun*. Life is relaxed—none of the pressure and
hurry of Australia, where a phone call may get through
first time or a letter be answered frantically by return of
post. No, you'll find a more leisurely pace here, as
expressed in the age-old wisdom of such folk sayings
as 'There'll be another one along in a minute,' 'You can
never find one when you want one' or 'Well, that's
what it's all about, isn't it? I mean to say.'

THE ECOLOGY
Britain can boast sensationally varied flora and fauna.
The first thing you'll probably notice is that so many
animals have no pouches! These are called non-
marsupials and they produce their young straight into
the open, just like humans. Go out for a drive in Britain,
and you will see along the roads such creatures as
hedgehogs, rabbits, pigeons and pheasants, and it
serves them right for not getting out of the way in time.
The most distinctive tree in these islands is the elm,
which stands stiffly, tall, bare and dead. There is no
dangerous wildlife in the British Isles; there is the
occasional stinging flower or toxic fungus, but the local
authorities always make a point of ruthlessly cutting
their verges and hedgerows in case any potentially
harmful wildflower should survive. There are many
different kinds of fish to be found, notably rock salmon,
skate, fishcake, saveloys and pickled onions.

CULTURE
The arts have a tremendously important place in
Britain. It's called the National Theatre and should be
finished before 2000, so you won't miss the Sydney
Opera House saga at all! Seriously, the theatre is in a
very advanced state in Britain. London's famed West
End can offer you up to thirty of that most famous of all
British genres, the farce. Plenty of fresh talent, too;
most farces make way after a month or two for another

A NEW LIFE IN BRITAIN!

new farce. If you want to see a serious play, you can also be catered for, though we can't remember its name off-hand.

Music? London is crammed with symphony orchestras, recitals, concerts, and you'll find plenty of room at all of them. The scene is very international; German, French, American and Russian works are performed every night of the year and British works on February 29th. Britain has a thriving folk music scene of its very own, too, known as rhythm 'n' blues. There is also a lively cinema industry. (For ease of reference, you can tell foreign films from British films by glancing at the title: if it's British, it begins with the words 'Carry On . . .')

MEDIA

British television is the best in the world, it's generally agreed, and the BBC's films on rare South American tribes have carried off prizes for films on rare South American tribes all over the world. In fact, a rare South American tribe is now defined as a tribe undiscovered by the BBC! Seriously, they're very good. There's also *Parkinson*, a programme for insomniacs.

There is a great choice of daily newspapers, from the somewhat right-inclined *Sun* to the somewhat right-inclined *Times*.

THEY'RE HERE ALREADY—AND THEY LOVE IT!

Rolf Harris 'There's a sort of feeling that you have to be pretty qualified to get work in Britain. Well, it's just not true. Look at me, for example. I've made a good living out of a bit of singing, a bit of painting, a bit of talking and a bit of comedy. Yes, life's pretty good in Britain for the non-qualified part-time worker. I came here a poor man without any special skill and now look at me—a rich man without any special skill. Britain's the country for me.'

And they're not the only Australians that have made the big time in Britain. Artist *Rigby* has become well-known as a kind of Australian Francis Bacon, with his distorted anatomy and caricatured bodies. *Sidney Nolan*, the well-known cartoonist, has made many people smile with his versions of life in Australia. *Joan Sutherland* sings. *Richie Benaud* has become a great favourite with children on TV, telling stories about the legendary spinners and famous batsmen of the past. These are just some of the Australians who have made it big over here. The other one is *Barry Humphries*.

Rupert Murdoch 'When I came over to this country I thought it would be hard to fit in with the average Britisher. But I very soon found he was interested in exactly the same things I liked—girls with no clothes on, sport, girls with not much on and sport. Once you accept that, you can make your way pretty fast in British society. I don't take much interest in politics, except if a local councillor gets caught in a secret Essex love nest, but I can definitely say that Britain's the country for me.'

Would you like to earn a quick few thousand quid at the expense of the soft, decadent Pommies? Then just write to the Come-To-Britain Board. We'll see you right. Between you and me, any hot-blooded Aussie could make a fortune here. Just mark your letter 'Willing To Work'.

You'll Never Walk Alone

GRAHAM is watching your every move

"Tom Bates . . . Wife Edna, two children Ann and Peter . . . semi-detached, £5000 mortgage . . . Ford Escort, 1972 . . . Works foreman . . . About £3,500 with overtime . . . Who is that, anyway?"

"Your father's got it into his head that the living-room's been bugged."

"Mr. Martin, our computer will want a little more information than 'comfortably off'."

"Since when did you need the dog's date of birth to issue him with a licence?"

Fifty-four last month . . . Anyway, I saw this car draw up at the bank, and . . ."

"Hullo, hullo! . . . What's this, then?"

"Strictly speaking, Mother and I are just good friends."

"He's been dodging around for days . . . Bert thinks he's got something to do with the Council."

Do You Qualify for Government Aid?
How Would You Like a Massive Subsidy?
Do Your Debts Total Ten Million Pounds?

If Your Management doesn't Know its Ears from its Elbow, if Your Work is of National Importance—that is, Employing over Two Thousand Voters—we can Help You

Civil Servants working overtime to write out cheques—one of them could be yours !

All you have to do is apply to us at the Department of Industry, where we have a special fund for people like you in trouble.

All we want from you is the answer to a few simple questions.

Are things so bad that : (a) the bank manager is on his way round to read the riot act ?

(b) the Official Receiver is looking up your address in the Street Atlas ?

(c) Neither can enter because of angry creditors hammering on the door ?

Do you manufacture (a) electronics for satellites ?

(b) notices warning "Toilet out of order" for Concorde cabins ?

(c) Squidgy plastic insects for export ?

(d) Other essentials for a mercantile nation ?

Then work out how much of the folding stuff you need to keep off the rocks, add a bit to be on the safe side, and give us a call. If business appointments or lengthy working luncheons make that inconvenient, get your secretary to telephone. State how you prefer to receive the cash—cheque, used notes, foreign currency of your choice. (We regret that this is not a good time for us to make any deposits to accounts in the Cayman Islands or Lugano.)

All we ask is that you refrain from writing letters to your employees telling them that Mr. Benn ought to have his head examined. And please do not conduct surveys among your employees that ask : "Do you think nationalisation is (a) a bad idea (b) an appalling idea ?" It's not much to ask, is it ?

And when you've cashed the cheque and drawn out your spending money, please try to sort things out so that the firm ticks over for a week or so without you needing to ask for more—okay ? (And if you can't last the week out and have to come round for more, for heaven's sake use the back entrance.)

But if it be a sin
to covet honour,
I am the most offending
soul alive!

**or at least, cries CARL FOREMAN,
Henry V and my wife are**

IF I AM NOT CREATED LORD HYDE PARK
Square or Baron Bayswater in the New Year's
Honours List, it will certainly not be for lack of
effort on the part of that damned Englishwoman who
bears my last name. I tell you, if certain persons in this
country gave their jobs one-eighth of the energy that
blasted woman and her miserable British brats have been
devoting to getting me into the House of Lords, the rise
in GNP and the fall in the balance of payments deficit
would give us all vertigo.

This sneaky elevation campaign, this conspiracy to get
me ennobled, began scarcely a moment after I had got
them on the last plane out of Portugal just before an
August airport strike. Suddenly we were in the area of
long silences, of whisperings in corners, of telephone
conversations hastily adjourned as I entered the room, of
furtive signals and esoteric gestures. I trod warily,
suspecting that these were simply the usual goings on
prior to breaking the news about our next holiday, a
fortnight in Calcutta, say, at the height of the famine, or
the Fiji Islands for the next French A-bomb tests.

The attack, when at last it came, took me, I must
confess, by surprise.

'Do you know,' she murmurs, sipping the chic new
Marks and Spencer red plonk she and all her girl friends
have suddenly become enamoured of, 'that Ted Willis
is 472nd in line for the throne?'

'He what?' I riposte brilliantly. 'Ted who? Audrey in
Chislehurst's Ted? From the Writers' Guild? Our Lord
Willis? What throne?'

It develops that our dear Lord must have had an extra
pint or two at the last Writers' Guild Awards Nosh-up,
and has leaked to my romantic Englishwoman that if, God
forbid ten thousand times, something should happen to
the entire Royal Family and all their kith and kin, the
succession passes to the Peers, and if something should
just happen to happen to the 471 who are ahead of Ted in
the queue, then, by gosh almighty, guess who gets to
be King.

'Say!' I say. 'That's nice. King Ted. I don't know how
Audrey would like it, but it would be very nice for the
Guild. Admittedly, Philip is a dues-paying, card-carrying
member, but, no question, there's something about a king.
Could come in very handy when us writers have to go into
negotiations with them producers. On the other hand,
assuming we are able to avoid the catastrophe you

25

"Don't worry, Sire. I'll get someone else for the legs."

hypothecate, we're bound to get Charles into the Guild, when the time comes. I mean, after book reviews the next step is always a BBC2 documentary about miners or old age pensioners, then some coaching from Barry Took, followed by his very own comedy series, 'Upstairs, Downstairs and Down the Garden Path,' and the first thing you know he's writing sequels to *Percy's Progress** for Nat Cohen. So I really wouldn't worry, beloved,' I say.

If I thought I could talk her into a coma, which had been, I admit, my hope, no soap.

'What about Hugh Cudlipp, then?' she says as soon as I have stopped for breath.

'Oh, God,' I say. 'What about Hugh Cudlipp?'

'Hugh Cudlipp is no fool,' she says.

'Granted,' I say. 'What is your point?' I ask stupidly.

'You didn't see him stay a knight very long, did you?' she says. 'Into the House of Lords, very first vacancy, quick as a bunny-rabbit, he was. He must know something.'

'I think I'll go lie down, dear,' I say.

'I mean, it isn't as if you've got a hope in hell of getting a knighthood before Dickie or Bryan or Leslie or Kenny or John, or Nat for that matter, or even Bill Davis,' she says.

'Listen,' I say, 'I haven't got a hope in hell of getting a knighthood, period. Even Richard Burton has a better chance than I have. You'll be happier once you learn to live with that, beloved. Why can't you be content with a nice little honorary CBE?'

'Big deal,' she sniffs. 'Nobody knows what it means in the first place, and nobody calls you Commander or anything. I mean, darling, what good is it, really? That's what I told Philip at the Guild dinner and he said I had a point there.'

'Oh, God,' I pray in vain.

'It's true,' she insists.

'That's fine,' I say. 'Just don't be surprised if one fine day someone comes around from Buckingham Palace in a golden coach and asks for their CBE back. I've been expecting it to happen anyway, as soon as they find out they gave it to the wrong fellow.'

'There you are,' she says. 'That's exactly why you ought to try for a knighthood.'

'You don't try for a knighthood, darling,' I explain. 'You just hang around and wait for the Queen to step into a puddle of mud, and then you hurry and put your mac down for her to walk on, and the first one—'

By pure accident, she spills her Nuit St. M & S into my lap.

'Look,' I tell her, 'once and for all, you have to be British to get a knighthood, and I am A-mer-i-can, get it? even Doug isn't a real knight, you know.'

'If you loved me, you'd become British,' she wheedles.

'Greater love hath no man, baby,' I vow, 'but do you remember what happened to poor Jules Buck when he opted for British citizenship? Special Branch tailed him for three years, and that was way back when we never had it so good. If I asked to become British now, right in the middle of the Social Contract, they'd probably put me away in a booby hatch somewhere for life. Is that what you want to have happen to the father of your children, woman?'

'All I want for my children is a better life,' she sobs quietly, 'and an equal opportunity with everyone else. Is that too much to ask? Forget about a knighthood, then. What about a peerage?'

I should have known the knighthood bit was just the old hidden-ball play, her own perfidious-Albion version of the Viennese camouflaged dagger-spiel. Before I can regain my balance, she is sailing fast and free along her predetermined course.

'You get eleven pounds a day, tax-free, for life,' she enumerates. 'Everyone says the food is excellent, considering. The library is noted throughout the world. Your credit cards are honoured everywhere. You can go on the lecture circuit in America whenever you're not working. The wine cellar has maintained its standards even in these uncertain times, and the bar prices are competitive. It is truly the world's most exclusive club, notwithstanding that the United States Senate has a smaller head count, and membership in the Lords, bear in mind, is for life. You could give up the Garrick and the Savile, and we could save a hundred and sixty-five pounds annually, plus VAT, right there. You could see a lot more of Ted and Arnold and Jenny and Sidney and Dennis, and Alexander would probably start going again if you were in it. We could have tea-parties on the riverside terrace. The children would be Hons. People would call me the Lady Eve, and at last our day boat would have a right to its name. If nothing else, we owe it to the boat, have you thought of that? Darling, please?'

Wow.

But I fight back. Patiently, I explain that the citizenship requirements are the same for both knights and peers, and as a result I am included out.

'Oh, that,' she says happily. 'Not to worry, lover. I fixed it all up with Philip that night at the Guild thing. Knowing how much your American citizenship means to you, I suggested that perhaps you could be an honorary Lord, with guest privileges and everything inclusive, naturally. He said he thought it was a very interesting idea.'

'I see,' I say hollowly, 'so that is why, when I escorted him to his car, he ran the last fifteen yards.'

She pretends not to hear me, but I know her, not to mention her miserable pommy brats. So, oh, my friends, and oh, my foes, the die is pretty damn well cast, let me tell you. For myself, I can take the House of Lords or leave it alone, and no doubt the feeling is mutual. But when my demented Englishwoman, fighting for what she has made herself believe is her birthright, as well as a good investment, sets her mind to rearranging one of our oldest, if not one of our most cherished, institutions, I can only promise you all that you face a constitutional crisis unparalleled since practically anything. She will stop at nothing, believe me. Do not think of her as the simple English rose she pretends to be, but rather as the elemental force she is. Visualise King Kong,** or perhaps more aptly Godzilla,*** laying waste to Westminster, or the Juggernaut reducing all Whitehall to rubble in its remorseless progress, and you will have an inkling of what may be in store for us all. You have been warned.

And so, in place of strife, bring us together. It is not yet too late. But there is only one way out: abolish the House and thus divert her fearful energies into other directions, like ending inflation or recycling all that damn money, or remembering to clean the goldfish tank every now and then.

I rest my case.

*Check with Mr. Benny Green.
**As above.
***Once again.

"Somehow I've lost all my old enthusiasm for bird watching."

THE REPORT ON THAT REPORT

The research organisation called the Hudson Institute (Europe) – which is linked to the mighty American 'think tank' of Herman Kahn – says that Britain faces a smiling death and that by 1980 the British worker will be no better off than his counterpart in Spain. But who knows what terrible fate may overtake the Hudson Institute? Here it is . . .

By 1980 fifty per cent of the population of the 'prestigious' Hudson Institute will be working a nine-hour day stuffing cotton wool into the tops of aspirin bottles.

Thirty per cent will be employed as menu-wipers in pizzaramas. The remaining twenty per cent will be scratching a precarious living as unqualified pregnancy-testers in Sri Lanka.

These are among the remarkable forecasts of the long-awaited Report on the Hudson Institute (Europe). It was commissioned by the Albion Group, a body of patriotic Britons who, in their own words, were 'tired of assumptions of deity by a camarilla of inadequate ticks who seem unaware that Britain has been on the edge of the abyss since the days of Richard II.'

The Report is the more valuable because of its studied moderation. Mildly, it sums up the Hudson Report on Britain as 'a *réchauffage* of curdled pessimism marinated in green bile and drenched in Sauce Gomorrah.'

Here are summarised extracts from the Albion Report:

What Is The Hudson Institute?
It is a chance accretion of politico-economic adventurers who, at some time and in some place unknown, conspired together to call themselves an Institute, in the same way that ambitious hacks, dissatisfied with their role in the cosmos, band together to call themselves 'The Tribune' or 'The Clarion'. By this means the members of institutes give the impression that they are a

supra-human body of received wisdom and authority and do not wear Y-fronts like the rest of us. It cannot be repeated too often that in practice, every institute, every world council, every international fellowship is either a man called Charlie or an adenoidal Left-wing female scold.

What Has The Institute Done Before?
It has reported on the prospects of France. This nation wisely ignored the unsolicited advice to pull itself together and has continued to give first priority to reconditioning its liver.

What Is The Future For The Institute?
This will be conditioned by the following factors:

(a) the ever-accelerating run-down in the world's stocks of credulity;

(b) the limited number of Great Powers willing to be insulted in depth by gangs of nonentities;

(c) the existence of a substantial residuum of persons who prefer to take their futurology from astrologers;

(d) the uncertain world demand for pessimism;

(e) the talent displayed by the Hudson Institute in cozening the media into publishing its conclusions;

(f) the growing output of half-educated riff-raff from the universities who now regard the forming of socio-economic institutes as an easy option;

(g) the steeply increased price of printing paper, which is needed for essential purposes like publishing books about the Bloomsbury Set.

Can The Institute Withstand Internal Fission?
When the Institute has finished its task of analysing and rebuking the major Powers it is probable that frustrated elements in its ranks, discontented with the uneven distribution of wealth accruing from their labours, and disliking the quality of life within offshoots of 'think tanks', will break away to prepare reports on the Republic of Andorra, the Corporation of Blackpool and the Metropolitan Drinking Fountain and Cattle Trough Association. This process is not one that can continue indefinitely and the members of the Institute are likely, by 1980, to be driven by pressure of circumstances into honest employment, however menial.

How Will The Hudson Institute Rate in 1980?
It will rank immediately after the Incorporated Institute of Postal Masseurs. Its influence in the world will be equivalent to that of the Public Relations Officer of the Association of Frilled Paper Cutlet Holder Manufacturers of Great Britain. It will be the Sick Man of Peoria, Illinois.

" 'Mafia' . . . that's a nice name."

" . . . and when you've been in the service six months you're promoted to the heavy horn-rimmed kind."

When Irish Eyes are Hiding

COOKSON's paramilitary fashion parade

"You're a disgrace to the uniform!"

"Actually, they're the wife's— I couldn't find mine."

" . . . and get your flamin' lenses polished, laddie!"

" . . . above and beyond the call of duty . . . losing a lens in a skirmish in Kilburn . . ."

The incredible shrinking Police Force

by MILES KINGTON

I COULD TELL THE COMMISSIONER OF POLICE WAS in a bad mood. He jumped up on to the stage, slammed his papers down on the desk and started speaking without even looking at the audience.

'Right, you know why we're all here today. It's the staff shortage again. Undermanning and poor recruitment are now so bad that we can barely fulfil our normal tasks let alone take on extra duties. In a moment I shall ask you all for ideas on the problem; meanwhile let me give you some figures.'

He looked up, and stayed looking up. His gaze went round the room till it came to me. Except for him, I was the only person in the room.

'What's your name?'

'Sergeant Smith, sir.'

'And where is everyone else, Sergeant? The Deputy Commissioner, the Assistant Commissioners, the Deputy Assistant Commissioners...?'

I cleared my throat unhappily.

'Well, sir, as you say, we're very short of people. Some of them have been called out suddenly, some have resigned because of the pay and one or two are being held pending charges. It was my day off, so the general idea was that I should take notes of what you say and let them know. Sir.'

I'll give him this. The Commissioner isn't easily thrown. He started again, grimly.

'Right, you know why we're both here today...'

Things certainly were bad, worse than I'd ever known them. I joined the Force thirty years ago and was what you might call an experienced copper by now, which meant I had developed a few extra instincts. You get a sort of sixth sense which enables you to pick out in a crowd the one man who isn't a regular civvy. Something to do with his blue helmet and uniform, I expect. And when I see a man in a striped shirt and black mask

*"Won't keep you a minute, Jackson—
just like you to participate in the following decisions."*

climbing out of the window with a bag marked 'SWAG,' there's a little light which goes on in my mind and I think: 'Hallo, hallo, hallo – they're shooting another series of *Monty Python*! Wonder if they got permission?'

And you get a few ideas at grass roots level about how to organise things. I mean, the high-ups in the police are more interested in administering the law than police work, but ask any copper if he's administered the law today, and he'd laugh at you. He'd never get further than the first five illegally parked cars. Which gave me an idea. Normally, you don't get to put ideas to the Commissioner if you're a Sergeant, but this seemed my chance.

'Sir,' I said. 'We all know we're never going to get the men to do the jobs. So why don't we cut down the jobs to fit our numbers?'

'Meaning?' he said, which showed he was listening.

'Well, we get lumbered with an awful lot of things which aren't really to do with crime at all. Picking up drunks, manning state occasions, sorting out traffic jams, being amateur psychiatrists, attending Commissioners' lectures, if you'll pardon the liberty. Why don't we announce that we will only deal with real crime from now on? Then they'll have to look after the rest themselves.'

By 'they', of course, I mean the Government. It isn't generally known that the police have a lot of slang of their own. When a copper (a policeman) says 'him', it's a convenient way of meaning 'that man over there'. 'Shop' is what we call a place that sells things to the public and a 'nick' is the thin red line left on the chin after shaving, if you shave anything like me. A 'villein', of course, was a medieval peasant, though we hardly get any trouble with them nowadays.

Anyway, the Commissioner went all thoughtful and it didn't come as much of a surprise to me when he announced two months later that the Police would henceforth deal only in crimes such as burglary, assault, riots or murder. It seemed to take the rest of the station aback, though – that's Constable Black I'm talking about. Just the two of us run the station these days, though back in the 1970s there'd be as many as ten or more.

'Should make things easier, Sergeant,' he said.

'Inspector now,' I reminded him.

'Sorry, sir. Forgot you'd been promoted.'

'That's all right, Constable.'

'Sergeant, sir.'

I'll say this for the Police Force. The fewer there are of us, the quicker promotion is. Mark you, it's just that touch embarrassing for a Chief Inspector to be out on the beat, but if you haven't got the men, what can you do?

Just then there was a commotion outside, and Black went to have a look.

'Nothing to do with us,' he reported. 'Some drunk or other has stalled in the middle of the road, causing a big tailback. Couple of blokes fighting, but they don't seem to be doing any grievous harm. One of them's got an untaxed car.'

'You'd think they'd crack down on that sort of thing,' I grumbled. 'Now, what's new?'

'Backlog's cleared up a bit, sir,' he said. 'Remember

the Thacker Road jewel robbery?'

'1974, wasn't it?'

'That's it. We've been working on it for nine years off and on, and there's been a fresh development. Everyone involved in the case has died or emigrated. So I've struck it off. That leaves us free to deal with the 1975 stuff. Interesting murder case in Exeter Square.'

We were round there in a flash. Being eight years later, the fingerprints were covered up and the body disposed of, but everything else had been left exactly as it was. The widow opened the door.

'You've taken your time!' she snapped. 'Eight years I've kept the dining-room locked, waiting for you. It's been most inconvenient having dinner parties in the kitchen. Well, you'd better come in.'

'Lord bless you, mum,' I said. 'We haven't come to take statements or view the scene. We've come to make an appointment to come. We've got a pile of work as long as your arm to get through first.'

That's the trouble with the public. They don't seem to realise that a policeman can only work twenty-four hours a day. And the police force doesn't expand to embrace the available crime, whatever Parkinson says, not that I ever watch TV. In fact, the Force contracts and gets further and further behind, as the Commissioner freely admitted at his next lecture.

'Well, Chief Superintendent,' he said, 'had any new ideas about undermanning?'

'As a matter of fact, I have, sir,' I said. 'I think we ought to specialise more.'

'We've tried that, with the Fraud Squad and Special Branch,' he said, 'but it never really worked. Any news about Special Branch, by the way?'

'No, sir, we haven't found him yet. Actually, what I meant was that we should be more selective about the crime we agree to investigate. If we limited robberies to anything over £3,000 and refused any riots that didn't hit the headlines, we could increase efficiency 100%. We could also give priority to mass murders, and perhaps phase out single murders as we go along.'

The Commissioner said he'd think it over, and sure enough a month later we got our new directive, leaving us free to concentrate on the big villains. They're a funny lot, criminals. Most of them are just ordinary blokes like you or me, working long hours in not very good conditions, but now and again you get a bent villain who's up to no good, and you have to put him away if you can. Well, it stands to reason there'll be a rotten apple in every barrel. The one that me and Inspector Black had our eye on was Joe Teacher, an East End villain who was guilty of every crime in the book. Well, he wasn't exactly guilty of them all, but we reckoned that if we could get him sent down for them all, it would clear up an awful lot of backlog.

So we went out on a raid. I gave the instructions over the radio.

'Z Victor Four. Proceed to arrest of Joe Teacher.'

I raced outside and got in the car.

'Wilco,' I said over the radio, 'and see you soon.' Keeps morale up, you see, if you feel you've got a back-up force. Anyway we pulled Teacher in for questioning, and he wasn't saying anything. Actually, after about an hour

"Well, we ought to take them something."

I noticed he was asleep, which made me cross. Normally, I don't go in much for violence, but this time I nudged him awake and told him I was arresting him for the Exeter Square murder, and for 17,869 other crimes. He went pale.

'You can't pin all those on me.'

'I know,' I said. 'You're going to ask for them to be taken into consideration.'

'Bloody coppers,' he said. 'How did you ever get into this business, anyway?'

'I blame it on my background,' I said. 'I am a victim of an unbroken home and two understanding parents. I was bound to drift into a life of crime detection. Now, do you plead or don't you?'

'Well, what's in it for me? 17,870 pleas of guilty is a lot.'

'One, you'll make the Guinness Book of Records. Two, I won't oppose bail. What you do then is up to you.'

He saw the point of that all right. Three months later he skipped bail, and I had the satisfaction of knowing we had cleared all the crimes on Scotland Yard's books. I say we. It makes it seem more chummy, somehow, if I feel there's more than one of me. Commander Black's retired now, and the Commissioner has gone back to wherever he came from. I went along the other day for the new Police Commissioner's morale-boosting talk. Though I say it myself, I thought I made a very good speech. Pity, really, there was no-one there to hear it.

"The difference between me and the Impressionists is that they explored the nature of light, whereas I'm into stripes."

TWENTY WAYS THAT YOU CAN SAVE POLICE TIME

1 If you see a party of Japanese (or similar) tourists approaching a policeman, run up to them and cry: 'It is 11.37 am, the Tower of London is first left, second right, and the height of the Monument is 246 feet!'

2 Paint on the side of your dog/cat/budgie/newt: I HAVE ESCAPED FROM 14a OSBALDESTON CRESCENT, WILMSLOW, LANCS. (Or, of course, your own address, if you have no reason to visit Wilmslow).

3 See that any small boys you possess carry a small tub of margarine at all times. Either that, or ensure they develop narrow heads (sleeping between mahogany planks will do it). *Merely instructing them to keep away from railings is not enough.*

4 AVOID ABSOLUTELY saying any of the following to a police officer:
'Rubbish! This car can't even *do* seventy miles per hour!'
'What yellow line?'
'Smell? What smell? Oh, do you mean the joss stick, ha, ha, ha?'
'I happen to be a ratepayer, you know.'
'I was just about to put it back.'
'The Chief Constable and I are like *that*!'
'Come on, can't you take a joke?'

5 Watch *Match Of The Day* instead. One team is, after all, very like another.

6 Put it in your pocket and shut up. Most police stations have more muddy cigarette lighters/school scarves/hubcaps than they know what to do with.

7 If you are 8½ months pregnant, try to keep within staggering distance of a telephone.

8 Following a collision in which your tail-light is shattered, as a result of which the other car's wing-mirror is pushed askew, try to avoid involving Scotland Yard.

9 It may well be that the young lady turns out not to be a schoolteacher who has wandered in by accident and that the whisky she has been shifting at a quid a shot is actually cold tea, but do try to leave quietly. It's a funny world, some you win, some you lose.

10 Try to ascertain whether the man mightn't be merely a householder who has left his key in his other suit. The best way to do this is to shout up: 'IT'S IN YOUR OTHER SUIT, I EXPECT!' If he starts ripping tiles off and hurling them at you, he is undoubtedly the householder.

11 Remember the one basic rule about burglar alarms: they only go off by accident. It is when they do not go off that the premises are probably being turned over. You could, of course, try dialling 999 and saying: 'There's a burglar alarm not going off in the house across the road,' and see where that gets you.

12 Remember the one basic rule about the description of wanted men: they all sound like the man who came to the door to see if you wanted any trees lopped. Yes, of course he had penetrating eyes. Almost everyone has penetrating eyes.

13 Try to think of other places to make love than open-air pop festivals.

14 Having two plain-clothes men walking round the marquee does not automatically ensure that your daughter's wedding will be written up by Jennifer/Hickey/Chatterbox of *The East Drayton Bugle*. If an EPNS toast-rack *does* get nicked, it was probably your cousin Esmond from Cockfosters, anyhow.

15 It is true that Chile has a repressive government. Shoving your banner-pole between a police horse's legs, however, may not bring South America to its senses.

16 While it may well have been in order to make the world a better place for cocky young policemen to live in that you fought at El Alamein (from the reunion dinner for which you are returning), you are in a better position to point this out to them if you have not just been sick on their new uniform.

17 Or in that cab.

(*Printer's note:* Well, there were bloody twenty when I started, that's all I can say. I don't know what happened to the other three. I've run out in the street, but there's never a bloody copper around when you want one. I've dialled 999, but God knows when they'll turn up. I suggested they drag the river, send a couple of dogs over, that sort of thing, you think they'll take a blind bit of notice? I don't know why I pay rates, I swear I don't! They sit around all day in the bleeding canteen, playing cards and – hang on a minute. Oh, here they are. I was sitting on them. Bit late now. Oh well.)

THE CHILD CRIME BOOM

by ALBERT

"*. . . and have you cleaned your teeth?*"

"*He'd better be good—he's costing us two pounds of jelly-beans and a conker!*"

THE BOARDROOM CANNIBALS

by WILLIAM DAVIS

ONE OF AMERICA'S LARGEST COR-porations maintains a small suite of offices in New York's Pan-Am Building for about-to-be-dismissed executives. When the company decides to terminate your services they transfer you to one of these rooms. You keep your title and your secretary goes with you; nothing is said about a termination. But when you arrive, you find that you have no duties to perform. Most people take the hint fairly quickly: the average stay in this corporate version of Devil's Island is about four months.

A variation of this civilised technique (which is by no means unknown in Britain) is to promote people to posts which sound impressive but mean absolutely nothing and, worse, are known to mean nothing. If you can stand the non-pace for more than a year (and British businessmen tend to be more thick-skinned than their American brethren) they will generally find a way of telling the world that you have been forced to leave because of 'the pressure of other commitments'.

Whether companies will be able to afford such niceties in future is open to question. Life in the corporate jungle looks like being a good deal tougher than in the past. Industry is no longer expanding, falling profits will produce unsettling mergers, 'rationalisation' (always a magic phrase in times like this) will wipe out whole departments, older directors will try to postpone retirement until an answer is found to inflation, and chairmen will need even more scapegoats than usual. So the restless struggle in the nation's Boardrooms is likely to have a different emphasis: instead of the normal in-fighting about the size of offices and desks, length and wording of minutes, titles, car park places, keys to washrooms, expense accounts and seating at the Top Table, we shall see a cunning and ruthless battle for survival.

The basic rules of Boardroom survival are well known: flatter the boss, don't talk unless you have to, arrange out of town trips whenever important decisions are taken (so that no-one can blame you if things go wrong), and never offer to resign because there's always a good chance that your resignation will be accepted. Marrying the chairman's daughter is, alas, no longer a guarantee of safety because most companies nowadays are run by managerial types who may themselves have reason to feel insecure.

There are, however, a few other well-tested gambits which should improve the odds. It helps, for example, to be black or a woman, because no-one wants to be accused, in the *Sunday Times* or by some publicity-conscious Labour M.P., of harbouring prejudice. The next best thing is to get close to one or more of the big institutional shareholders. When a company runs into trouble, it's the City which forces changes in management. If you are a personal friend of the chap who runs the insurance company, investment trust, or pension fund concerned, he can make sure that someone else is chosen as the sacrificial offering. If you can arrange to be his watchdog on the Board you are even more secure – everyone, from the chairman down, will be terrified of you and no-one will risk accusing you of incompetence or cupidity.

Another ploy, which has proved increasingly effective in recent years, is to build yourself a reputation – inside and outside the company – as someone who 'gets on well with the unions'. It makes you far more useful than, say, the marketing director and, given the power of shop stewards, should ensure that the whole plant will be shut down for an indefinite period if the chairman as much as hints that you might like to consider retirement or running a subsidiary in Iceland.

If you can't stand the unions (or they can't stand you) there may be some mileage in a trick which works well in America: discover some fancy-sounding new management techniques. Company boards everywhere will be looking for miracle cures this year and it shouldn't be too hard to convince your colleagues that you have the answer. Providing you stress that your ideas will take time to work ('long-term' is always a useful phrase on these occasions) and providing you make sure that no-one else really understands what you are on about, this should keep you safely occupied, as the company's resident whiz-kid, until the storm is over.

Not least, it pays to make friends in the Department of Industry or other Ministries which hand out Government money. It doesn't have to be Tony Benn; these things are usually arranged by a discreet civil servant. Don't forget, though, to promise him that when he retires from Whitehall, twenty or thirty years hence, he can walk into your Boardroom. Civil servants can be awfully generous with the taxpayer's cash but they naturally want something more out of life than MBE's.

It could happen that, despite all these precautions, you will still find yourself the would-be victim of a hungry Boardroom cannibal. It's important, therefore, to know what makes a man unpopular (and therefore vulnerable) and to be aware of some of the more sophisticated methods used to cook his kidneys. Unpopular directors are easily recognised: they are the people with ideas, imagination, enthusiasm, ambition, and a dreary capacity for hard work. If, in addition, they have the misfortune of being young (and thus representing a threat to every colleague who is a day older) they are natural candidates for the pot. Conspiracies to get you there are generally organised by the colleague you suspect least: every company director in Britain has read *Julius Caesar*. But the most dangerous enemy is the man who, on paper, holds the most power – the chairman and/or chief executive. He didn't get to the top by being soft, and he knows what it takes to stay there. One of the smartest stunts in his extensive repertoire is to have you lured away from your own company by a better offer elsewhere. The way it's done is to tell other chairmen and/or chief executives at the club, or on the golf course, what a brilliant fellow you are. If this doesn't produce the desired result the next step is to approach a 'headhunter' and offer an attractive fee if he succeeds in finding you another job. When you bite at the bait he will act the part of the surprised and rejected suitor – and send his secretary out for a clock or some other parting gift before you have a chance to change your mind.

None of this matters very much, of course, if you have managed to fix yourself up with multiple directorships. The non-executive director is one of those British inventions of which the City is immensely proud: it is a comfortable, well-paid extension of the old boy network. The way into this peaceful corner of the business jungle is generally through a bank or City institution: some of the bigger ones scatter them around like confetti. A non-executive director doesn't have to do much except question everything done, or about to be done, by the working executives. And because he is not actually involved in production, or selling, or anything else that really matters, no-one can ever hold him responsible for mistakes.

In troubled 1975 the people most likely to collect these plums are company doctors. The title is not an official one: it was bestowed by financial journalists because it seemed appropriate and fitted neatly into a headline. The company

Hallo . . . Hallo . . . Is Anybody There?
With characteristic unthinking extravagance, the US Government is about to spend at least three years and countless millions of dollars in an effort to break up the American Telephone and Telegraph Company before it becomes a total telecommunications monopoly. Why don't they just take a leaf out of our book, let it become a total monopoly, and watch it break up all by itself?

Utterly Frank
Most people read Prince Charles's comments on the creeps and Mafia men that surround Frank Sinatra, but not many seem to have come across Sinatra's indignant reply:

'From what I read, this guy ain't got no business calling any pot any kind of colour. How come he's such a big wheel in England and not with any regular kind of job or anything, and all that money coming in? Real estate, too; right now I can't fix Wales, Cornwall and Lancashire on my map, but it sure sounds a whole heap of development area to me, and no-one can explain where he got it. Came down the family from a relative, it says here, but the American tax people wouldn't swallow that, I can tell you. Still, you got to admit he's well looked after – I ain't denying *I* got the occasional bodyguard, but I sure as hell ain't got a regiment of horse outside the house. And talk about trying to get close to him; relations everywhere in the way and most of them German from what I can tell. I ain't heard him sing yet, though.'

doctor may be an accountant, lawyer, management consultant or simply a chap with a proven track record or smooth tongue. His chief characteristic is an impersonal regard for facts – not for him the luxury of wondering what happens to a middle-aged executive when the carving has been done.

If you want to become a company doctor (and there is no law which says cannibalism is reserved for your enemies) the obvious course is to get your name known among likely creditors: banks, finance companies, owners of debentures and loan stock, disgruntled family shareholders, the Inland Revenue. But be warned – this is a job which, as a rule, involves a tiresome amount of work. An easier move is to convince people that you have all the makings of an expert liquidator, or to take a crash course in asset stripping. The stock market values the shares of many well-known companies at far less than their assets are worth and 1975 should be a fine year for strippers who know their way around a factory and are not too fussy about people.

J. Paul Getty, that great humanist and public benefactor, has noted that business depressions are splendid because they offer the chance of easy pickings. The main thing, as he would no doubt wish me to add, is that one must have the knack of being in the right place at the right time – of knowing instinctively when the owners, or directors, are about to jump from the eighteenth floor of their head office and to have one's cheque book out before they hit the pavement.

I suppose it's possible that some of you, reading this, will think me guilty of exaggeration. All your Boardroom colleagues are dear friends; they wouldn't dream of indulging in such sordid manoeuvring. Well, I hope you are right. But remember this – next time a dear friend pats you on the back he *may* simply be trying to find the best place to insert his knife.

*"For God's sake! We're **all** worried about defence cuts!"*

A Yawning Chasm

The Government has just set up a new department to look into boring jobs. Their job will be to investigate routine jobs and find how they can be made more exciting and fulfilling. We asked one member of the team for his interim findings.

'We go into factories from 9 till 5 and ask people questions. That's all we do really. We say things like "What happens to the grommet after you've fitted it into the pin?" and they say things like "Dunno, really". It's a job, I suppose, but really it's very boring and none of us feels we are reaching our true potential at it. The daily grind of going round factory floors which all look the same and talking to people who all sound the same should not really be allowed in a very civilised country and the main recommendation in our first report, we've agreed, is that we should immediately be switched to asking film stars, stunt men, masseuses, gamblers, oil sheikhs and jazz musicians about their jobs. It won't help the factory worker much, but at least it will have solved our problem. It's been lovely talking to you for a change, too.'

"Well, we have a tradition of hospitality to wayfarers and as the steeple was falling down . . ."

Blessed are the Efficient

A new organisation is applying business efficiency methods to churches and monasteries. Brother DICKINSON reports

"Our St. Sebastian line of vests are completely moth-proof, madam—the holes are an integral part of the design."

"Hallelujah—we've got the McAlpine M3 contract!"

"For a penance, say three Hail Marys and do four night shifts on the drop-forge hydraulic hammer."

"Keep going, Ignatius—the last hundred went round in twelve minutes flat."

OPERATION OILKILL

As American sabre-rattling grows ever louder over the Middle East, and President Ford murmurs "it is difficult to discuss the oil problem without lapsing into doomsday language", can anyone doubt that the Pentagon already has a contingency plan well advanced for military intervention against the tiny oil states?

STATE DEPARTMENT

From the desk of The Secretary of State

To: The President

Dated: October 15

Mr. President,

Thank you for your enquiry. It is good of you to take an intere Kuwait is the one we have marked with the arrow. The arrow is the lo thing with the pointy end.

As you can see, even with the naked eye, Kuwait is pretty damn small. This presents us with certain difficulties. As you know, it hard for the United States to go in anywhere with less than around ha a million men. It is true we could start small, with ten thousand advisers, say, and work up, the way we have in the past, but that take time and time is something we do not have much of. I know these Arab if they think we're going to bomb the shit out of them, they may star blowing things up, and then where are you? As it is, we are going to have to go damned careful: the USAAF, as you know, tends to like to drop more bombs on things than were dropped in all the previous wars up to that moment in in time, and this could mean we end up with a big hole.

Of course, half a million troops means, logistically speaking, three million personnel, and I do not think they could all stand on Kuwait, let alone have cinemas, airstrips, whorehouses and so forth. This means we shall probably have to move in on Saudi Arabia, on account of the space.

And possibly Iraq. Iraq is the one to the North, i.e., at the top of the map as you're holding it. If that's the way you're holdin it, of course.

You will appreciate I cannot go into all the details here about why this step may prove necessary. Suffice it to say that we thought of other things, like building smaller cars etcetera, but the Pentago rightly thought this would spell the end of democracy as we know it. Anyway, we have a moral obligation to the Free World.

I know what you're going to say. You're going to say you haven had a war of your own yet, and shouldn't we wait awhile. All I woul say to you is: don't worry. Kennedy and Johnson and Nixon all had wars without any previous experience, but they didn't let that stop them. Wars are like swimming, the toughest part is getting in. You just have to take the plunge, and after that it sort of takes care o itself.

I'll keep you posted.

Your friend,

Henry

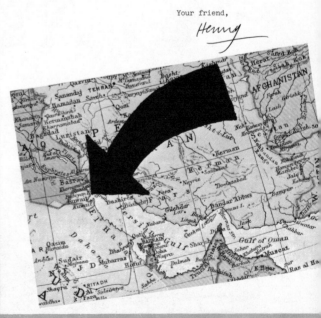

UNITED STATES NAVY

MEMO

From: Chief of Naval Operations
To: Secretary of Defense

What I wish to be apprised of as of this moment in time is who is putting out all this shit concerning the saturation bombing of K*w**t, to be followed up by airborne landings at division strength? I have had personal guarantees AT THE HIGHEST EXECUTIVE LEVEL that if there was going to be any saturation stuff then it was the Navy that was going to lay it on. Also, if anyone is fixing to put personnel in, then that personnel will be the United States Marine Corps.

I do not have to remind you, Mr Secretary, that the Marine Corps has had considerable experience in this field compared with some people I could mention who have the habit of ending up dangling from some goddam church spire, or in this case minaret, or else floating in the goddam sea where the enemy can pick them off like fish in a barrel. I would like to know if anyone in your Department has taken a good look at a map of the region lately: this K*w**t is about the size of a dime, and my considered view is that where the Airborne is going to wind up is somewhere in the nature of Eth**p**, and if they start emptying ordnance into the Eth**p**ns, all hell is going to break loose.

Don't think I am not aware of what is behind this snub, Mr Secretary, but no-one can say the Gulf of Tonkin louse-up is down to me, this Department has had a major shake-out since then, and we are are all geared up to go out and saturate something and this K*w**t could be the start of a real comeback. As for my Marine Corps, Lieut. Calley as you know has paid his penalty and deserves another chance, and anyway you have my personal guarantee that he will be accompanied by a senior officer at all times. I know there are pernicious rumours flying about that the Marine Corps is under strength at 197,000, but I am sure I do not have to remind you that we have fifty-four (54) nuclear submarines in our arsenal, and the Persian Gulf is only two hundred (200) kilometres wide, for Chrissake! At four kilometres apart, nobody's going to get lost, Jesus, they can practically *see* each other!

I look forward to your early observations.

THE COCA-COLA CORPORATION

Peach Tree · Centre Station · Atlanta · Georgia

The President
Washington, DC

October 15, 1974

Dear Sir:

re: *Military Take-Out Of Mid-East Oil States*

I think I speak for all of us here at Coke when I say that the above item has taken us completely by surprise; and further, with respect, that we are not a little affronted at the fact that the news when it did finally come was conveyed to us by Mrs J. Cleveland Hominy of Arlington, Va., and not by your Office. It is really coming to something when we have to rely upon vital information getting to us via people who sweep out the Pentagon.

Of course, it may just be that non-experts have no idea of the forward planning necessary to put down four million crates of Coke on a makeshift military airstrip in the middle of the desert in temperatures of up to 120°F. Nobody, of course, has seen fit to tell me the exact dimensions of the operation you have in mind, but looking at my executive globe and bearing in mind our experience in the South East Asian theatre, I do not see how you can do it with less than two million combatants, i.e. four dozen million bottles per week, not allowing for breakages.

Even this estimate may be on the low side. According to our New Jersey computer, which has been re-programmed out of its S. E. Asia parameters, the mean mid-day temperatures obtaining in the Persian Gulf could involve a man-Coke ratio in excess of 9:1 x S, where S equals the number of survival days per involvee. In order to meet this, we would have to take on at least 10,000 new personnel, and open two, possibly three, more processing plants.

On these calculations, your planned invasion cannot be mounted before January 3, 1975, at the earliest. Looking forward to your observations,

I remain,
Yours very truly,

Emmett Dunlop III

Executive Vice-President.

ZCZC AGL 394 2-012812E2B1

GWL D CO UWNX 018

FROM THE OFFICE OF THE SUPREME US ARMED FORCES COMMAND KOREA STOP COPY TO ALL CHIEFS OF STAFF STOP ANYONE STARTING THIS GODDAM ARAB SHOW WITHOUT REQUESTING MY PARTICIPATION IS GOING TO HAVE TO ANSWER TO ME PERSONAL STOP I GOT MEN BEEN OUT HERE FIVE YEARS WITHOUT KILLING NOTHING STOP IT IS NOT RIGHT WHERE YOU ARE ASKING MEN TO WATCH OLD CLINT EASTWOOD MOVIES OR CATCH A DOSE FOR THEIR COUNTRY AND YOU DONT GIVE THEM THE CHANCE TO EXPEND LIVE ROUNDS ON LIVE PEOPLE STOP I BETTER NOT GET NO FUNNY ANSWERS TO THIS ELSE ME AND THE GUYS IS GONNA GO RIGHT IN AND TAKE OUT RED CHINA STOP SEE QUESTION MARK

NOT THE CENTRAL INTELLIGENCE AGENCY

c/o General Delivery . Washington . DC
Somewhere in America

October 15, 19--

Dear Grey Squirrel,

Following your instructions, I took Rabbits Hammerstein, Griswold, Jefferson, Muldoon, Kristofferson and Kowalski to see L******* Of Arabia yesterday, and they are now pretty fully briefed on what to look for, i.e. people in kind of sheets with towels around their heads. It was noted the sand is all over, and if you want to get about there are these big deformed animals they have. Kowalski was a bit dubious about passing unnoticed, mainly on account of he only has Polish, but my view is at least he's a foreigner, and as the top Arab yesterday had blonde hair and blue eyes, the Rabbits feel they have a lot going for them.

As far as the political destabilisation is concerned, I am fully confident in the sophistication of our planned modus operandi, especially as wearing these long sheets you can carry an automatic shotgun and nobody notices a goddam thing until you're right up close and blasting, except maybe you have a stiff leg or something, and I hear the M***** E** is full of cripples anyhow.

Thank you for your good wishes,

Yours very truly,

Mickey Mouse

P.S. I enclose a pic of the guys.
P.P.S. Eat these enclosures personally.

To Henry —
from
Duke
A man's gotta
do what a
man's gotta do.

POTZ & WIFE'S BROTHER (Tailoring) INC.
1465a Alameda Boulevard · Pasadena
California 100876

The Secretary of State,
c/o Pentagon Building,
Arlington, Va.

October 17, 1974

Dear Mr Kissinger,

You should pardon the delay in getting in touch, but I only heard last night from my nephew Harry the cabdriver. It's just possible I know where I could lay my hands on ten million yards nice khaki mohair, only a six ounce material, you could walk about in a hundred degrees centigrade you wouldn't even know you got a suit on. Believe me, more tropical lightweight than this you don't find.

I hope you'll agree with me where this gets the absolute top priority. This country's in enough trouble already, the last thing we need is a sloppy-looking invasion.

Hoping to hear from you at your earliest convenience, please God, you're keeping well,

Yours truly,

Jack L. Potz

Jack L. Potz,
President.

This letter Belongs to Gerald Ford, the Wite Houze, Pensilvania Avenue, Wazhington, United Statez the World, the Univerz.

Dear Henry

I wold like Kwait + Zaudi Arabia + Iraq + Bahrane + a cowboy zuit + a Magik ring + a real Wotch, pleeze.

Gerald

Senator Mike Mansfield
1788 Canyon Drive
Georgetown
Washington DC

October 12

Dear Mike:

This changes everything!
I mean, I may well run now.
No, really! Well, possibly, anyhow.
Or at any rate, maybe.
No, make that probably.
Okay, definitely! Well, almost
definitely, I think.

Ted xxx

MEMO

From: Chief of Staff of the Army
To: Secretary of State

Look, Henry, I'm only, you know, spitballing, but I have been taking a kind of straw poll, and the general consensus among the military personnel who, like, count, is that we have a de-confidence situation vis-a-vis President Ford with regard to the operation currently under review. I mean he is a regular guy and all that, and a dummy, but we have to set against these plus-points the fact that he may show a shortfall in, you know, nerve, when it comes to pulling all the plugs out.

Believe me, Hank, nothing undermines the military morale like the feeling that when the chips are down and the greatest army the world has ever seen is getting zapped by a bunch of bare-assed tribesmen, there is no thermonuclear back-up contingency policy. I mean, I have *been* in Vietnam, Mr Secretary, and I have seen crack troops suffering terrible embarrassment that could so easily have been overcome with a few kilotons pitched in at the right spot, or near it.

What I'm getting at, Hank, is how about getting Ford to step down? What we need in the White House at this moment in time is a homicidal madman with nothing to lose. The people would rally to someone like that in a time of low-profile peace, and would be prepared to forgive previous peccadilloes. You only have to look at Churchill or Hitler. What we have in mind is someone who would come back in his country's hour of need and lead us to, you know, victory. I mean, he only has phlebitis, for God's sake, and only in one leg, and I've seen men crawl the length of Iwo Jima beach with everything blown off below the waist; is this too much to ask?

From Our Ugandan Correspondent

HUM, it lookin' like Destiny callin'. It lookin' like Dame Fortune on de blower, not to mention de Lady Luck comin' up wid de tap on de shoulder, also Fate takin' a hand.

I referrin', o' course, to de fac' dat de collapsin' Britain spawnin' de paramilitary organisations on ev'ry side wot comin' up wid de plans to save de crummlin' remains o' democracy, an' wot dis but a example o' history lookin' fo' De Right Man? An' all it gettin' at de present is de wizzened ol' retired colonels an' gen'ls in de tatty bowlers an' de arfritis in de knees sittin' aroun' in de Brit Legion halls wid de ninety-year-ol' ex-corporals an' sim'lar an' workin' out wot they havin' on de blazer badges an' wot colour they paintin' de regimental mini-van an' whose turn it bein' to write a letter to de *Daily Telegraph* an' de exac' date fo' gittin' India back, weather permittin'.

Wot kine o' coo you callin' that? Wot kine o' pop'lar support fallin' in behine a bunch o' wore-out toffs in de gardenin' trousers? Wot chance they standin' wen de Boilermakers Union start swingin' de spanners an' puttin' de fearful boot in? It all very well bein' a dab hand at sittin' in de basement underneaf de Somme an' workin' out where de nex' consinement o' turnip jam comin' from, but it not much help wen de TUC lobbin' de mortar shells into de elegant premises o' de Dorking Tennis Club.

Britain clearly in de market fo' a progressive young officer wot commandin' de respeck o' de popperlace, also a man wid de deep political wisserdom wot capable o' takin' a sophisserticated view o' de sensitivies o' de delicate sitwation: nex' time de notorious workin' to rule gittin' pulled at de Ford Motor Company, fo' example, it no good de private troops jus' rushin' in an' lashin' out wid de batons. Dis jus' invitin' trouble. Fust thing you

got to do is sort out de prominent shop stewards, talk to 'em man to man, an' stick their heads up on long poles outside de factory gates. After that, you sendin' de fast jeeps roun' de local housin' estate an' burnin' it to de groun'.

Nothin' shuttin' up de lef' wing troublemakers like gittin' de fambly charred.

Natcherly, wid de threatenin' o' de breakdown o' de law an' de order, you havin' to be dam sure de judiciary takin' a firm line; de bes' way to make certain o' this is to bung de present lot in chokey, an' pass de wigs out among de reli'ble NCO's wid a card fo' 'em to learn off by heart, sayin': 'GOOD MORNIN' YOU RED BUGGER I SEE YOU PLEADIN' GUILTY. DE PENALTY IS GITTIN' HUNG BY DE NECK. WHO NEX'?'

'Course, de media gotta be handled right, it no good simply droppin' napalm on de shop-stewards or settin' de dogs loose in de universities, it necessary to woo de popperlace wid a bit o' de smart propaganda an' winnin' 'em over to de cause. De leader gotta turn up in de offices o' de innerfluential *Times*, fo' example, an' explain to de Editor wot line he takin' f'om now on. Natcherly, he replyin': 'Piss off, nobody muckin' about wid de inner-dependence o' de press!' whereupon you pointin' out dat de big bang wot jus' knockin' his monocle into his tea comin' f'om de *Daily Telegraph*, on account o' you got a missile frigate moored off de pop'lar Tower Bridge an' how about a headline sayin': GUMBOOT DIPPER-LOMACY MAKIN' BRITAIN GREAT AGAIN!

Anyway, dat about as much as I revealin' at de present time. All I attemtin' to point out to de British people is de fac' dat de Walkers an' de Stirlings o' dis worl' jus' a bunch o' amateurs compared wid de high professional standards o' Uganda. If their supporters really wantin' de job done right, it jus' a question o' droppin' a nice note.

No room in the middle

ALAN BRIEN in a class, darkly

'WE ARE ALL MIDDLE CLASS NOW' AS Edward VII would undoubtedly amend his only remark in the *Oxford Dictionary of Quotations* (itself borrowed from Sir William Harcourt) if he were still padding the corridors of power looking for the way back to his own bedroom. Instead, *The Times* has been saying it for him, coming to the conclusion that 'the middle class is at least half our society.' Well, it only bears out what I always say, the majority always get the dirty end of the stick, usually in the eye.

Thirty years ago, perhaps up to fifteen years ago, I could have instantly identified them. The middle class boy, for instance, was recognisable as being the sort the rest of us only saw in children's books. Even in our comics, they were the heroes of a world I long thought make-believe, perhaps historical romance, where you toasted muffins in your study, kept a tuck box under your bed, and had masters with mortar boards. Richmal Crompton's William, despite his concertina stockings and hangman's-knot tie, dirty neck and scruffy hair, went to a private day school. If he had ever been allowed to reach fourteen, I reckon Mr. Brown would have sent him off as a boarder to have his character built and his morals impaired.

The Browns were middle class all right, not quite so posh as Christopher Robin's people, but well off enough not to have to live in a street in town, or a semi in the suburbs, but in a detached house, with a driveway, a shrubbery (infallible sign of m-c status) and a car, on the fringes of some Home Counties village beauty-spot.

They had the Vicar to tea – they had tea yet, with cakes and scones and triangular sandwiches – and knew the doctor by his first name and Mr. Brown would go to an office and come home cleaner than when he left – something no fathers around us ever did until the long-delayed opening of the pit-head baths. Middle class parents never went out to 'work', it was always 'business'. It was rather common to have a 'job', and even 'profession' was rarely used except in an intimate circle of equals. If you were a solicitor, or a dentist (and that was not-quite – 'only a dentist, I'm afraid') or a parson, or an accountant, or a politician (a bit suspect for pushiness – 'for my sins, I'm an M.P.'), it was never suggested that this was an achievement for which you might have had to study and sweat and scrape. It was like an hereditary title – The Solicitor – which appeared to have descended upon you by right of blood and birth, though with privileges came duties of course, *largesse oblige*, and you would perform your functions with probity and dedication, and a bit of charity on the side.

Nobody was first-generation middle class. You weren't safely inside the pale until the oldest living inhabitant had forgotten what your great-grandfather's name was before he changed it, or how your grandfather wiped his nose on his sleeve. The self-made man (like Mr. Bott, the sauce-manufacturer) could only hope to live to see the rank granted to his grandchildren, and only then if his son and daughter married the right sort. Self-made men were often jerry-built, if not actually jerry-builders, and rarely knew when to say 'when'. They lowered the tone, and could never be trusted not to revert to type. After all, they had already swapped allegiances once. They had the rather ambiguous role of the bench-hand-turned-foreman among the working class.

The point about the old, traditional, middle class family was that they *wanted* to remain in the middle. They liked it there, and they asked nothing other than that life should go on the same – the lawn be rolled, the tulip tree bloom, the Boot's library books returned on time, the tennis club dance and the amateur theatricals as great a success as ever, Christmas tree ornament unbroken, the towel rail kept hot, the church bells ringing out over the crispy bacon, the daily woman as much a character as her old mother was, in Betjemanland. So long as the pound remained steady, you could afford to sympathise with the unemployed, not all of whom were shirkers, and be tolerant of the teacher next door who joined the Left Book Club, of Uncle Jeremy who was a bit of an agnostic, and Aunt Sylvia who liked to think herself a sculptress.

If there was some guilt, it was not so much that the poor got poorer when the Government, sternly realistic, slashed the wages of public servants and reduced the dole, as that you were getting gradually more prosperous. (Between 1918 and 1938, through two Depressions and a General Strike, incredible as it seems today, the pound in your pocket, if you had one, increased in value from 100 pence to 160 pence.)

The middle class didn't expect, or aim, to be rich, or famous, or ennobled. They were critical of the morals of the Bright Young Things. They wouldn't, like their Roundhead forebears, cut off the head of a king, but they pushed King Edward VIII off the throne, rather than put up with hanky-panky with American divorcees. Neither – and who can blame them? – did they want to sink to the council house, the employment exchange, the jug of beer

47

from the off-licence and the fish and chips in newspaper. They prided themselves on treating everyone as if they were equals, upper class or lower class it didn't matter, so long as it was clear it was just an hypothesis. Prosperity for all was just around the corner – a corner *they* had turned already, with no state subsidies or handouts, though perhaps an occasional scholarship, a couple of generations ago.

This is the middle class as I saw it, the middle class as it continues to see itself reflected in *Times* leaders. But then it was small, compact, homogeneous, easily recognisable, especially by itself, through its clothes, its customs and ceremonies, its idioms, its prejudices and its ideals. All its ways of describing itself emphasised its centrality – the backbone of the nation, the heart of business – and it was usually cultured, honest, kind, worthy, respectable. If its wilder spirits broke out to anywhere, it was to Marxism, not Fascism. It voted for Chamberlain, but its true archetype was Churchill. It was at its best in war to preserve an England it held dear and it had much to hold dear.

But where the reality and the myth diverge is in numbers. There were always half a dozen layers of middle class – lower-middle, middle-middle, middle, upper-middle-middle, and upper-middle. All of them at some-time or another, for protective colouration, out of modesty or snobbery, claimed to be just 'middle'. When *The Times* says 'at least half the nation', it is gathering in all sorts of the *nouveau-riche*, not to mention an occasional *Nouveau Richelieu*, expense-account bounders, backstreet twisters, small shopkeepers, door-to-door salesmen, supermarket executives, property developers, used-car dealers, publicans, journalists on the *News of the World*, scrapmetal merchants, bookmakers, mini-cab proprietors, garage managers, and other upward aspiring outsiders who have profited from the age of affluence. None of these would have been allowed to call at the front door of the old middle class, let alone jump the queue ahead of them at the hospital, join their clubs, turn up at their speech days, enter their first-class carriages, buy their houses, pinch their taxis, and not only marry, but later on divorce, their daughters.

If these are all in the middle class now, no wonder those who joined before the rush are getting angry. If *The Times* is correct in regarding this motley mob of privilege-hunters as the majority, who have they got now to fear except each other? By *Times*-style qualification, their ancient enemies, The Workers, are in a minority second only to their ancient enemies, The Capitalist Rich.

To be middle class, apparently, means wanting a house of your own, the best education available, money in the bank, a job you enjoy and can be proud of, and the chance to give your children a better start in life than some other children. What makes *The Times*, and all the commando groups enrolling under the middle-class banner, think that the shrinking, status-bereft, working class don't want these things too? The trouble with the middle class is that there are too many of them. We are all middle class now . . . alas. You can't run a country with a thousand backbones and one right hand, a million hearts and only one left foot. Some of them will just have to go.

"All right, next Thursday, when maybe he won't be wearing his armour."

S.McWerey.

The One-up, Round-the-World Gourmet

ROBERT MORLEY
keeps one jump ahead!

HE SAT BESIDE ME AT THE BAR and, when I enquired idly about his plans, he announced he was off to Strasbourg to eat a goose. So many travellers attempt too much. His reply encapsulated a singleness of purpose altogether admirable. I don't now remember to whom I was talking, only that it was in Buck's where such affirmations are—or at least were—listened to without distress.

How far is one prepared to go for a good meal?

I posed the question to several acquaintances. A number demanded elaboration: Do you mean a free good meal? How good is good? Myself, I would be prepared to go a long way, but then, of course, I like travelling, let alone food. Clutching my Michelin, how often have I sought out the rosette and crossed spoons and demanded the speciality of the house and, strangely enough, how often have I been disappointed.

There is a *Café de Paris* in Biarritz which serves, for a few golden weeks of the year, a sort of special white truffle with apples, which I found as nasty as tripe and couldn't finish. The baby lamb at *Les Beaux* is, to my mind, altogether too babyish—a veritable slaughter of the innocents. Reminding me of a celebrated restaurateur in Gerard Street—now, alas, retired—who would explain the ritual murder necessary to prepare the feast he had in store for me. 'Mr. Morley, you take a baby frog just as he utters his first bellow, and cut off his head. You must do it in the moonlight, otherwise it is no use, and then you throw away everything but the tip of the heart where the coralete is' (there was always, in the description, a word I could not catch) 'then, later, you bake this for a dozen hours on a slow peat fire, turning it over and over, and then you butter it at the table.'

'If you want a really first-class moussaka,' I heard myself announce the other day, 'you'll have to go to Newbury.' The fellow who was unlucky enough to be within earshot hadn't even mentioned moussaka and, as far as I know, never touched the stuff.

We each have a Gourmet Guide hidden on our person and long to expose it. 'Don't be put off by the Formica table-tops,' we urge each other, 'the chef used to cook for Onassis before he took to the bottle.' We are speaking of the former chef, naturally—for we all know, Aristotle was teetotal.

The impression we seek to leave is of a blue tit which has already skimmed the cream. When the milk-bottle is taken inside it will not be the same. The eateries we extol today will, tomorrow, be ruined by the hoi-polloi—places we would not be seen dead in. 'Not quite what it was, is it?' we enquire of the still-faithful customer. 'I hear the *ptarmigan à la façon de Président Giscard* is pre-cooked and frozen.' Once the hat-check girl and the diners' club take over we are off, once more, in search of the little restaurant in Shrewsbury where the firemen eat because the captain's wife comes from Bayonne and does a mincemeat tart which is out of this world.

I have two distinct approaches when eating out. Quiet confidence, as host —a hint of formality in my manner of greeting the staff. I try to impart a sense of occasion to the ritual of seating my guest and choosing the food and wine, adding a touch of originality by asking for the salt to be taken away until we have need of it. 'I don't know if you feel as I do,' I remark to my friend, 'but I cannot bear a cruet with the apertif.' The use of the word *cruet*, here, is, I flatter myself, not without courage. Occasionally, before ordering the meal, I will summon a waiter and enquire about his wife. 'Better, I hope?' I tell him. I don't actually know whether the fellow has a wife but he will not care to correct me, though he may look a little puzzled – but I am confident that my companion will mistake his bewilderment for gratitude. The impression I wish to give – and, I have no doubt, succeed in giving – is that of the late Noël Coward in charge of a happy ship: the crew's troubles are my troubles – up to a point, of course. Before choosing the wine, I always say quite simply and, indeed, truthfully, that I know nothing whatever about it. When the others have suitably expressed their disbelief, I suggest we take the wine-waiter's advice. 'Something you want to get rid of,' I tell him encouragingly. 'Perhaps a Sancerre 1958, or Sauvigny de Clos Montard

'49? I usually give a little chuckle as he departs. When he returns with the bottle I am careful not to taste it – this is a privilege I reserve for my guest.

When our roles are reversed, of course I am a totally different creature. I go for the overkill. 'What a delightful bistro!' I exclaim. 'Blue beams! I don't think I've ever seen blue beams before *and* brown paper napkins! So convenient for the Natural History Museum – it's just round the corner, surely? How did you find it? Let's stick to the set meal, shall we? It's sure to be excellent . . . I'll have what you're drinking – half a carafe will be ample. How long has this place been going? . . . And I've never heard of it. What do you suppose they're having at the next table? Who would you say the people who come here are, mostly? . . . Students? It's so jolly and unpretentious. I am reminded of a little place half-way up the Bosporus on the right-hand side – you know it, of course – I was taken there by our Ambassador to eat yoghourt, and then we discovered this perfectly marvellous way they cook kid – in a blanket. You must try it next time you're there; just mention my name – or even the Ambassador's.'

Stored among the disorder of my memory is a positive armoury of food bombs to demolish the culinary one-upmanship of others. I always insist, for instance, that the *millefeuilles* at the *Château de Madrid* is worth negotiating the hairpin-bends of the Grand Corniche. 'I don't know why being circular should make all the difference,' I tell anyone who is listening, 'but somehow it does. Kobe beef in Tokyo is best, really, at the Hilton. They seem to have a particularly skilled masseur. You know that the Japanese massage the

We Don't Want To Die, But By Jingo If We Do!

No other paper seems to have picked the story up, but by chance our own reporter was on the spot last week in a side-alley behind one of London's major hospitals when a line of frail citizens in pyjamas began filing carefully out of a back door. Some were on crutches, some with little more than limbs in plaster were pushing trolley cases, some were merely crawling along in the gutter, assorted tubes and drips trailing behind them. Never slow to sniff a possible story, our man approached the figure at the head of the pitiful group, who said (as best he could through his nose-clip): 'We, the members of the National Patients' Union, have decided to withdraw our support from the hospital service. If the NUPE lot won't stoke the boilers and process the forms, and if the consultants won't do the operations, we see no reason why we should lie there and get cut about and have things jammed in our bums and down our throats just to keep this mob in work. Without us, the National Health Service and the private sector would come to an end overnight. Unless we get some sort of satisfaction, we shall have no other course open but to snuff it.'

"You were always the intellectual of our class, Bill. I'll bet you've read every book on these shelves."

50

"At least we've proved one thing pretty conclusively . . . the Polynesians were a race of raving lunatics!"

beasts on the hoof? I can't think why we don't do it here.'

No experience is too horrific to go into my book and be subsequently translated into a trap for the unwary.

The journey up-country from Bangkok to the Temple of Divine Light is seldom undertaken by train – at any rate by tourists, who prefer the river-steamer, or bus. I, on the other hand, went by rail, and have never forgotten the breakfast. I can still taste the cold fried egg, nestling in sago and topped with Soy sauce. 'Worth all the boredom of the Jade Buddha,' I maintain, stoutly. 'Be sure and catch the nine-twenty, and insist on the restaurant-car.'

One of the legends of travel I like to re-tell to anyone thinking of returning from Australia by air and re-fuelling in Teheran, is that if they hasten to the Transit Lounge and take the small door on the left, next to the gentlemen's lavatory, they will find themselves át the back of the Imperial Caviare Emporium, where they have only to rouse the attendant, who sleeps under the counter, to secure enormous quantities of sturgeon roe at knock-down prices.

It may well be that the store exists, but I have not, after numerous attempts, ever discovered it. I am not sure I want to. It gives me something to look forward to on the flight.

How dull the world would be if we all knew the mystery of Glamis Castle – which reminds me of a little teashop on the left as you leave the Keep, where they serve a really excellent Scotch pancake.

Hymns to New Gods

From The Daily Telegraph

Mr. Ford, 57, was stopped while driving in Santa Barbara, California, on Saturday night. A 35-year-old Detroit model was with him at the time.

Let's see, 1940, she'd be the one with the short chassis and the manual shift, right?

And Sidon

Pirelli may have stopped producing their famous calendars after ten years, but the boom goes on. A complete set has been auctioned in London for over £400 and Pan are bringing out the whole lot in book form. Where next?

'The stage, that's where next,' said mighty American movie mogul Darryl K. Helmutberger during a fifteen second stopover in London yesterday. 'I aim to turn the Pirelli calendars into a mammoth musical stage show. See, my office has bought the rights and my writers have come up with this great story about these twelve girls who travel the world every year – no, wait a minute, that's the sex movie I'm making out of the calendars – the musical is all about this shy photographer who falls desperately in love with Miss August, and it's great. Hey, did I mention about the spectacular Vegas show I'm putting on, "The Pirelli Girls"? Well, it's great. At the moment the only problem I've got is figuring out a way of using the days and months, which we also bought with the package. Maybe a History of the Sixties, I don't know. Oh, and don't forget to mention about my new disaster film. What? It's about this great tyre company which is headed for a cataclysm and no-one can save it and there are these twelve girls, see, and . . .'

Never bow to gods of granite,
  Never kneel to fire or soil,
Pray not to the distant planet,
  Let the sacred mountains boil.
    North Sea waters,
    North Sea waters,
These shall bring you holy oil!

Never bow before the phallus,
  Shun the ancient myths that coil
Round the mind of man. Be callous!
  Start anew and kneel to oil.
    North Sea waters,
    North Sea waters,
These shall bring surcease from toil!

Hushed was the Comrades' hymn.
  The temple courts were dark.
The lamp was burning dim
  Before the Sacred Ark,
The Ark of Public Ownership,
Concealed by years of candle-drip!

The Grand Old Man of Truth,
  The Priest of Albion, slept.
His watch the earnest youth,
  The round-eyed Tony, kept.
And what from Harold's sense was sealed
To Tony was that night revealed.

O give me Tony's heart,
  A heart that beats for me,
A heart that forms a part
  Of all humanity,
A heart so patient and intense,
Immune to reason, fact and sense.

O give me Tony's mind,
  A tiny mind and quaint,
So preciously designed,
  So free from worldly taint,
Whence all may learn, with hushed surprise,
Truths long discarded by the wise.

The Nation's one foundation,
   Its strength through years to be,
Is Labour's own creation,
   Endorsed by One in Three!
Conceived in face of scoffers,
   Matured in bitter gall,
The Social Contract offers
   Eternal bliss for all.

Though schisms rend asunder
   This angriest of lands,
Though folly piles on blunder,
   The Social Contract stands!
Ineffable! Transcendent!
   Thy Word no man may see!
On thee are we dependent –
   O perfect Nullity!

Rise up, have done with praying!
   The Contract is our Grail.
It's time to go round saying
   That Good Sense Will Prevail.
Bite not the hands that feed us,
   Destroy not Freedom's pen!
O Social Contract, lead us
   To perfect peace. Amen!

Now the day's long anguish ends,
Now the dreadful dark descends.
Who can doubt there's worse to be?
Help us, Chemotherapy!

What but thee can e'er control
Dark encumbrance of the soul?
Swift to our salvation come,
Librium and Valium!

We are children of the dust.
Quicken, and restrain, our lust.
Keep our errant steps from sin,
Help pure joy to enter in.

Mark and Matthew, Luke and John,
Tried their utmost and moved on.
Where is Heaven's golden key?
Open, Chemotherapy!

E. S. TURNER

"Murphy gives the bomb warnings and Father Ryan runs the 'Dial The Last Rites' Service."

"Try to get it right this time—I'll smile just once more!"

53

I Got Plenty o' Nuthin'

With the arrival of the wealth tax, owners are keen to minimise their assets. R. G. G. PRICE watches the effect on the stately home business

GOOD MORNING, LADIES AND GENTLEMEN. This is the Entrance Hall. It is impossible to heat, very difficult to light and completely useless.

Next we have the Banqueting Hall. Have you ever seen a room better designed to serve cold food in maximum discomfort? The table is laid as it was when the eleventh Duke entertained the Czar. The service is mock gold-plate. At one time, some dishonest dealer faked hallmarks. They have, of course, been removed. The ceiling used to be attributed to Sir James Thornhill. Now it is attributed to a pupil of a pupil of Rex Whistler.

The Rotunda. Really there's nothing much to the Rotunda except rotundity. The statues are plaster casts brought back from the Grand Tour by the seventh Duke. The joke is that you will still find pictures of them in books on Greek Sculpture as though they were originals!

The ante-room is a silly little space. The walls are panelled in some cheap fabric which is badly showing wear. It is probably a silk-substitute. In Stuart times they were not very expert on substitutes.

Now for the Library. Have you ever seen more unreadable volumes in one place? Here's a typical shelf-ful, put out on the table for visitors to inspect . . . sermons, early Victorian children's stories, chessboards disguised as *Paradise Lost*. Ugh! We used to boast a First Folio but there has been a recount and it's only a Tenth.

Now we retrace our steps to the Gold Drawing-Room, the ugliest room in the house. Don't trip over the plastic covering on the carpet; it's there to hide the patches.

"It started off as a family reunion, but I'm afraid it's turned into a plague!"

All those photographs of royalty clutter the place up. At least, the signatures are probably authentic, which is more than can be said for the silver frames. The chimney-breast is crammed with an elaborate carving of fruit, a slapdash attempt at the style of Grinling Gibbons. Our Head Gardener says that the grapes are a very poor rendering of the real thing. In fact, they represent cheap, imported grapes used as ballast. The picture over there shows an Italian landscape after a storm has passed. His Grace's optimistic parents managed to believe that it was a Giorgione! Modern research, organised by our consultant, Mr. T. Potter F.C.A., attributes it to Surbiton School of Art Copyists' Class.

There's nothing much to detain us here. Brace yourselves for a climb. You can't see any hotel or school taking a place with a staircase like this. The first-floor rooms open out of one another and are quite useless for any practical purpose. The last one has some old portraits on cracking wood. They look as though they have been produced by unsuccessful painters of inn signs.

Now for the State Bedroom. Elizabeth I did not sleep here—at least, we are almost certain that she didn't. There are some paltry washing utensils and a very short bed, which looks horribly uncomfortable. The tapestry of *A Satyr Surprising a Nymph Batheing* was the work of a Miss Entwhistle, a governess of former days. The resemblance to Gobelin's work is purely coincidental. The letter from Sir Alex Douglas-Home thanking His Grace 'for his interesting communication' is genuine.

Now down to the charnel house. The tomb of the third Duke is so encrusted with grime that the very poor bas-reliefs are invisible. The statue lost its head in the Commonwealth and suffered other alterations when Australian troops were billeted here during the first World War. The flat slab covers the remains of Lady Alicia. It is said that, if Gallows Copse is ever cut down, she will resume the performances on the spinet which were thought to have been responsible for her defenestration in the time of Duke Peveril le gai.

The Chapel is too small to sell for a parish church and too large to clean. His Grace almost persuaded a firm of straw-hat-makers to take it off his hands for warehousing; but the deal fell through during the probationary period as the mice ate the stock. The blackened canvas over the altar is thought to represent *The Martyrdom of St. Sebastian*, a subject often treated in better pictures. A less critical generation managed to make themselves believe that it was by Raphael. If anybody would like to throw a coin in the font . . . ? There is a legend that donors are safe from a return visit.

And now, ladies and gentlemen, I will let you out by the north postern. Nothing will grow in the park except grass which is useless for hay or grass skirts. If you all feel able to buy a pot of honey, or even try the set tea, the Ladies Felicity, Tara and Deborah will be able to have another week's music lessons. Well, no wonder the present Duke and his Duchess prefer to live modestly in the tropics.

"*I don't know why we keep coming here, the service is so slow.*"

NASTY WORK
IF YOU CAN GET IT

After the Swiss referendum rejected the suggestion that foreign resident workers should be chucked out, we talked to just a few of these unenviable folk who do all the filthy jobs their Swiss hosts would never touch . . .

JULIE ANDREWS "I feel sure that the reason the Swiss voted to keep me is because I sing on mountains. It is very hard to get a Swiss to do this on account of the cold; they prefer to stay under a blanket in the bank, eating Toblerone and entertaining themselves with pocket calculators. There was, I believe, a Lugano girl who once volunteered to sing *The Hills Are Alive With The Sound Of Music* from the saloon of a centrally-heated steamship, but a sudden breeze blew up on the lake and she made for the shore and retired. The record eventually came out, but the producers felt that *The Lake Is Alive With The Sound Of Music*, which is what they were forced to call it under the Sale Of Goods Act 1953, would not be a goer, and it was withdrawn."

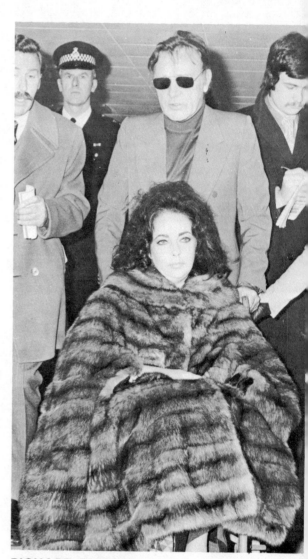

CHARLIE CHAPLIN "I came here many years ago because Switzerland didn't have anybody prepared to have a stove fall on his head. The authorities had also noticed that I was happy to have people hit me in the face with various desserts, and that if a man was required to fall down a drain or get his arm stuck in a lion's throat or hang over the edge of a precipice, I was always ready to oblige. Also, they were led to believe I lived on old shoes. I have not been called upon to engage upon any of this for some time, but I can see why they want to keep me around. There is little worse than needing someone to get stepped on by a moose and not being able to find him."

RICHARD BURTON "Well, of course, the result was a relief, but I'm bound to say I'm hardly surprised. The Swiss are a canny people, bach—*In Wales, man sagt noch 'bach', nicht wahr? Gut, gut!*—and they realised that a vote to chuck the foreigners out would mean having to do some indescribably awful and unrewarding jobs themselves. I mean, can you imagine some stodgy Swiss burgher rolling up his sleeves and getting down to the terrible business of marrying Elizabeth? All that shrieking and chucking the furniture about, boyo! All those damned flea-ridden mongrels yapping round your ankles! All that jetting round the world to every bloody auction room God made to cough up your hard-earned—well, earned —nest-egg on great chunks of polished rock! Of course, I myself am now in the process of changing jobs, but does any of us seriously believe a Swiss would look twice at what I'm letting myself in for again?"

JACKIE STEWART "There's no getting away from it, it *is* a filthy job, it *is* a dangerous job, it *is* an incredibly difficult job, and you'd not find a single Swiss from Geneva to Zürich prepared to take the fearful risks involved. I'm sure that one of the main reasons for them voting to keep me was quite simply born of amazement that anyone existed who was crazy enough to tackle it! They like having me around to remind them of what they don't have to do, d'you see? What? No, no, no, I've retired from *that*, what made you think I was talking about motor racing? I'm talking about endorsing British products."

ROLF HOCHHUTH "I would not waste your approval on the Swiss, if I were you. As always, selfish motives prevailed; they are a cowardly people—you realise, of course, that William Tell actually planned to shoot his son in the head rather than pay taxes to Gessler, but missed? It's all in my forthcoming play and letter to *The Times* —and would never risk exposing themselves to the terrible hazards of libel suits and injunctions that are an inevitable part of my courageous and dangerous work. I am currently planning two more fearless documentary dramas, one proving that it was, beyond any question, Winston Churchill who assassinated President Kennedy, and one explaining why Franklin D. Roosevelt, acting directly upon instructions from Pope Pius, bombed *Pearl Harbour*. I ask you, can you imagine the stolid, unimaginative, meticulous, dreary Swiss doing something like that?"

BERNIE CORNFELD "Very few Swiss ever go to jail for fraud. On the other hand, they have this enormous fraud squad, a giant organisation, cars, buildings, electronic equipment, top grade accountants, agents, it costs a fortune a set-up like that! So they look round, and all the Swiss are maintaining this very low profile, they stay in nights, they invest in gilt-edged at 11%, they buy gold, they take out a lot of respectable insurance, they subscribe to pension funds—where's the percentage in that for a progressive fraud squad? Who are they going to go to work on? Who are they going to fill their expensive jails with? How many Swiss would do what I do, take the risks I take? Believe me, as long as Switzerland has a fraud squad, they're going to be looking for people of my calibre."

Throwing the Hammer and Sickle

ALBERT's preview of the Moscow Olympics

"*. . . remember the old doves?*"

"*A real woman would change that tractor tyre in twenty-one seconds!*"

Genuine Repros?!

For one day only they plan to recreate Portobello Road in New York, which makes one wonder if they quite realise the problems involved. Where will they recruit the three card trick men in time, the pickpockets, the unwashed fake-American singers, the genuine British traffic wardens? How much will it cost to transport all those Union Jack chamber pots, those second-hand Guy Mitchell 78s, those pictures made from the insides of watches, those dirty sheepskin coats, and who will buy them? Do they realise the enormous quantities they will need, for real authenticity, of trampled *Daily Expresses*, squashed fruit and veg, abandoned English hot dogs, picturesque plywood flotsam, forgotten bangles, sweet papers, crisp packets, melted ice-cream cones, dirty straw packing . . .?

Still, at least they'll have the milling crowds close at hand—the shuffling hordes of American tourists that really make Portobello Road what it is.

COMING SOON

IN FABULOUS INFLATOSCOPE!   IN NEW ECONOMIC MONOCHROME!

In 1974 the Republic of Italy, the greatest empire of corruption and tax evasion the world has ever known, began its rapid slide towards ruin as the armies of creditors massed on its frontiers. NOW we bring you the whole awesome, sensational, incredible story.

THE FALL OF THE ITALIAN REPUBLIC

The Crash of the Lira!

The Stampede of Stranded Tourist

The Collapse of the Market!

The Horror of Fellini's Latest Epi

SEE THE CRAZED MOB DEMAND PASTA AND CIRCUSES!
WATCH LORD CLARK FIDDLE AS VENICE SINKS!
GASP AS THE GERMAN SUBSIDIES POUR OVER THE ALPS!
THRILL TO THE SIGHT OF ITALY'S GREAT MASTERPIECE, THE PIRELLI CALENDAR, ABANDONED FOR EVER!

starring **CHARLTON HESTON** as the power-crazed Prime Minister who leads a Christian/Democrat/Liberal / Communist / Fascist coalition government for two and a half days...

starring **FRANK FINLAY** as the Pope, desperately trying to stem the orgy of divorce and trial separation that sweeps a stricken nation...

starring **SOPHIA LOREN** as the woman who waits tragically for a letter from her lover, unaware that it has been lying in an Italian post office for six months...

starring **BARBRA STREISAND** as the kooky, wacky kid from Naples who gets up to some of the darnedest currency speculations at her local branch of Lloyds...

with guest stars MARIO & FRANCO, SIR CHARLES FORTE, ENZO APICELLA and FRANK SINATRA as the ones that got away! also ORSON WELLES as the sherry salesman.

THE CHILD IS FATHER OF THE MAN, WHATEVER THAT MEANS

KEITH WATERHOUSE on the eternal problem of fatherhood

MY FATHER HAS GOT A NEW BOOK, IT BOUGHT for him by My Mother. It is a Present, but, it not his Birthday. She buy it for him, because, she Hate him, because of me. (Why are you always picking on Him, it pick pick pick all day long) my Mother vouchsafed. To which that worthy volunteered (He want a good kick up the Back side.) Just because of Lego in, his Whiskey Decanter. So, therefore, she have brought him a New Book.

It is entitled, (How to Father). The author is a Dr. His name is, 'Dr. Fitzhugh Dodson'. It, the Book, is printed by 'W. H. Allen'. It cost Six Pounds. For this she could have bought, 2 sets Royal Canadian Mounted Police, 1 set Confederate Army, also 4 matchbox Cars. It relates how to bring up your children, if, you are their Father.

I have Read this book, Unknown to my Father.

It says that, you should not Hit them, but, if it make you feel better, you can Hit them. This was on p.52. I have Torn it out.

Also, that, you should Praise your child for Tidying up his room, but, it says (do not expect adult standards of room cleanliness from a nine-year-old!) I have underlined this Bit with my red porous Pen. I have done this, neatly, with a ruler. He will think it done by, the Printer, 'W. H. Allen'.

Also, that, Fathers should not Punish your child for Swearing. Instead, they have to use (extinction technique). That is, when you Swear, he not go purple, he just pretend that, he is Not Bothered. This is the (extinction technique), it stop you Swearing because, you have not made him go Purple. I have not underlined this Bit, as, I do not believe it.

The Book 382 pages long, it very interesting. If you are My Father, you should read it. It say, (Fathers tend to believe that 'all that kid needs is a good hiding.' If this naive belief were true, our prisons would not be so full of adult criminals, many of whom received a large number of 'good hidings' when they were children.) This on p.47. I have Written in the margin, (This very important, signed, The Author). He will think The Author wrote it, but, he not take any notice. He sorry when I am in Prison. I will not write to him, I will just write to 'Dr. Fitzhugh Dodson', and, he will put it in his Next Book. Just because I left my Roller Skates in, the Grand-father clock, he gave me a Good Hiding. This mean that I will go to Prison. It will make my Mother cry, but, she will bring me things. I would like, 1 pie, 1 box plastic Warders, 1 Colditz book, also 1 Bottle of poison.

It, the book, is Very Good, because it tells you, how make your Father go Purple. If you are called Jane, you are supposed to say, ('Bye, I'm off to school). Notwithstanding, your Father ripostes, (Darling, it's raining and you don't have your raincoat on). (I don't want to wear my raincoat, I hate to wear a raincoat), expostulates Jane, whereupon her Wretched Father explode, (You march right back to your room and get that raincoat. I will not let you go to school without your raincoat on a day like this). This proves that He, your father, is Loony and also Moony, because, he Go Purple.

Also, he is still Wrong, if, he say (Oh, I give up! Go on to school without your raincoat – you win), after she has Sobbed (I hate that raincoat. I won't wear it. If you make me wear it, I'll be mad at you). Her Father not go Purple but, she has still won.

But, if you are a Good Father, you Must say (You Sure

sound like you definitely don't want to wear that raincoat). You have to sound like, John Wayne. Then she say that, she does not, as, it is Tartan. Then Your Father Must Say, (I see. Well, we really have a conflict here. You don't want to wear your raincoat 'cause it's tartan, but I certainly don't want to pay a cleaning bill, and I will not feel comfortable with you getting a cold. Can you think of a solution that we both could accept? How could we solve this so we're both happy?) I not know any Fathers who talk like this, except our Scoutmaster, but, he is not a Father. But, it make your Daughter exclaim, (Maybe I could borrow Mum's car coat today). The Famous Author say this mean, that nobody has lost, but it does not, it means that Jane has won, because, she not wear her raincoat even although, it raining.

I have not underlined this Bit, as, it is about Girls. Also, I have left my Raincoat at the Swimming Baths. My Father does not know this, he would be mad also sad if he did know. He would say (You dozey little specimen). He would not say (Well, we really have a conflict here.)

Also, the printer, 'W. H. Allen', have printed that, your Father is supposed to play Educational Games with you. He supposed to ejaculate, (Here's another new game for you, Terry. It's called What Is The Best Thing To Do? Here's how it goes . . . What is the best thing to do if you accidentally break a friend's toy when you are playing at his house?) Answer: you should say, It Was Not Me. But, my Father would not play this Game. He would just say (Why you always picking your nose). I have Torn this page out. It page 103. I have put in red, This Page Missing Owing to Shortage of Paper, 'signed', W. H. Allen. He will think it was them, the printers.

Also, it, the Book, tell your Father how to make boats. This my Father would not do. He say (He already have enough Things to stock a blessed Toyshop).

If I had three wishes I would wish that, I was the Famous Author of (How to Father) I would write in this Book that, Fathers should give their children More Things, also, that when they put your Lego in the Dustbin, they should buy you some More, also, that they should not Ask you about your raincoat. This, this book does not do. It therefore Potty and also Grotty. But, it does not matter, as My Father will only throw it in the Fireplace, whilst in the same instant expostulating (This my money you have been spending, then you say I not give you enough Housekeeping). When I am in prison, I shall write a Book entitled (How To Child). It will tell you, how to Get Your Father. The printer will be 'W. H. Allen.'

Lady of Spain,
I Have Gored You

Spain has finally allowed women matadors.
HONEYSETT throws a rose

"I thought having women matadors was bad enough."

"She shows promise, eh Manuel?"

"Not bulls' ears again?"

" . . . and by then he was really dangerous so I decided to forego
the third banderilla and go straight for the kill."

The Times

A TIME TO HALT

So once more the Crown Jewels have been lost in the Wash. Yesterday's disappearance off Hunstanton of an aircraft bringing back these precious relics from a currency-earning tour in Asia calls into grave question the whole policy of "putting the Royal resources to work." We have gained a few pitiful rupees and lost an orb, a sceptre and a crown.

The public are rightly uneasy. They have hardly recovered from the shock occasioned by the disaster to the Royal Train, which was on charter to the American Bar Association. The fate of so many brave American lawyers may or may not be a cause for grief, but the loss of this Royal asset is irreparable.

Now there are reports that the Household Cavalry is being worked almost to death escorting film stars to West End premieres. Mr. Richard Burton appears to regard it as below his dignity to travel anywhere without a Sovereign's Escort. Many loyal citizens have been incensed by the spectacle of wives of American senators queening it from the Royal Box at Covent Garden. It is to be hoped that the proposal to hand over the Royal Enclosure at Ascot to Butlin's at a record fee is but the chimaera of a press agent's imagination.

Let there be no mistake. Such bruises as these to the national psyche can never be healed by financial receipts. It is no use taking desperate steps to preserve our national heritage when that heritage finishes up at the bottom of the Wash.

Daily Mail

Big Queues for Throne

"Sitting on the Throne" has become one of London's leading tourist attractions. The queue yesterday, when the rate was cut to £10 a minute, extended right round Buckingham Palace. It included a party of Eskimos with snow on their boots.

Lord Snowdon and Lord Lichfield, the royal photographers, were in attendance. They are believed to be grossing £5,000 a day each, photographing Throne-sitters. Ninety-seven per cent of their takings goes to the Treasury.

Tomorrow, at a special ceremony, "Miss World" will be crowned in the Throne-Room. The Queen will be in New Zealand for this historic occasion.

Daily Express

Sauce for the Queen!

It had to come!

From tomorrow the North Front of Buckingham Palace will carry a gigantic poster showing a bottle of tomato sauce beside a plate of sausages.

Tens of thousands of the Queen's subjects already have sauce bottles on their gable-ends. The knowledge that the Queen has turned her home into an advertisement hoarding will forge tighter the links that bind the people to the monarchy.

The Press Officer at the Palace said, "The Queen was impressed by the argument that advertising is the lifeblood of industry, so she decided that the Palace should do its bit. She was a little disappointed that the first poster had to be a sauce bottle, but it was either that or a gigantic plateful of peas."

Mr. Cyril Brash, of Brash, Topper and Garlick, advertising agents, said the sauce bottle had been specially painted by a leading Royal Academician.

"We are very pleased with the Queen for renting us this prime solus site," he said, "but not nearly so pleased as we are with ourselves."

The Morning Star

In this shameful picture gunners of the Royal Horse Artillery are firing a 21-gun birthday salute in honour of the visiting chairman of General Motors.

At £100 a bang this new facility is proving an irresistible attraction to wealthy tourists, many of whom are arranging their visits to London to coincide with their birthdays.

Workers throughout Britain are protesting at this squandering of the nation's gunpowder to gratify the vanity of capitalist bloodsuckers.

Evening Standard

LONDONER'S DIARY

Bed Service

To test the facilities in the new Paying Guests Wing at Buckingham Palace—the Queen's latest ploy in the drive for foreign currency—I sent my Girl Reporter to spend a night there. Here is her report:

As soon as I reached my gold-and-white room I rang for the Lady of the Bedchamber. For a long time nothing happened, then the Duchess of Bristol bustled in and asked what I wanted. "To be put to bed, if you please," I said. She seemed taken aback and tried to tell me that her post was really a sinecure, but I pointed out that for £100 a night I expected a bit of help with my zips.

Two Fivers

I suppose the Duchess is quite an old dear, really, but frankly she hasn't a clue on how to fold a pair of slacks. She kept rattling on about her great days in Royal service and hardly disguised her belief that she had come down in the world. She would have stopped brushing my hair at the twentieth stroke had I not instructed her to continue up to a hundred.

She told me she had never done any ironing in her life and did not propose to start now. I gave her my smalls to be washed in Malvern water and that was the last I saw of them. How much does one tip a duchess? I left two fivers on the dressing-table, with the feeling that they had been easily earned.

Daily Mirror

A Shake-up at the Castle!

The American Legion descended on Windsor Castle yesterday—and the fun was fast and furious.

For the right to hold its five-day convention at Windsor the Legion paid a fee of £50,000. So awed were many of the veterans that it was two hours before the first water "bombs" were dropped from the windows.

At night the Castle was lit by flickering flames as the Legionnaires set fire to each other's shirt tails. The sound of rapid explosions alarmed many of the Poor Knights of Windsor, who fled into the Great Park. They returned shamefaced to be told that the cause of their alarm was —exploding cigars.

Wrecked!

"Jeepers! This kinda makes up for the time you British sacked the White House," said a Korean veteran, Al Limburger, as he surveyed the wreckage in the State Rooms. "The difference is, we pay for the damage. But we don't grudge a cent, if it helps to put Britain back on her feet."

An elderly member of the Household said, "I have seen nothing like this since the days of Edward III, unless you count

The Tatler

After opening a £1 Million Tupperware Week at Kampala, Princess Anne poses with a couple of friends whose names we did not catch. As unofficial trade ambassador the Princess is utterly fearless.

the Knights of Columbus last week. The old place needed a bit of a shake-up, if you ask me. We're looking forward to the Kiwanis next week—a tribe of wild Red Indians, aren't they?"

"The Life and Loves of a Monarch," caught the guttural accents to perfection. Vanessa Redgrave twittered adequately through the roles of Mrs. Langtry, Mrs. Keppel, the Countess of Warwick and a dozen others.

The lighting up of innumerable windows to suggest naughty goings-on became both tedious and confusing.

Sound effects were at their best in the pheasant *battue*. The audience heard the birds screeching overhead, followed by salvoes of shot, and then the sound of crashing carcases, seemingly close at hand. Several of the audience claimed that they had been hit on the head by dead birds.

Daily Telegraph

Ghosts Return to Balmoral

Nearly 50,000 tourists fought their way into the grounds of Balmoral Castle, at £2 a head, to hear the first Royal *Son et Lumière* performance in aid of the National Debt.

The two-part performance featured, firstly, "The Romance of Queen Victoria and John Brown," which was a little too tepid for modern tastes and earned good-natured barracking. As Brown, Andrew Cruikshank sounded too like Sir Harry Lauder.

Orson Welles, as Edward VII in

As up go the costs of motoring again, drivers will have to face reality with

PARK

The magazine for the spent-up motorist.

INSIDE THIS ISSUE:

Car Test

ON A TORTUOUS HAIRPIN IN THE CARINTHIAN ALPS WE TEST THE NEW HOT FIVE-SEATER FROM DETROIT

EXPECTED to be launched next spring on the UK market—perhaps sooner if the weather picks up—the Pandora GT heads the list of new-generation family convertibles for 1976. It is every inch an enthusiast's car, built for the man who wants to spend time in his motor, not just house the cat or keep the anthracite in it. It's a beautiful-looking job, designed to blend in with modern traffic: equally at home and certain to turn heads among pedestrians and cyclists whether parked racily alongside the sleekest of the European competition on the outside lanes of the autostrada or just pulled up for the summer on a quiet, country lay-by.

In a gruelling, three-week programme of road tests, we put the Pandora through its paces in the municipal car-park of Rüdesfeld-im-Gleistal, two hundred metres above the tree-line and a stiff stroll of a twisty three kilometres off the notoriously crowded Flugelhorn by-pass, where three-quarters of the village is now housed for the winter in the big-engined saloons of the Bavarian carriage-trade motor industry. It's a tough test of any car's suspension and grip on the road. In the bumper-to-bumper traffic which fills this Alpine beauty spot, if just one car starts to slither the whole lot could be over the edge and into the Oppenheimer Falls. The Pandora hardly budged, though the all-independent configuration may be just a shade spongy for sports-car drivers with a perceptible tendency to rock gently in

a stiff breeze or when the nearby funicular rumbles by.

The weather, too, is exceptionally rough out there—flogging the demisters and searching out the slightest weakness in the rubber door seals or in the basic aerodynamic resistance to snow. Corrosion for drivers in these parts is a constant nightmare.

Without doubt the Pandora is a family car, with bags of room for dad, mum and the kiddies to tumble about the richly-upholstered interior without any of those irritating cricks in the neck or stiff backs which are such an embarrassment in cheaper cars after the first week or so of sitting on a motoring hol. Through-flow ventilation sees to it that there's no claustro-phobic sense of being cooped-up during an outing and the doors open smoothly if anyone should want to break the monotony and go for a stretch. The accessories are a delight with nostalgic touches like the horn which emits an authentic ''poop-poop'' and

(cont. page 44)

CLASSIFIED

1968 CORTINA, mech. unsound but good weather-proof interior in much sought-after lay-by off Paddington, conv. West End. Would swop for similar model in Abersoch or Cardigan Bay. Box 44.

WHY PAY swingeing road tax? Hit back at the Chancellor by parking on your lawn. Skilled operators will winch any saloon from the kerbside on to your property without fuss, without mess. 01-246 8090.

TWIN QUARTZ-HALOGEN matching lamps for dashboard fitting. Fills whole interior with warm light, ideal small parties, poker groups, interior picnics, etc. Most stockists.

LARGE, COMFORTABLE Bentley limousine, Wigmore Street, W.1, would make spacious bachelor flat. £25 monthly plus 5p every two hours.

Water works wonders

**A one-man tasting by
BARRY TOOK**

FOR THE WINE DRINKER TO BE TOLD that he must stop drinking wine is like telling Jimmy Hill that the FA have banned football from TV or telling David Frost they've stopped printing money.

It can happen though and sometimes does, although as an elderly friend of mine, a choleric old buffer, said when I suggested the idea to him, 'What – not drink the club claret? Why, it rinses the vital parts. Bad for the liver? Nonsense. I've had my liver hanging over my head for 25 years. Waiter, another carafe.'

And with that he expired.

Actually he didn't die from over-indulgence but from a poison-tipped dart fired from a blowpipe manipulated by a Sumatran loony in the next but one armchair.

Throw another log on the fire and I'll tell you the rest of my grisly tale. (Sound effect of log being thrown on electric fire.)

What happens when you're told you can no longer drink is that you either continue but *pretend* you've given it up, or give it up and become a 'water bore'. (Choir sings: 'Water bore where are you hi-iding.')

Water bores are as bad as wine bores but at least they have fresher breath. Their language is much the same, a mixture of jargon and lying.

'It's an impudent little water but I'm sure you'll be amused by its pretensions.'

'A couple of chaps and I have invested in a little well in the Dordogne.

The side of the valley that just soaks up the dew. Old Pierre manages it for us. Doesn't need much cultivating – they throw a dead sheep in every so often – helps the bouquet' – and so on.

Truly, people who are 'into' water are crashing bores, and in the wake of the bore comes the bottler.

As the man who blows up septic tanks for a living said, 'It might be effluent to you, mate, but sewage is my bread and butter.'

So the bottler of water.

Here the British have lagged far behind the continentals. We've all been brought up to look upon a bottle of Vichy, Vittel or Evian as de rigueur when eating in France. Malvern water has taken longer to catch on. Perhaps it's because you get it free in bars which isn't quite the same.

Some years ago French wine growers got quite angry because the government subsidy wasn't as large as that on water – to the point where one half of the population of Provence (the peasants) threw stones at the other half (the police) who retaliated with tear gas and, ironically, water cannon.

I have a photograph of my wife who was with me at the time, soaked to the skin and her eyes red with tear gas. An incident which prompted her to remark that it was a considerable improvement on most of her holiday treats. But we all have our problems, you, me and the viniculturists.

It's surprising, really, the amount of mineral water that's consumed in France, particularly when you consider the sources. Vichy evokes thoughts of Pierre Laval who admittedly looked as if he was sub-aqueous. Evian is on the shore of Lac Leman, which is a stretch of water not without charm but is roughly the consistency of mulligatawny soup.

A bleary-eyed English journalist during the recent festival of television at Montreux was heard to observe à propos the lake, 'If Christ staged his second coming here and did the walking on the water routine, the locals would say, 'Fair enough. Now let's see you try and swim in the bugger'.'

It is to be hoped that the good bottlers of Evian strain the water before they ship it out.

I'm a Perrier man myself, although I do miss Professor Hake who used to be quoted on the label, as saying words to the effect that it was jolly good stuff. I always imagined Professor Hake as a wizened, goatee-bearded yankee rather in the style of Woodrow Wilson and who while publicly supporting the Volstead Act secretly mixed his Perrier with Scotch.

Where we fall down, that is to say where the British water-bottlers fall down, is in their labels. There's no mystery, no allure in the simple statement

*"He **had** to be exhumed—we forgot to flaunt the body."*

"He came rushing up to say he'd just invented something or other and then that rolled over him."

Malvern Water – or indeed, if it exists, Budleigh Salterton Water or Bath Water.

What sells wine? Not the gunk in the bottle but the label *on* the bottle. (I commend you to Miles Kingston's piece on the subject of wine labels in Punch, September 5, 1973.)

'Château Bottled', 'Mise en bouteille dans nos caves', 'Grand Cru' and so on are fine wines even if they *are* concocted in a shed near Dunkirk. But what of water? Let's have a bang at one or two ideas for labels. How about –
'Petite Tamise; mise en bouteille dans Teddington Lock'
or
'Chateau Rotherhithe'
or
'Grand Eau de Gravesend'
or
'Putney Fumée'
or
'Mersey – Côtes de Birkenhead'
or, as an apéritif
'Ouse-o'.

And how will the water snobs describe these fine table waters – 'A trifle flinty'? – 'A young water good for laying down'? If it came from Lake Windermere perhaps they'd say, 'The 1970 rainfall produced some superlative waters in the classic style. They have depth and elegance; while they are already fine waters they will keep and develop further.' Or if it comes from the Grand Union Canal, 'An enormously full, rich water.' The Severn? 'A big, robust water with a very distinctive flavour . . . round . . . upstanding . . . a deliciously dry water.' That's the one that everyone will go for obviously, the ultimate in chic – dry water. Once the marketing campaign is under-way, Water merchants will spring up everywhere. There'll be a water supermarket in every high street and the famous Fleet Street pub El Vino will be renamed El Eau. (I know it should be El Agua but El Eau sounds sillier.)

Every good restaurant will boast its water waiter, his status being denoted by a small silver divining rod on a chain round his neck – and everybody will slosh round full of water, alert, healthy and as dull as a Comedy Playhouse.

The last word on water should go to the late Richard Dimbleby, who at the end of a long and fascinating TV programme on the subject stood in the laboratory of a Thames-side recycling plant. He watched the purified liquid dripping into a glass, picked it up, sniffed it, sipped it and drained the glass. Then he looked up and said – 'I wonder who drank that last?'

Cheers.

Black And White Minstrels

After a lengthy attempt to turn up something catchy for the citizens of Rhodesia to sing, hum or drum-beat by way of a national anthem (now that the original *God Save The Queen* is suspected of a certain irony), the Salisbury government has hit on the stirring bit from the end of Beethoven's ninth symphony, the choral. Now the search is on for an apt set of lyrics, something which, in the words of the official statement, 'reflects the spirit and determination of Rhodesia and the characteristics which pertain to the national attitude and outlook on life.' The tune, which was of course the theme from *A Clockwork Orange* and is widely expected to be of enormous appeal to Africans everywhere, does already have a set of words, those of Schiller in his *Ode To Joy*. Unfortunately, though, it is so much misguided guff and shows no understanding of a vigorous and emerging nation. It's full of stuff about all men embracing and becoming brothers and the breaking down of barriers erected by a strong-arm society. And in any case it's all in German.

You too could run a Postal Service

"First or second class?"

"That's the lot for America, Fred. Good luck."

If Sir William Ryland can play at Post Offices, why can't we? asks HONEYSETT

"Take a letter, Miss Simpson. To our Manchester office."

"Are you going to make every stamp yourself?"

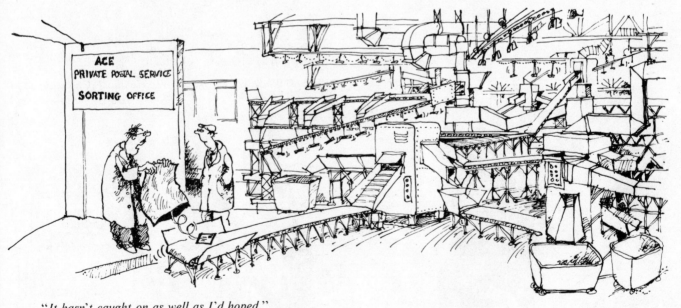

"It hasn't caught on as well as I'd hoped."

HEATH:
I'm Dreaming of a Gay Christmas

****

"When will my mother realise that I don't want to be irresistible to women!"

"And when you stick your chest out it spells 'butch'."

"Anyone we know?"

The Exotic Art of British Cooking

for Asian housewives

**With immigrant children now clamouring for
British food in the home, BBC-TV will be telling
Asian mothers this summer how to cook it.
Here's our introductory guide**

Forbidden Foods

Although British cooking may seem at first sight very different from Indian cooking, they have a lot in common. As in India, we British have our own traditional animals which it is absolutely forbidden to kill for eating. The most sacred animal of all is the horse; if anyone in this country is found eating horse meat he is subject to the most severe penalties such as raised eyebrows and a visit from the R.S.P.C.A. Other taboo animals include frogs, snails and octopus. Curiously, the taboo does not apply if other names are given to the forbidden meat, such as 'braised steak' or 'scampi'.

Sauces

Again, British cooking, like Indian cuisine, makes great use of spices, exotic herbs, dyes and other fragrant ingredients. The ones you will use most often are saffron breadcrumbs (especially for fish fingers), aromatic binding agent, permitted preservatives, artificial colouring, monosodium glutamate and added flavouring. But the genius for highly spiced cooking comes out most in British sauces, a dazzling but bewildering array of which are normally left on the table for the diner to mix his own selection from – salt, pepper, vinegar, Worcester, Dad's Favourite, HP, mint, chutney, pickle (brown and yellow), paper napkins, ketchup and mustard. Mustard, by the way, will come as a shock to anyone used to nothing hotter than a Madras curry, so be careful.

Ketchup is made from the tomato, used, apart from sauces, to give the flavouring and colour to the popular baked bean, to accompany spaghetti rings – not to be confused with an Italian dish of similar name – and to make the one soup native to Britain, a deep lustrous crimson broth known as Soupe du Jour.

Any list of normally reliable sauces would not be complete without a mention of the incredible variety of sauces available for puddings. They are called custard.

Meat and Potatoes

The great majority of British main courses are a mixture of meat and potato, which regional and historical factors have moulded into a wonderful range of possible permutations. It would take a lifetime to master all the variations, but some of the most common are:

Lancashire Hot Pot, in which the potatoes are sliced and lie on top of the meat, thus disguising it.

Irish Stew, in which the potatoes sink to the bottom.

Shepherd's Pie, in which the potatoes are mashed and slashed and left on top.

Cottage Pie, which is yesterday's shepherd's pie.

Sausages and Mash, in which the meat is served separately from the potato, in a small edible balloon.

Rissole, in which the meat is indistinguishable from the potato.

When the British feel the need for a change from meat-and-potato dishes, they turn to a meat-and-flour dish. The most famous are roast beef and Yorkshire pudding, pork pie, toad in the hole, steak pudding, Forfar bridies, veal and ham pie, Cornish pasty.

Eggs

It would be wrong to assume from British cafes that eggs can only be deep fried in black oil. The British housewife will also boil, scramble, bake, beat and soufflé them; the result is called an omelette. We also have an equivalent to the Chinese hundred-year-old egg, though the Scotch egg is normally left to age longer.

Scottish Cooking

The Scots have an ancient and quite distinct tradition of their own, which is to do what the English do but substitute oatmeal for potatoes; hence 'oat cuisine'.

Vegetables

It is often said that the British divide their vegetables into two categories, those that are green (which they boil) and those that are other colours (which they boil). This is most unfair; British housewives are well aware of other techniques for cooking veget-ables – for instance, stewing and simmering. Try cooking leeks, the extremely flavoursome national plant of Wales. (But do not cook daffodils, thistles or shamrocks. These are usually served cold and called green salad.)

Further Reading

Like your own *Kama Sutra* and *Bhagavad Gita*, we too have our own sacred books of British cookery and it is customary to have a shelf filled with the works of Elizabeth David, Theodora Fitzgibbon, Ambrose Heath and the blessed Robert Carrier. Like your own *Kama Sutra*, these are left unread, and unpractised.

Meanwhile, see you again in the summer, when you will learn how to cook such classic British dishes as Warmed Up Motorway Service Area Roast Lamb Slices, Paella TV Dinner For Two, Hamburger in a Basket, Fresh Garden Dew-Picked Minty Peas i' th' Packet, Handy Quik 'N' Easy Toad i' th' Hole, Sliced Bread and Marge Pudding and that greatest of all British classics, Golden Fried Fish with Crispy Style Potato Slices. Till then, good-bye and good luck!

"Are we still supposed to be in ferment?"

ПРАВДА

Газета основана 5 мая 1912 года В. И. ЛЕНИНЫМ

Орган Центрального Комитета КПСС

№ 89 (20693) • Воскресенье, 30 марта 1975 г. • Цена 3 коп.

LEONID MURRAY: MASS MURDERER AND 'TUC' BOSS!

Keep this man out of Russia!

From London Correspondent MILOS KINGTONOV

"THE MOST WICKED man in Britain". "A symbol of all that is evil". These are just two of the epithets lavished on Leonid Murray by such fearless English commentators as Peter Simple and John Braine. At considerable risk to their own safety, dissident British writers in their own independent newspaper the *Daily Telegraph*

have exposed the mass terror methods used by Leonid Murray in his iron rise to an impregnable position in the British system. And now we learn that this man may be trying to visit Soviet Russia. *It is a visit we cannot allow to take place.*

Russian readers who may not have heard the name of this vile man before should realise that Murray is the head of the feared and hated TUC, the apparatus which rules the workers of Britain with an iron hand. Outwardly, the TUC is merely an association which exists to safeguard workers' rights, but it has developed over the last few years into a highly efficient machinery which first started dabbling in politics and then established such power in the land that both the main political parties tremble in awe of it. (Britain, remember, has two political parties. This seeming impossibility is explained by the fact that they take it in turns to rule, being at an earlier stage of development than Russia. Britain is basically already a one-party state; the difference is that it is occasionally a different party.)

A comparison between the TUC and Soviet workers' associations is of no help. We in the USSR think of trade unions, quite rightly, as associations which work endlessly for better conditions for workers, to help implement the wishes of our leaders and to promote efficiency and understanding between different industries. The TUC—and my readers will find this hard to believe—

seeks to impose its own will on the government by promoting nation-wide "strikes" (an English word meaning to sabotage production by staying at home, for which there is no Russian equivalent), by infiltrating its members into the political parties, by undermining the national effort and even by refusing to obey British laws. And the man who controls this unlawful and monstrous power is Leonid Murray, the man who wishes to visit Russia!

But this is not all. In a personal capacity, Murray has been responsible for the ruination of harmless, prominent individuals in British life, driving them into bankruptcy and sometimes premature death. Ruthlessly he drove his predecessor, the statesmanlike Viktor Feather, from office and sent him into exile in the so-called House of Lords (an "old people's home" in London where men with independent ideas and views are sent out of harm's way). Over several years he implacably fought for the toppling of the popular leader, Edward Heath; Heath is now a broken has-been exiled in Spain. It is even rumoured that TUC agents may have been behind the sinister disappearance of British ex-politician John Stonehouse. He has brought terror and destruction to State industries in Britain, halting production and bleeding the economy. Is this the kind of man we seriously wish to listen to?

His defenders will smilingly tell you

that he is a worker, elected to serve workers, interested only in the working man's problems. The facts are rather different. Murray has never been a worker. He was educated in a socially privileged grammar school, he spent three years at the elitist University of Oxford, and he went straight into the ranks of the TUC from college. This man has never done a day's work in his life. He is no more equipped to speak for the British worker than Attila the Hun (a famous German revisionist). Beneath the bloodstains on Murray's hands you will find, not callouses, but the soft white skin of the dictator. His election was brought about by the inner secret workings of the apparatus. To talk of a democratic election is to mock words.

Let me leave you with the verdict of the British poet and philosopher Bernard Levin, scourge of abuses in the British gas industry, tireless fighter for nobler English prose and indomitable critic of some aspects of South African society. "This man represents a danger to all we hold dearest and finest in British culture." Those words were in fact applied to a British TV announcer, but they hold equally good of Leonid Murray, tyrant, bully and saboteur. Let us hope that if ever he does dare to set his feet in Moscow, the peace-loving peoples of that great city will show a massive demonstration of disapproval.

UNDER THE GREENPAPER TREE

Home Economy for the Very Rich

Baking your own bread, brewing your own beer, isn't much use if you're trying to save thousands of pounds. Here is the first ever luxury do-it-yourself guide.

MAKING YOUR OWN CHAMPAGNE

Imported champagne has become so expensive that you should think seriously about producing champagne, at a great saving, on your own estate. Home brewed champagne kits are now available at good chemists such as Harrods or Fortnums, but you will also need to open up that old unused cellar to stock with the bottles which you will save from your next party. For corks, get a friend with a Spanish address to look round his property; there are bound to be enough cork trees to supply you.

The process is simplicity itself—a couple of fermentations, a gradual tilting of the bottle to remove the sediment and a final addition of sugar to make it *brut* or *doux*. Voilà! Your own champagne at half the price, and the innate satisfaction that comes from knowing that it wasn't made in a French factory but in your very own home, by your very own staff.

Remember, it is illegal to call it champagne if you sell it. If your home is open to the public and you are thinking of installing an "Estate Brewed Champagne Kiosk—As Drunk From The Eighth Duchess's Slipper", it would be wiser to call it Gettycham.

HOME-GROWN CAVIAR

The sturgeon is a friendly little fish and would grace any spare pond or converted indoor swimming pool with its antics. In winter, simply remove the female roes and serve as an hors d'œuvre. If you are not used to this procedure it can be tricky and it may be necessary to kill the fish first. Send for our free booklet: "Sturgeon Breeding for Fun, Profit and Being One Up on the Lichfields".

Remember, it is illegal to call your product Beluga Caviar unless of course your name is Beluga.

SMOKING YOUR OWN SALMON

Even if you do not have your own salmon stream, it is still cheaper to buy fresh salmon and smoke it yourself than get the expensive shop-sold version. All you need is a spare oak tree, to make the fragrant woodfire.

Smoked salmon needs little attention; if you have Lord Lucan hiding on your estate, it's the sort of thing he could easily fill in his time with.

Remember, it's illegal to call the result Best Scotch Smoked Salmon, unless of course you have soaked it in Scotch first.

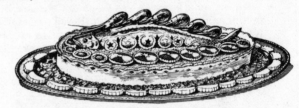

DOING YOUR OWN PUDDING

Set aside a small corner of your kitchen garden for a fruit bed and a small cow, and you can have instant strawberries and cream the summer through.

BE YOUR OWN CHAUFFEUR

A considerable saving can be effected by dispensing with your chauffeur and driving the car yourself, which is done from the front right-hand corner of the inside. (There is a special door provided for access.) The usual objection is that this wastes valuable *Financial Times* reading time, but this has now been met by our new daily FT Cassette service, which provides you with all the world's main financial news read by Peter Ustinov and John Gielgud. It also includes the main points from other papers, on request. When sending in this form, indicate which extra services you would like:—

- ☐ Ten-second summary of the point Bernard Levin is making today
- ☐ Best *Guardian* misprint
- ☐ Weather forecast for Jamaica, St. Moritz and Morocco
- ☐ Market movements in Impressionist paintings

HOME-SPUN TWEEDS

Now is the time to think about making your own clothes; the cost of importing ten old crofters' wives from the Hebrides will be more than offset by the cheapness of their tailoring. Be careful not to land yourself with Gaelic-only speakers, which also applies if you are assembling your own gramophone.

"Your financial advisors have arrived, Mr. Jeremy."

TEN FURTHER HINTS

★ Why not turn that abandoned conservatory or studio into a greenhouse and grow your own mangoes?

★ Safeguard your favourite Van Gogh or Constable by putting mirror glass in front of it. Result: a beautifully framed mirror, a masterpiece safe from the burglar's gaze and an investment quietly growing in value.

★ Install an artificial ski-slope down the back staircase —save £££s on winter holidays.

★ Give up trying to buy that knighthood.

★ Don't get eggs from the shop—set up your own quail or seagull range.

★ Register your yacht under the Panamanian flag and get good tax discounts on your next "business" trip to Cannes.

★ Grow asparagus in the Sèvres showcase.

★ Keep healthy with good, old-fashioned exercises. I recommend the "Tzarist Air Force Keep-Fit Course" (from all good emigré bookshops).

★ Convert an unused pair of spinets into a tasteful pair of stereo speakers.

★ Turn over the roof garden to the cultivation of *cannabis sativa*, a delicate bloom with a pleasing scent.

"He's not to be disturbed until after The Magic Roundabout!"

Transfer
in Haste,
Repent
at Leisure

Those fond fathers who rushed to beat
Capital Transfer Tax by putting everything in their offspring's name may be
living to regret it, warns MAHOOD.

*"What did we **do** today? Traded in the
company Rolls for **that!**"*

"And this, God help us, is the boardroom!"

CONTINUED OVERLEAF

"And you can tell the shop stewards there's plenty more where that came from!"

"I'll come in when Mr. Rodney has finished *his* dictation!"

"And now, those against?"

Stand up for Women's writers!

KEITH WATERHOUSE'S autumn book catalogue

A MAJOR AMERICAN PUBLISHER has struck a blow for women's rights (announces a major American publisher). A set of guidelines has gone out to each of its 8,000 authors – more authors, you might think, than there are in the world – designed to encourage the equal treatment of men and women.

Said guidelines list the kind of patronising phrases it is now considered that no self-respecting major American publisher can be doing with, such as 'the fair sex,' 'his better half', and 'sweet young thing'. The line is also drawn at 'scatter-brained females,' 'fragile flowers,' 'goddesses on pedestals,' 'hen-pecking shrews,' 'frustrated spinsters,' 'women drivers,' and 'nagging mothers-in-law'.

This edict is not aimed, as you would imagine, at romantic novelists, who are free to go on putting goddesses on pedestals until the cows come home. Surprisingly, the ban applies only to writers of reference works, text-books, children's books and educational manuals – all 8,000 of them.

The question that swims into the mind is: what kind of reference works, text-books, children's books and educational manuals have this major American publisher's 8,000 authors been writing, for heaven's sake? Sweet young things? Fragile flowers? Henpecking shrews? The mind, although ever-eager to improve itself with reference works and educational manuals, boggles.

I have none of these volumes to hand and have been unable to buy any (they were probably all pulped when the house turned over its new leaf). Luckily, however, I was able to salvage a copy of the major American publisher's last catalogue before the new leaf was turned over, and I append a few extracts. Eight thousand authors must be sighing for the halcyon days when a little woman was only a little woman, but a good history of the struggle for women's rights was a text-book . . .

The New Etymological Universal Dictionary. THE dictionary for dumb broads. Everything is arranged in alphabetical order so that any peanut-brained chick can look up all the long words she's too stupid to understand. If she can't spell (and what woman can?) the man in her life should be happy to help out, provided she moves her ass and fixes him that d-r-y Martini. P.S. for dum-dums: don't worry about what 'etymological' means, honey. It's just a word the fellas kick around in the locker-room.

The 'Edison' Electricians' Encyclopedia. Does your mother-in-law nag? Bat her over the head with this superbly bound, 2000-page comprehensive manual for the home electrician. Includes diagrams of alternating and direct current circuit, cross-section of an ordinary storage battery, detailed explanation of Faraday's Law of Electrolysis, and full-colour gatefold of a Playgirl Of The Month hugging a Hertz Oscillator between her bosoms. Boy! Does she ever try harder! And a bonus for electricity buffs – there's a special section for the little woman, under 'Fuses.' It says: 'DON'T TOUCH!!!'

Careers for Women. A MUST for frustrated spinsters who are too frowdy-dowdy to get a man and so have to get their kicks from holding down a man-size job. Weird! But too, there's plenty here for full-blooded femmes who need pin-money. Read how YOU can get to the top by hitching up your skirt. How Harriet Beecher Stowe's pillow-talk made her a best-selling author. How Marie Curie wiggled her derriere and won a Nobel prize. How Florence Nightingale fluttered her eyelids and became a world-famous nurse.

The Lady's Bible. Limp leather. Same as our regular Bible, but with all the cuss words missed out.

Gas Turbine Theory, new revised edition. Fellas! Are YOU married to a henpecking shrew? Show her who wears the pants by getting ahead of your rivals in the gas turbine game. Yes sir! Testimonials show that *Gas Turbine Theory, new revised edition* has saved hundreds of marriages. Professor Alvin Shoemaker, head of the Thermodynamics Department at Nixon University (Fla), writes: 'To me, my wife was a goddess on a pedestal. It came as a shock when I heard she was fooling around with the janitor. But I guess I had it coming – I couldn't afford to buy her the pretty things she wanted. Then I studied *Gas Turbine Theory, new revised edition*. It changed my life. Karen came back to me as soon as I got my professorship. I earn so much from knowing about gas turbine theory that we're a two-home, two-car family. And guess who's back up on that pedestal!'

Potter's '*Diseases of the Fair Sex*.' The established medical textbook on all the ills the little woman is heiress to. Covers every female complaint, real and imaginary, including: Frigidity. Convenient Headaches. So-called Labour Pain. Obesity. Hysterics. Fainting. Shoplifting. Blackheads.

Gibbon's *Decline and Fall of the Roman Empire Re-told For Women*. Simplified version of the classic, printed in a special flimsy paper edition so that the fragile flower of the family doesn't strain anything when lifting it down from the shelves.

The Sweet Young Thing's Advanced Driving Manual. Everything the woman driver needs to know, including: How to back up off a lawn. Hand-signals explained with easy diagrams a kid of three could understand. How to park in a 60-foot gap. What rear mirrors are for. How to break it to your better half that you've been in another pile-up. Difference between petrol tank and water tank explained. How to get a cut-price re-spray by wearing a V-neck sweater and no bra. Windscreen wipers made easy.

The Dizzy Dame's World Atlas and Gazeteer. Proves with coloured maps that Africa is NOT in Europe, how West Berlin comes to be in Eastern Germany, why you cannot drive from Dublin to Stratford-on-Avon, and how to remember where Naples is by imagining Italy as a cute little boot. Difference between latitude and longitude explained. Published in association with the Ladies' Coffee Morning Committee of the National Geographical Society.

The Hussies are Coming, the Hussies are Coming! Is the day dawning when women will demand equality in a man's world – joining our clubs, sharing our locker-room jokes? A major American publisher thinks it is. Read his crackpot theory for laughs – but keep this hilarious book out of sight of you-know-who's baby blue eyes!

"You mean we'll never know the ending?"

"How old hat it seems now."

"By being a criminal you have disgraced yourself,
disappointed your family, and made a lot of
people think of you as a very rotten person. I feel
that you have suffered enough."

Even as the cinemas fill to the sound of Walt Disney's intrepid voyagers to *The Island at the Top of the World*, there sets out another expedition to an island altogether closer to the bottom of the world...

VOYAGE TO WEIRDLAND

A tradition in my native Norway tells of an island to the south-west where our ancestors used to go and trade with the natives, or marry them, or eat them, according to their fancy. I decided to duplicate one of those early voyages and see if there really was such an island, inhabited by— as the legend suggests— people of taste and breeding.

We set out from Bergen in one of our funny old ships, powered by solar energy just like in the old days before oars were invented. There were five of us: Nils, Trygve, Aage, Haakon, and me, plus a beautiful dish named Turid — ostensibly for her grasp of anthropology, but really because you can't go anywhere nowadays without a beautiful dish.

After three days, we sighted land. So there _was_ something there! We were terribly excited and ate a lot of herring.

The place seemed at first to be uninhabited. Presently we met a lonely psychiatrist under a tree, who invited us to go mad for the sake of our sanity. Otherwise, we might go crazy.

Further south, he told us, were a great many knot cases whom he had personally driven sane. Eagerly, we set sail.

Several hundred herrings later, we entered the southern part of the island. Yes, there were people here, and yes, they were the same people! No, they had not changed over the centuries! We heard again those terse cries that had so impressed our forefathers.

Turid was kidnapped! Of course, that always happens when you take a dish to a primitive island. Natives never have respect for women.

We learned that she had been taken by unscrupulous black-and white slavers called Eric and Julia and was even now taking part in some hideous tribal rite.

Happily, it was not Turid who was selected for sacrifice. The unlucky maiden was led away, weeping. Sometimes, these poor girls have to wear the crown of shame for a whole week! Incredible barbarism...

CHEERS! CHEERS! CHEERS! CHEERS! CHEERS!

The islanders are in the habit of congregating at certain sacred establishments which are set to explode periodically. While waiting, they work themselves up to a kind of aggressive religious fervor, drinking a local concoction which they call beer. It bears little resemblance to real beer, being both stronger and weaker if you know what I mean.

After the explosion, a high priest evaluates the destruction. If it is a very great destruction, he utters the magic word "deplorable" three times.

DEPLORABLE DEPLORABLE DEPLORABLE

Both commerce and sport can be found at the many "supermarkets", where shoppers attempt to outrun a man with a rubber stamp. In another game, the merchants hide the food and the customers try to guess how much it will cost when it comes back. The merchants then pretend to be very sad.

Who ruled this island? Not "The Queen"— her subjects all seemed to be horses. We concluded that there was no one...

ARISE SIR SAUSAGE

We found the climate pleasant —nothing like as dark and cold as Norway. The aborigines like it, too; at least, it pleases them to talk about it.

NOT VERY NICE!
DREARY!
HORRIBLE!
WICKED!

The tribesmen were busy with "defence cuts", which as far as we could tell meant throwing away weapons which were no good to them anyway, being mostly in other countries or floating about uselessly in the sea. They remain, however, a warlike people, judging by the way they drive their chariots.

What, then, does the future hold for this appalling — sorry — this appealing race? Ought we to leave them in their present condition of lovable savagery? We thought so. Something has to be preserved. In any case, we had eaten all our herring and had to leave — alas, without Turid, who had fallen in love with a stockbroker. I have not explained about stockbrokers, have I? But this is only the trailer. See the film (U).

NÅR GÅR BÅTEN?
HVOR ER SPISESALEN?
HVOR FÅR JEG RØKESILD?
KAN JEG BLI BEDØVET?
SO LONG, CHAPS!
KAN JEG FÅ BYTTE KØYE?

So, as the pound sinks slowly into the sea, we say farewell to Weirdland — not much wiser and very, very hungry.

THE SAVE-GREAT-BR

Will You Let This Wonderful Old Country Decay and Crumble? It *can* be saved.

THE PROBLEMS

* infested by unions
* north and west sides in poor condition
* unable to pay its way
* open to rain, damp, cold and scattered showers
* present owners inexperienced to cope
* £5,000,000,000,000 needed at once

This is an age when the old and the beautiful come under attack every day. Now, more than ever, it is urgent to preserve what we have not yet lost. Many fine and handsome old countries have been destroyed and are no more—Serbia, Styria, Bohemia, the Austro-Hungarian Empire, Latvia and the Ukraine. Now Great Britain, one of the oldest and finest, faces the very real danger of decay or demolition.

LIVING HISTORY

Not one of the biggest or most imposing of countries, Great Britain nevertheless has a unique charm all its own. Standing near the main route from Scandinavia to France, but hidden from it by a large moat, Great Britain has been the home for generations of the Windsor family (previously known as the Hanover, Stuart, Tudor and Plantagenet family). The buildings themselves go back to Saxon times, though there are numerous Industrial Revolution and modern additions, such as the world-famous slums of Glasgow and the amusing folly called Centrepoint. The grounds, which are some 800 miles long, are unique; unlike the grounds of nearby France or Germany, they are completely unplanned and retain a fresh lack of pattern. If one is lucky, one may spot a herd of disgruntled farmers grousing under the trees.

TODAY

But in these hard times it is becoming increasingly difficult for the Windsor family, and their staff of some 56 million, to keep the place as it should be. Crippled by European taxes, increasingly indebted to Arab creditors, the occupants of Great Britain are no longer in a position to carry out even the basic repair work that the place needs. In twenty years time it may be too late to save what an earlier writer has described as "a sceptred isle". The millions of visitors who come every year to pay their £326 air fare to shuffle round the hallowed precincts of this old country are not enough to subsidise even its running costs. This winter the lights are low and the heating turned off in a desperate effort to save that little more.

Help must come now.

"*A mighty rescue operation is needed to save this wonderful and romantic spot*"—**Herman Kahn**

"*Unless something is done now, the whole place will fall to the ground at 11.35 on July 14, 1981*"—**Hudson Institute**

"*I cannot stress too strongly the need to preserve this very ancient, very unique and very convenient stopping-off place*"—**Henry Kissinger**

"*I have given generously. Will you too, please?*"—**The Shah of Iran**

AIN APPEAL FUND

The fabric is not beyond repair. Action now could save it for poste
But we must act fast and start rebuilding _now_.

THE SOLUTIONS

✳ inject massive reinforced capital _now_

✳ replace old-style laissez faire (crumbling badly) with central support

✳ remove remaining coal deposits

✳ modernise the Great Hall of Westminster (badly out of date)

✳ restock grounds with foodstock

✳ pay the staff a living wage

These are just the things that must be done now. They alone will cost a zillion pounds a day. But if Great Britain is to be saved in the future for the world to enjoy, we must look ahead. We must, for example, eradicate the unions which even now are gnawing at its foundations. In moderation, they are friendly little creatures quite welcome in the house, but in quantity they can become rapacious and highly dangerous. We must restore the gold to the old country, at present at an all-time low. We must replace the antiquated and inefficient machinery serving Great Britain's demands—even now Lord Stokes, ancestral head of the estate's transport fleet, is asking for another billion pounds an hour simply to stop it rusting while out of use. But above all we must stop Great Britain simply falling down and this can only be done by supporting the edifice with lots and lots and lots and lots and lots of money.

What can I do to help save Great Britain?

Easy. Join the Save-Great-Britain Fund in one of the following capacities.

Full Life Member Send a trillion pounds now and become a permanent life member, entitling you to a badge saying "I've Visited Great Britain", a photograph of one of the Windsor family and a daily newsletter reporting the dangers to the place called the _Daily Telegraph_.

Honorary Life Member For a billion pounds, you can receive a knighthood and free parking space in many parts of Great Britain. Your money will be used to shore up the underdeveloped north-east wing.

Annual Member If you send a million pounds every year, you will receive a vellum, gold-illuminated, hand-written receipt.

Associate Member For a mere hundred thousand pounds, you can have a play staged in one of Great Britain's many famous theatres, for about four days.

Temporary Associate Member This entitles you to advance booking facilities for some of the many famous products home-grown on Great Britain's own estates, such as bread, sugar, beef, coal and cheap pound notes. (There may be delays of up to nine months in delivery.)

Temporary Associate Twenty-four Hour Membership Necessary, unfortunately, to see our daring, adult programme of films such as "Too Hot To Handle" and "A Very Serious Grown-Up Film About Sex For Education Purposes Nudge Nudge".

Send your money _now_ to: Save-Britain-Fund
PO Box 41a Cayman Islands

Passing through
David Taylor talks to Telly Savalas

'YEAH? That's nice. For me also *Kojak* has been terrific. Just so long as I don't get to spend the next five years of my life sucking lollipops in my sunspecs and a sharp suit, asking half of New York *who loves you, baby?* The thing has to develop, in order to stay real, am I right?' Yes indeed, Theo. Telly (which is got from Aristotle, don't ask how) Savalas has already developed the US make-believe TV cop away from the bolt-together run of world-weary, fat, blind or lame investigators and created in the earthily human, ugly but cute Detective Lootenant Theo Kojak an authentic 14th Precinct tough with a sweet tooth and nature, with a head like a turnip and a wise-cracky line in Graeco-Yiddish Brooklyn patois, however that shapes, pussycat. You figure this is getting hard to follow, catch *Kojak* any Monday. It is police documentary played for laughs, a

witty sit-com with stiffs. Telly has spent time with New York's Finest: 'They're as likely to bump you on the head as lend a dime for the Subway. It could go either way.'

It is a little after nine and starving cold outside in Curzon Street where he's doing a short take for a feature movie, *Inside Out*. It has him cast as a smart opportunist of the nice kind which is easy because that's pretty well him for real. His mother (who keeps on telling him he's gorgeous) married Nicholas who made the fortune in tobacco, lost the lot and made another pile in the bakery business. They lived at Garden City, Long Island with grandma who lasted till 108, Telly's four brothers (George it is who plays Stavros) and a sis. Telly majored in psychology at Columbia after the war and joined the US State Department Information Service, only they weren't that eager to inform on the foreign service wireless the way that Telly figured they should. 'It was Moscow had the real professionals who could have made it big on Madison Avenue. There was no way we could push, or slant, and, such is the world, that kind of sweet innocent naivety makes you look one sucker and that really burns me inside. So I leave and I'm with ABC suddenly doing my kind of Voice of America and by now what you're trying to figure is where did this guy learn to act?' By accident is the answer, by being asked to find somebody for a theatrical buddy to do a European judge part and, thwarted, turning up for the audition himself. 'You'll be a glorious actor,' said ma.

Burt Lancaster recognised it too and gave him the big break in *The Birdman of Alcatraz*. It got him an Academy nomination and Savalas, a natural gambler, was on his winning streak. 'Today I have a home in California (bought off Frank Sinatra) because I'm obliged to be there, or else sitting it out in New York, and it is London I want to live in. There's not much speculative about that, I'll be here.

'If you really want to know where I got stuck on the English it was at the UN watching some little guy from the UK delegation—he'd be about fifth banana—put down Vyshinsky with some devastating, caustic and witty invective of the kind was really needed. I wanted my kids brought up in his kind of country.'

Savalas has been married three times and still gets on, determined that whatever he can't be as a husband doesn't mean he can't stay friends with the people he's made children with (four so far). We pause for him to be photographed with a bunch of primary school admirers – 'How old are you, sweetheart, sixteen? Oh, you're seven, well that's nice. Here we go, be sure to look sweet now, boom. Good-bye, gang.' Reaction and affection from the UK he loves, it's special. When a take outside is ruined by a cab-driver stopping in the middle of the shot ('Happy days, Theo, seen you on the telly last night!') it is Savalas who takes it in best part, 'because without some lucky breaks, what is there? I don't mind all of the razzmattazz. You keep right on going till you collapse, you owe fate that much. I love all of the mail from the UK. It isn't all asking where you can buy those stick-on red beacons ride with me on top of the Chrysler. You have to live by your wits in the movie business and, well, it suits me. You don't have to forget the responsibilities – like to make sure the villains are good and nasty so the kids don't imitate, push it home that schizophrenia and villainy go hand in hand – but of course it's a lot of fun and if *Kojak* comes across real I'm delighted.'

Telly Savalas, who loves you? Yeah? Terrific.

...and Victor Borge

VICTOR BORGE, who also has trouble with his spelling, which is why, perhaps, he gets so very few letters on occasion, is an accomplished pianist since childhood who spent three hours only with the Berlitz Language School, after which his teacher spoke much better Danish than he did English. So he turned to practising by himself in a darkened cinema, mouthing the sound-tracks of an unintelligible, three-feature, fifteen-cents programme until today, when he could be taken for Humphrey Bogart with the wrong set of teeth in. Neither has Victor Borge been disposed to pursue his music with a sober seriousness; he finds that dull. And so, to pianists especially, who are familiar with the hazards which surround, for example, the opening chords of Tchaikovsky's Piano Concerto when tackled from a highly-polished stool, anticipation alone of Victor Borge at full stretch losing the necessary purchase on his trouser-seat and skidding clean off the treble end is enough to have them helpless even as they're booking the tickets for his show. Box-offices have remarked on this.

Victor Borge swears that he's seen this particular mishap occur in concert, for real. He has witnessed, too, an unfortunate soloist collapse after five bars and pass away; the world is not yet ready for such a routine. And so his own is confined to trapping his fingers beneath the lid, to larking about with much-revered melodies, to performing through a series of carefully-paced interruptions, off the cuff, off the script, the product entirely of his own extempore wit and talent for slapstick, blended with skilful mimicry and a genuine dexterity on the keys. It is, in short, an hilarious turn and one that has had him made a knight three times in Scandinavia so that 'already I am a

89

a valley whether it wouldn't have much preferred to be a river or what I might have done if I'd been born in China. For some reason I don't know, when I put my fingers on a piano keyboard they go to more or less the right places; and so I either have to be a pianist or a piano-tuner. I don't think you can decide so much in life. You can't decide to be tall for instance. Neither, of course, can you hope to persuade everybody that what you are doing is what you ought to be doing. There are people who are colour-blind, there are people who are tone-deaf. You cannot argue with them. What I try to do is to mix in parts of my performance which will appeal also to those who know nothing of music. I don't believe in any élite. What I am chiefly aware of is the responsibility, especially in a television studio where you are obliged somehow to justify the provision of so much equipment. Generally I prefer to perform before an audience, live. It would of course look foolish to perform dead. I suppose that there is, after all, a special satisfaction in performing alone. Of course, just lately I am a one-man act with two people. It is very useful to have somebody else because there are just so many things you can do on your own with a piano. Just as in ballet you can go on your heels or on your toes, pick up the girl, it's still ballet. No, but the main thing was to get away from the predictable. For too long, also, it has been usual in music, during a concerto, say, just to sit and to play. Why shouldn't you talk also? It's more personal, more interesting. Excuse me once more because there is someone at the door.' Enter a bell-hop with a wardrobe case. 'That is my wife,' declares Borge, 'put her down please, I'll unpack her later.'

whole weekend.' Yet he insists that it isn't difficult.'If it were difficult, I couldn't do it. I don't believe that anybody does things that are difficult. Of course, for me it would be difficult to have been Winston Churchill. Probably he found it easy. Now what was I going to say just then? It must have been important, why else would I bring in Churchill? Excuse me, please, while I answer the telephone. Probably it is the White House.

'Ah yes, now, what everybody wants to know is whether I wouldn't rather have been a serious pianist. This I can't answer because it is like asking a mountain or

And so it goes on, nonsensically ill-disciplined, through a detailed chat upon his comic techniques and expressed, oddly, almost entirely in culinary terms; through a series of philosophical imponderables, assorted aphorisms much to his taste. And particularly refreshing was the total lack of any bogus star-quality sheen to Victor Borge, not a man to mention glamour, cash, or the basic happiness of his audience. The absent-minded dottiness is his nature, making him very good company indeed.

HONEYSETT.

UP THE MATTERHORN

with VINCENT MULCHRONE

I CONFESS I HAVE MIXED feelings about the decision of the Swiss Government to build a WC half way up the Matterhorn. It'll be a loo with an unrivalled view. But is this what travel has come to?

Take Whymper. Or, if you take the view that he cut the rope, don't take Whymper. When Whymper made his ascent a man had to do what a man had to do. If a chap was holding onto the Matterhorn with an ice-axe in one hand, and doing what he had to do with the other, it's obvious to me that he didn't have a hand spare to cut loose a couple of Swiss mountain guides.

But it's a long way from that controversy, which sullied fair Albion's name, to actually constructing a WC half way up the mountain. The Swiss, far and away more practical than their German cousins, say it is a sanitary necessity to cope with the sheer numbers of people conquering the Matterhorn with the apparent ease and density of commuters mounting the stairs of a No. 4 bus.

One gets the deflating impression that the Matterhorn has been reduced to a schoolgirl's PT exercise, and the WC the point where the Mother Superior says, 'Better make sure, girls,' much as my own mother told me to 'make sure' before embarking on a 70-mile coach journey to Blackpool.

The reassuring thing is that the Swiss generally know what they are doing. If they are building a lavatory half way up the Matterhorn it is because the volume of traffic on the easy slope needs a certain amount of relief in decent privacy. Red hot on privacy, the Swiss.

I have some sympathy with this view because I once found myself among an odd pack of tourists strung out on a jungle trail in Papua, cursed (me, that is, not the trail) with the local witch-doctor's revenge. With a speed which became legendary among my cannibal bearers I could take a tangent into the jungle and re-join the trail with my shorts buttoned up before being overtaken by a splendidly built lady who follows the Wharfedale Harriers. (Only a remarkable sense of sportsmanship prevents her from *leading* the hounds.)

Anyway, it's probably too late to worry about a loo half way up the Matterhorn. Climb a good way up Everest these days and what do you find? A first class hotel offering whiffs of oxygen should the final ascent onto the bar stool prove too much.

What most travel writers dare not tell, I shall now fearlessly reveal. It is that most of the 'wild' places on earth have already been blown. Take, if you care, Snowdon. It fell to my lot, as a young reporter, to acquire several

"Sorry—I'm fighting inflation."

doses of flu waiting through the special wetness of a wet Welsh night for rescue teams to bring injured climbers down from what seemed like a thousand different difficult ascents of Snowdon.

Those who made it found, at the summit, a caff dispensing tea and rock cakes and ice cream for people who had chosen to make the ascent by the well-proven railway. I came to understand both lots, though never the ones who climbed alongside the railway track, which somehow seemed sneaky.

Show me an adventure holiday, and I'll show you the loo, or the caff, or the safe, scheduled flight at the end of it. The ad says 'Get away from it all in little-known Zurp. Ride the wild Zurpian hills on sturdy Zurpian ponies. Join the Zurpian peasants as they dance their heady Zurpolkas, quaffing flagons of their fiery Zurpolsky.' The smaller print, intended for your wife, says that Zurp-Hols villas have mod. con. to Weybridge standards, and that your courier is a Cordon Bleu gel who can make you feel you've never left the Home Counties.

Cross the plain from Delhi to Dehra Dun, and climb to the old hill station of Mussoorie only to be told that Sunday's lunch is always roast beef and Yorkshire pudding, and you begin to doubt the legacy left by the Raj. From Peshawar to Pindi, in a technically dry Moslem state, you can still get a stiff burra peg, or something Simla, which sets at nought your efforts to secrete your duty-free hard stuff in your pyjamas.

Off you go up the Khyber Pass, where the old regiments chiselled their precarious presence, crests and mottoes, into the granite they fought over. You may tread the village street where Marco Polo passed, and watch the tribeswomen buy five .303 cartridges, bundled in an elastic band, much like the afterthought buying of chocolate bars at the check-out desk of any supermarket in Britain. What spoils the illusion is the next shelf, which is full of cans of tepid Coke.

Come in low over Ayre's Rock, a great, purple boil smack in the middle of Australia's face, and land at Alice Springs, a place very few Australians will ever see. Ah, the Alice. There's the dried-up river bed where they hold canoe races on foot. As there's no water, they quite sensibly carry the canoes.

"Apparently it's one of those very sadistic films."

"The strike weapon for increased pay for clergy is not something we would care to resort to."

There's the stockaded prison, a half-hearted sort of jail for half-drunk Abos, who are let out regularly to line the stockade to cheer any visiting dignitary. And what do you get? You get a modern motel with a swimming pool, and a giant Aussie who doesn't mean to let his swimming interfere with his drinking. He swims a length underwater and surfaces by a tube of iced Foster's from which he takes a swig. Then he dives, completes another effortless length and comes up with a hand reaching out for his other can of beer at the other end. And, disappointingly somehow, people at the Alice are far pleasanter than they are at, say, Frinton.

I think my first disillusionment in travel occurred on the Via Dolorosa. I had been suitably awed by the prison cell into which they had lowered Christ through a hole in the floor. That was, as you might say, the Roman Catholic cell. Emerging, blinking in the sunlight, and turning towards Calvary, I was accosted by a perfectly charming Orthodox priest who said, in effect, 'Psst, wanna see the *real* cell?' For all I know, his was the true cell. But I declined, having taken my first step in the Christian minefield which is Jerusalem.

Ashkelon, I thought, many years later, must be different if only because they publish it not in the streets. A quiet, mind-your-own-business sort of town, I'd reckoned, where a stranger could mosey into the saloon and call for whisky with no questions asked. You've gotta be joking. Ashkelon is a swinging town with a pub that sells Watney's Red Barrel and a landlord who clips off the end of any customer's club tie to decorate his ceiling.

I was given, and spoiled, one glorious, away-from-it-all moment. I was at 2,000ft, half way between Window Rock and the Grand Canyon, looking down on the hogans of the proud Navaho nation from the tribe's very own plane. Then I was caught short. The pilot landed alongside a modern school in the middle of nowhere and watched me sprint for the little boys' loo. OK. You forget about that, and I'll forget about the Matterhorn.

RONALD BIGGS
SINGS
THE BLUES

**The Great Train Robber has
just cut his first LP in a
Brazilian studio.
E. S. TURNER proudly
presents some
of the additional lyrics**

Oh, every day to England,
   Great aircraft, sleek as trout,
Go flying out of Rio
   (Fly out – fly out from Rio!)
And I'd like to fly from Rio
   Before my teeth drop out.
Yes, fly me back to England,
   The land of easy quids!
Oh, fly me out of Rio,
   (Fly out – fly out from Rio!)
For I'd like to fly from Rio
   Before I've fifty kids.
But we who live in exile –
   How hard our lot, how hard!
We cannot fly from Rio
   (Fly out – fly out from Rio!)
Who meets each plane from Rio?
   Why, Slipper of the Yard!

Never ask me where it went to!
   It is true we nicked a bomb.
Time rolls on and brings the question:
   Where's the next lot coming from?
Ronald Biggs's "True Confessions,"
Ronald Biggs: "My Flight to Fame."
Kiddies! Get your Uncle Ronnie's
Grand Exciting Hold-Up Game.
Never ask me where it went to!
   It is true we nicked a bomb.
Time rolls on and brings the question:
   Where's the next lot coming from?
Ronald Biggs, for discs and T-shirts,
Posters, stickers, shopping-bags!
"Ronald Biggs's Monster Cook-Book,"
"Ronnie's Super Book of Gags."
      (*27 verses omitted*)

Oh there ain't no extradition from Brazil!
It's a wonderland that packs a mighty thrill.
　　No, of course, they won't expel you,
　　But there's something I must tell you –
There's an awful lot of prisons in Brazil.
Oh there ain't no extradition from Brazil!
A land where man does almost what he will.
　　But they do have certain rules,
　　And the cops are tough as mules.
There's an awful lot of prisons in Brazil.
Oh there ain't no extradition from Brazil!
It's a perfect earthly paradise, but still
　　They can give it to you double
　　If you get their girls in trouble.
There's an awful lot of prisons in Brazil.
Oh there ain't no extradition from Brazil!
But they rather like to keep you on the grill,
　　Saying, 'Ron, it's time to go.
　　We suggest Fernando Po,
For we've filled up all our prisons in Brazil.'

✻

I know not whether Laws be right,
　　Or whether Laws be wrong,
I know that Fleet Street rings each night –
　　I know the Press is strong!
It makes me feel much less a heel,
　　I sense that I *belong*.
Oh each man writes the stuff he loves,
　　To each his little jeer.
Some handle me with rubber gloves,
　　Some slay me with a sneer.
The humbug rubs the moral in,
　　And does it with a leer.
Their ties are slack, their hearts are black,
　　Their livers are far gone –
They still troop in to flirt with Sin
　　And call the sinner Ron.
Oh sweet it is to rob a train!
　　It's sweet to sack and burn!
The quick man ends up on the plane,
　　The slow man in an urn.
But no man wins who dreams up sins
　　As the tape-recorders turn.
The tourists crowd to stare at me,
　　As if I were Bill Sikes,
To watch me brave the daily wave
　　Of deferential mikes.
An English chaplain called one day –
　　And that's a bloody fact.
He said I had a price to pay,
　　And left a little tract.
The man of God spares not the rod –
　　By God, I'll get him sacked.
Oh the wild regrets, the bloody sweats
　　Have left me now a wreck –
They steal my tears, my hopes, my fears –
　　First, gentlemen, your cheque!

✻

"*That's not fair! It was my turn to overreact!*"

HOW IRON WAS MY CURTAIN

A lecture by Mrs. Penny Pitfall
of Peekskill, with Mr. Handelsman
at the slide projector

I want to begin by saying that I have never been a member of the Communist Party, or even the Democrats, and neither has my husband, Robert J. Pitfall, Insurance. We joined the expedition sponsored by Détente Tours because heck, our government goes there all the time, and who wants to be more narrow-minded than their government? Click.

The Berlin Wall—that's what it's all about! This is where President Kennedy came and said he was a Berliner, but he wasn't—he was from Boston. Click.

On one side of Checkpoint Charlie, freedom; on the other side we went to the opera. *Fidelio*, wasn't it, Bob? So depressing! I mean, is Florestan innocent or guilty? In America, he would at least have had a fair trial. Click.

Bach played the organ in this very church in Leipzig, unless this is Dresden. People don't believe in God any more, of course, but they still go to church. Pretty much the same as in Peekskill, I guess. Click.

Friendly Prague natives in Wenceslas Square, where good King Wenceslas looked out, but some people think he was pushed. The Russians sent tanks to stop the Czechs from making good movies. There is a very old synagogue. They make you wear a hat. Click.

There is a place called Buda and a place called Pest, which is silly, like Wis and Consin. Hungarians always write their last names first, and they put paprika on everything. This is their Parliament building. Note the paprika on the dome. Click.

According to our learned guide, Doris (her husband's parents were Balkan), this is where the archduke was shot. The Yugoslavs split from the other Communist countries, causing bad blood, but later Tito and Khrushchev kissed each other a lot, causing good blood. There's a lot of rivalry among the national groupings: Serbs and Montenegrins always at each other's Croats. Click.

Albania wouldn't give us a visa. They worship Stalin and won't talk to anyone who isn't Chinese. We flew low enough to see an example of Albanian art. Click.

Doris is showing how to take off shoes at a Bulgarian mosque. So many different customs! Shoes off, hats off, hats on—it's an education. I had no idea there was so much diversity among Communists, and I almost regret having thrown a rock at Paul Robeson. Click.

Doris says the Romanians are descended from convicts, which may explain why they play tennis so well. Click.

At last—Mother Russia, the Big Daddy of them all! Let me give you a rundown on Russian history. Kiev was invaded by the Tartars, but Ivan the Terrible wouldn't give them the right time. Cossacks can ride under their horses. We went to the ballet and saw *Swan Lake*. Click.

So anyway, Ivan the Terrible's son, Fyodor the Saintly but Weak-Minded, was followed by Peter the Great, who forced the nobles to cut off their beards, whereupon Catherine the Great forced them to grow them back. Napoleon then set fire to Moscow, and Lenin took over. Did I leave out anything, Bob? Bob says I have a terrible memory. Click.

They keep moving Stalin in and out of Lenin's tomb, but it was quiet the day we were there. Bob, is this Lenin's tomb or the Moscow subway? We went to the ballet and saw *Swan Lake*. Click.

We visited the Hermitage Museum in Leningrad and got special permission to see the Decadent Collection (Impressionist and Jewish painters); then to the ballet and saw *Swan Lake*. Click.

You mustn't leave Russia without taking in the Asian bits. These people are Uzbeks. Behind them is a Steppe. The Gulag Archipelago is supposed to be nearby, but we couldn't find it. Instead, we saw *Swan Lake*. Click.

We returned home feeling that we had really learned something, though none of us could quite express what it was. If the Communists ever want to come over here, Bob and I will be glad to see them and even entertain them in our home. Right, Bob? That's a very different matter from having American Communists in the house, which I wouldn't tolerate for a minute. Click.

SOME
LIKE
IT
HOT

In particular the four sizzling writers we asked to dream up their own daft ways of keeping the warm in

SPIKE MILLIGAN

THERE are many ways of keeping warm. It all depends on how much money you have, let's start at the bottom, that is the bottom of the social scale. There are those gentlemen of the road who at midnight can be seen sleeping peacefully on the embankment in cold weather. The secret is the English Newspaper, which is wrapped around the inside of the outergarments, *The Financial Times* being a favourite, as one tramp said, 'Like bein' wrapped in dreams.'

I myself was working class and keeping warm was different in each room. The outside WC in winter was a formidable affair, so when I saw my father putting on Long Underwear, a heavy sweater, overcoat, muffler and gloves I knew what his next function was. My brother had his own method, he would do vigorous exercises until he was boiling hot, then rush to the WC, abort at speed and get back before he grew cold.

The only room with heat was the kitchen where a great iron stove glowed red, fed with all the rubbish in the house, on its hot plate kettles steamed and whistled, pots boiled, conkers hardened, chestnuts popped and socks and underwear steamed in the scarlet heat, and grandma's shins scorched in the inferno, no, there was no heating problem for the poor in the kitchen, but the rest of the home was clutched in Stygian ice.

The habit of staying up late only came into being when the people stopped sleeping in the kitchen or, to be exact, in pre-industrial times the kitchen, bedroom and living room were all one room. But came the age of the separate bedroom and late nights started. My own family would start to disrobe in the kitchen, start putting on flannelette nightshirts, pyjamas, bed socks etc., and finally, each one clutching a hot water bottle, would get on our marks and at a signal run screaming to our freezing beds, from where we would all groan and scream 'Oh Christ I'm freezin', cor stone a crow, Brrrrrrrrr, etc., etc.,' until the bed became warm.

Winter mornings were agony, the thought of getting out of bed was as pleasant as hara-kiri. So I would pull my suit into bed and when it was warm, undress and dress under the bedclothes; mind you my suit looked like a concertina, but I was warm.

Now the article is called how to keep warm, so let's bring it into the present. I give up. I don't know *how* to keep warm. Keeping warm with central heating is very difficult, because most of the time is spent roasting, as a result one spends the evening adjusting the thermostat, opening and closing windows, taking off jackets, or pullovers, so there is as much difficulty keeping warm with central heating as if you were in a freezing room. If it were up to me, I would abolish all central heating, it destroys furniture, floors, walls, and your respiratory system. No, a big cosy armchair, a pair of thick woollen socks, carpet slippers and a roaring coal fire (or logs) are the answer. In the street, people only get cold if they walk like cripples (as most of the English do). I walk very fast, as a result I arrive at work warm as toast and exhausted for the day.

TERRY JONES

THE only really sure way of staying warm this winter is to run about a lot, and this, of course, means keeping yourself young and healthy. And yet it is a fact that today more and more people are becoming elderly and infirm than ever before, and, as a consequence, ending their lives stationary in cold bed-sitters which they cannot afford to heat. And the simple truth is that in the present appalling crisis, which threatens the living standards not just of the poorest but of the very highest in the land, we simply cannot afford to provide heating *ad lib* for those who are too old or, in some cases, too lazy to run around a bit for themselves. Such people are not only a burden to themselves but a burden to us, as the late Sir Keith Joseph so succinctly put it.

But there is an even deeper and more philosophical point to be made. If every man, woman and child in this country, who cannot afford central heating, were to devote the winter to running about a lot, instead of remaining stationary and demanding more and more artificial warmth, then not only would this nation slash its fuel bills dramatically, it would also prove to the World that it can stand up for itself – that its moral fibre has not been totally eroded by years of walking about and sitting down. And if those who *have* allowed themselves to

become elderly or limbless should go to the wall this winter, it may be regrettable, but it can only improve our nation's stock, and ensure a young and healthy breed of Britons in the coming years of struggle for World Domination that lie ahead.

KINGSLEY AMIS

HE who cuts wood gets warm three times, once doing the cutting, again when carting the results to the hearth, and yet again through fetching the coal necessary to rescue his spitting, sizzling, smoking fire. He would do much better to leave the wood where it wallows in the slough and get down to some internal stoking: more effective as well as nicer and less laborious, though admittedly no good at all for raising domestic prestige.

Keeping warm is a drink called alcohol. Scientists say (the sort of thing they always do say) that alcohol actually lowers body-temperature; you simply *feel* warmer. Oh, I see. Heated alcohol lowers your temperature even more, I dare say, because you feel even warmer a good deal quicker. One bottle of cheap and nasty red wine brought near the boil with a glass of lousy port or cooking brandy plus some sugar will cause four or five people to open windows in January after about twenty minutes. It won't be nasty any longer; I don't know why. Scientists may know, but (for once in their lives) they don't say.

JACK TREVOR STORY

WHEN I was thirty-four and had just started staying out all night, a girl called Fifi set me alight by tricking me into chewing green chillis. Although I detected some kind of atmosphere, I had not realised that I had offended her by arriving at her flat in a lather of sexual anticipation and crying, when she opened the door, 'Knock twice and ask for Fifi!' Mr. Arrowsmith, our headmaster at Burwell in the Fens, once told us that girls called names like Fifi, Kiki, Lulu, Trixie and Topsy are trying to say something. After that I lived in high hopes of somebody saying, 'Let's go round to Fifi's.'

By the time it happened I had been married 15 years, already had about six of my eight children, had worked in factories for 20 years, had published two books and had come out into the literary world at last. So far I had had no sexual adventures, except Nancy Spain clapped me on the back one day.

This was about the time when somebody said, 'Let's go round to Fifi's.'

'Are you all right, Jack?' said Frank. Frank was my friend.

'You should not take things for granted,' said Fifi.

'Mm,' said I. 'Phew! Hahhh! Oh my God!'

'Your success with women,' said Fifi, herself steadily chewing with no discomfort, 'depends not on how many you fancy, but on how many fancy you.' Frank said: 'Give me some water!' The first one to drink water was a cissie. Fifi sat chewing without sweating or gasping, watching me like a bacteriologist who has found a new specimen and intends to destroy 99 per cent of it. What I didn't know was that she was chewing gum.

Since when I have had just enough love to get me through the winter.

ffolkes's History of Keeping Warm

"Inventing fire wasn't so hard, it's protecting the copyright."

"Warm, yes, but terribly, terribly guilty."

"Of course you have cold knees. Everybody has cold knees."

"I don't need you any more, Naneek, I've discovered blubber."

"Mark my words, Lavinia, in six months every home in the country will have one."

"Warming pan or Cynthia?"

"Please, Vickie, it's my turn for the damned dog!"

HELP CLEAN UP BRITAIN

PERSONAL CONFESSION
(For Parliamentary use only)

I, the undersigned, being to the best of my knowledge and belief a Member of Parliament, wish to confess to the following hitherto undisclosed indiscretions committed between the years 1870-1974:

```
accepting Moscow gold (1938);
frequenting certain saunas (1970-72);
transmitting bomb scares to the Speaker (1970-74).
```

I am willing: *(put tick in appropriate box)*
- ☐ to be questioned by self-righteous barristers
- ☐ to be interviewed by self-righteous broadcasters
- ☑ to make a self-righteous statement in the House
- ☐ to resign my seat

In extenuation of the above errors I wish to state:
- ☑ I was facing severe domestic trouble at the time
- ☐ It was the drink
- ☐ I thought the Ten Commandments did not apply in the North-East

(state any other explanation)

```
I do not know what came over me
```

My reason for making this confession is:
- ☐ I wish to see a higher standard of public life
- ☑ I would enjoy being hounded by the media

I did not confess before because:
- ☐ I saw little hope of publicity
- ☐ I was waiting for an old friend to denounce me
- ☑ There was never all this fuss about integrity before

(signed) *Arthur Bloodstone*

Do not BEND or MUTILATE this form, or you will have something else to confess.

FORM OF DENUNCIATION (General)
(A separate form must be used for each accusation)

I, JAMES GUMBOYLE, Editor hereby denounce the following person RORY O'GORY, Author and Broadcaster   for the following offence committed in 1950-55

Mr. O'Gory, then a prolific but unsuccessful free-lance, used to bombard my office with unsolicited manuscripts. Each was accompanied by a return envelope with the stamp positioned in such a way that it missed the franking machine. He would then use the envelope again and again until it disintegrated. By this cunning means I estimate he defrauded the Post Office of up to £50 a year by obliging them to carry his rejected articles for nothing. When I taxed him with the fraud he justified himself on the irrelevant ground that the Post Office defrauded him of six times as much by misrouting his telephone calls. He is now an established writer and appears regularly on television, where he browbeats politicians and impugns their good faith.

I certify that this communication is inspired by the purest dictates of conscience and has no other purpose than to rehabilitate standards of behaviour and to expose wrongdoing wherever it may be found.

(signed) *James Gumboyle*

FORM OF DENUNCIATION
(Vague and Unsubstantiated Charges Only)

I, being a person of sound but wandering mind, and anxious to stir things up a bit, hereby state that I could say a thing or two about the individuals listed in Schedule A, about whom I have heard discreditable stories from time to time, notably from:

Mrs. Amelia Sock, of The Dredgings, Buncombe
George, the milkman

I solemnly and sincerely declare my belief that the individuals named are no better than they should be, and that the authorities would be well advised to inspect their marriage certificates, income tax returns, television licences and other documents. In addition I believe the authorities should:

Turn over their back gardens to look for missing spouses

I promise faithfully to communicate any further unsubstantiated stories that may reach my ears.

I understand that I shall receive the protection of the Royal Commission at all times.

(signed) *R. Gamboge*

ROSALINE GAMBOGE (Mrs.)

From The Commission's mail-bag

Dear Sir or Madam,—In March 1944, at a black period of the war, my father, Albert Fridge, a butcher by trade, was fined £100 under the regulations of the day for putting too much meat in his sausages.

My father thought he had lived down this unhappy episode, but the other day the *Slopton Gazette*, under the headline "Slopton 30 Years Ago," reprinted the report and my father has again become a target for obloquy. The editor of the newspaper did not have the common journalistic courtesy to tell my father that he was reprinting the item.

As this matter will doubtless be brought to your attention in garbled form by my father's political enemies, in an effort to show that he is unfit to be Chairman of the Ways and Means Committee, I am endeavouring to get in first and set the true facts before you, coupled with a plea for sympathy and understanding.

What a terrible age we live in, to be sure!—Yours truly, **EMILY SHREW (Mrs.)**

PS. It is a foul lie that he tried to bribe the inspector with half a pound of sausages.

Gentlemen: As Duke of Durham it has come to my notice that the Council of Little Clumping has by false and unscrupulous representations, and much financial jiggery-pokery, secured possession of a quarter-acre plot of valuable agricultural land on which it proposes to erect a family planning clinic.

The ownership of land is a sacred trust and its transfer, for whatever purpose, should be subject to the most stringent safeguards.

I am advised that I should disclose my interest. It is well-known that I live on 25,000 acres of former monastery lands which were presented to my ancestor, the first Duke, for hanging a number of abbots. I do not conceive that this requires either justification or apology.— I remain, Gentlemen, Your obedient servant, **DURHAM.**

Dere Royal Commission, Five years ago my Unkle Tom put a dead mouse in a harf-loaf of bred and took it along to the bakery and got £50 for it. He is now standing for the Counsel and says he will expose disshonesty wherever he finds it. If you send me £10 for this informashun I will send you some more.—**Toby Snout** *(aged ten), 10 Railway Cottages, Burstholme-on-Sea.*

Dear Sir,—While riding on a No. 16 bus in London a fortnight ago I found myself without any money and my fare of 7p was paid by a courteous but fanatical-looking gentleman sitting beside me. At the time his face seemed familiar but I could not place it. Judge of my surprise when, on opening today's newspaper, I found a photograph of my benefactor, who is none other than Mr. Anthony Wedgwood Benn, the Left-wing revolutionary. I now feel ashamed and contaminated. What I thought was a simple disinterested act of kindness looks suspiciously like a bribe to win my acquiescence in the nationalisation of British Leyland and other mischievous endeavours of the kind. I have tried to give Mr. Benn his 7p back but he refuses point-blank to accept it and laughs in what he evidently thinks is a disarming manner. How many more innocent citizens has Mr. Benn been trying to subvert in this cunning and brazen fashion? Yours faithfully, **Albert Peavey,** *Flat 1a, Silverside Court, Putney.*

Dear Sirs,—You will be surprised to hear from a common old dustman, I should say refuse orderly, but I have evidence of attempted corruption by Mrs. Biggs, of The Moorings, Bathwater, who gives herself airs because she is on the Housing Committee. If you ask me, Mrs. Biggs with a name like that could probably tell you where the money went from the Great Train Robbery. Well, to cut a long story short Mrs. Biggs put out an old mattress with an envelope containing 10p inscribed "For The Dustman". I could hardly believe my eyes. As you know the Council rules are that dustmen must not accept gratuities and I speak for dustmen everywhere when I say that not one of them would dream of accepting such a bribe. So kindly pull Mrs. Biggs in for questioning, and oblige, **Jim Gulley,** *Rose Lawn, St. Mary Kray.*

Edited transcript of tape supplied anonymously to the Royal Commission. The postmark on the package was "Clockwhistle-le-Pump".

Jim you old *(expletive)* this is *(expletive)* serious. They've traced twenty-four of the Council's paper clips to employees' homes and the *(expletive)* auditors are going to *(expletive)* surcharge us. We've got to get those *(expletive)* clips back, Jim, and you know my *(expletive)* thinking in these matters. Burglary is morally wrong, Sir, but in this *(expletive)* context it makes sense. The trouble is we're *(expletive)* amateurs at break-ins.—Get the *(expletive)* dirty tricks boys on to it but I don't want to *(expletive)* know.

The writing on the wall

as read by
WILLIAM HARDCASTLE

IT'S PROBABLY A FAIRLY COMMON occurrence in Chinese family life these days. The master of the house dons his cap and raincoat, puts the leash on the dog, and announces, 'I'm off for a read.' And down he toddles to the Street of the Revolutionary Committee to see what the latest wall posters are saying.

In Britain we have lots of pleasant parks for strolling. The Ramblers' Association will provide you with pointers to plenty of public footpaths. There's even the Pennine Way. But scenery isn't everything. What is there to *read* while you perambulate in this country?

I'm probably influenced by a deprived childhood. On my walk to and from school each day I used to pass one of those 'Wayside Pulpits' which were fine as far as they went but, after a fortnight of the same brief excerpt from Ezekiel V, the message began to pall. Otherwise, and even today, there are graffiti, whose creativity, I believe, is grossly overestimated. 'Crystal Palace for the Cup' and 'Pam loves Cyril' are opinions that fail to grip the mind for long.

We have advertising, of course. Why a certain stout is good for you, how a particular motor oil increases your attraction to the opposite sex – such messages have a passing attraction as you pause to let your dog inspect a lamp post. But just imagine the lift that could be given to your evening stroll if you came across something like this in bright yellow lettering:

An open letter to Chairman Wilson:

My sister Sheila has been falsely accused of having illicit sexual relations with the foreman in the plastics factory where she works.

These lies have been propagated by a senior member of the regional party committee whom I'm prepared to name.

Please do something about it;

Her brother Fred.

Believe it or not, that is the sort of thing that is going around Peking, and other Chinese towns and cities, these days. The above is a rather inept parody of the apparently true case of Chao-Pao-Fang. Her brother travelled all the

". . . furthermore we find it intolerable that you should be playing several instruments when so many musicians are out of a job!"

way from Honan province to put up posters to the effect that she had been falsely accused of having an affair with one Chang Hsing-yi. The fuzz moved in, beat her up and in despair she killed herself. Chao's brother said the man guilty of telling all the lies about her was a senior official of the Honan Communist Party, Mr. Wang Hsin. What are you going to do about Mr. Wang, Chairman Mao Tse Tung? was the essential message.

And so it goes on the walls of Peking these days. I wonder what the Chinese is for 'All Human Life is Here.'

I will grant you that the Chaos and Changs and Wangs of the Chinese world do not enjoy what we consider to be our considerable freedom of expression through many outlets. If they knew about it they might envy our decadent capitalistic choice which offers *Reveille* with one hand, the *Investors Chronicle* with the other and the *Socialist Weekly* with the third. The Chinese scene, in this context at least, is not tempting. I doubt if even Mr. Rupert Murdoch would find the Peking *People's Daily* an attractive proposition for acquisition.

There is also probably something fundamentally artificial about the rather primitive form of free speech that is currently being permitted on The Street of the Revolutionary Committee. The subjects vary from the particular and the personal – *vide* poor little Chao-Pao-Fang – to the Communist traditional, such as a poster complaining about a serious shortfall in a tractor factory at Kiangsi. There are tales of dark deeds, factional strife and killings. There's even a rather corny character who's been using the paste pot in Peking lately and signing his posters with the John Creasy-like signature, 'The Golden Monkey'.

Some posters go too far. A group of girls turned up outside the Peking International Club recently and put up a poster to the effect that party worthies were using the place for *pleasure*, for heaven's sake. The club's swimming pool was being *enjoyed* by people whose minds should have been on more serious matters. That was too much. The fire brigade turned up and hosed the girls, and their posters, off the sidewalk. In other words there are clear limits to the odd Chinese exercises that have been going on.

The authorities in their characteristically inscrutable Chinese way are

"I was here long before you!"

"If you ask me, what some of them need is a good dose of conscription."

allowing the folks to let off a bit of steam, just as long as they show no signs of blowing off the lid. Even so – and even if we all have instant access these days to countless hours of radio phone-ins – I wonder whether we couldn't do with a bit of wall-postering ourselves. With all the outlets we possess I would still like to see a personalised and passionate poster complaining about the culpability of the South Shields Watch Committee appearing on the stately walls of Pall Mall.

In other words, and in this increasingly complex world of ours, the Chinese, however cynical their motives, are reviving a simple and forcible means of self-expression. We are satiated with modernity, we yawn at the prospect of staying up for *Midweek*, we go out to the pub instead of listening to *The World at One*. But give us a mix of flour and water, a clean wall, and a bit of paper to scribble on and what wonders we might perform!

I have this idea of erecting one long billboard around the boundaries of the Palace of Westminster. Just to make the exercise more intriguing I would have it labelled at frequent intervals with 'Stick No Bills' signs. My guess is that it would be necessary to ban traffic from Parliament Square, so great would be the surge of individuals and groups anxious to stick their opinions around the decision centre of our democracy.

The laws of libel would be difficult to enforce. To serve a writ on a group of indignant herring-gutters from Aberdeen who had slapped notices about their grievances outside the entrance to the House of Lords would put an excessive strain on the police. In any case the message from Aberdeen would soon be overlaid by a querulous demand from the Darby and Joan Club of Lytham St. Anne's who want to know more about the role played by Marcia Williams at No. 10 Downing Street.

Eventually every town hall, every rural district council office, would be surrounded by billboards and paste pots would litter the grass roots. We could run a 'Billposter of the Year' competition with official awards under the headings of a. political, b. sociological and c. sexual, and may the best man win. Damn clever, these Chinese.

Here Are The Groovy Fantastic Headlines Again

The BBC has announced plans for a children's TV News . . .

'Hello, and welcome to News at Five. Fighting broke out in Cyprus again today, where the Greek gang were having a punch up with the Turkish gang. The Greeks say that the Turks should keep to their own area, but the Turks won't, so the Greeks have ganged up on the Turks, but the Turks have got the best fighters and are winning for the moment.

'There was a super train smash in Bulgaria today, when the morning express left the rails leaving Sofia and really made a sensational flying leap into the fields, with ten of the coaches going Kerash Kerump Smash one after the other. Here are some pictures of it.

'In London, Prime Minister Harold Wilson told TUC leader Len Murray that he could have 40p more pocket money a week if he agreed not to ask for more. Len said, Well, what if the price of liquorice goes up, what then? Harold said, I'll make sure the price of sweets doesn't go up and that goes for cinema tickets and bikes too, OK? Well, said Len, OK but I'll have to ask my gang first, you know what Scanlon is like. OK, said Harold.

'Also, there was torrential rain all over Britain today and here is a shot of the North Circular Road under water, so if you live nearby get your home-made rafts and snorkel tubes round as fast as you can.

'Well, all the rest of the news is boring so let's forget it. There'll be another Late News at 6.30—and remember, if you want any special news items on this programme, just write to Children's News, BBC, London W12, England, Europe, the World, the Universe, Infinity.'

General BILL TIDY
invades the south

me and my JUNTA

THE PLACE HAD BEEN BUZZING WITH RUMOUR FOR THE LAST COUPLE OF DAYS SO I MADE IT OFFICIAL AT THE FINAL BRIEFING

LADS, HINCHCLIFFE FORCE IS HEADING FOR...

LONDON!

THE COUNTRY WAS IN A MESS SO I'D FORMED 'H' FORCE TO KEEP THE MEN OFF THE STREETS.

IT WAS ONLY LATER THAT I REALISED WHAT A POWERFUL WEAPON I HAD IN MY HANDS. DISCIPLINED, NORTHERN AND UNEMPLOYED.

GENTS

WE HAD BEEN LAUGHED AT BUT NOW THE JEERS WOULD STOP. THE INVITATION TO MARCH SOUTH HAD COME FROM LONDON ITSELF. I MOBILISED.

HUH! ONLY ONE FELLER FROM THAT STREET!

CONTINUED OVERLEAF

OUR ROUTE WAS SIMPLE. M6-M1-LONDON! OVERTURNED LORRIES, ROADWORKS, NO HARD SHOULDER FOR 2 MILES— NOWT COULD STOP US!

REMEMBER EXIT 26!

EXIT 26. BEER WAGON CRASH 1971.

FIRST SIGNS OF THE INSIDIOUS ENEMY WHICH FEASTS ON OUR VITALS. NO PRISONERS.

LONDON

LONDON

LONDON

SHOOT THEM!

MARCHING AND DRILL DEMO AT 'GREY BUN' MOTORWAY RESTAURANT. NO MORE PARTISAN ACTIVITY IN THIS AREA

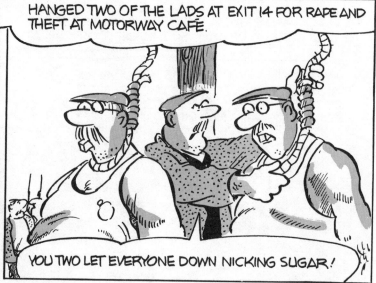

HANGED TWO OF THE LADS AT EXIT 14 FOR RAPE AND THEFT AT MOTORWAY CAFÉ.

YOU TWO LET EVERYONE DOWN NICKING SUGAR!

PRESS AND T.V. INTERVIEW AT HENDON TO ANSWER ATROCITY CHARGES.

ABSOLUTE FABRICATION...

...NONE OF MY CHAPS HAVE THROWN TRIPE INTO CROWDED CELLARS. NOW GENTLEMEN, IT IS TIME...

...FOR OUR FINAL THRUST. FORM THE MEN UP, WE'RE GOING IN IN STYLE!

AYE, AYE SIR!

THE JOHN PLAYER 'WHO REPRESENTS OUR COUNTRY?'
ALL ENGLAND
PRIVATE ARMY FINALS '74

Labour Oriented

A whole management team is being sent out from Britain to create a new car industry in South Korea. Only trouble, it seems, is that the workers out there are used to working long hours and weekends without protest...

Report from TGWU (South Korean branch)

In this report I am handing in my resignation. The reasons for this are as follows:

The workers at the factory are all members of the TGWU, thanks to a big recruiting drive. I therefore thought it was time to take action to improve conditions and rates of pay, which are not good.

I therefore demanded from the management a twenty-minute tea break morning and afternoon. This, after some argument, they granted. My members, however, seem not to understand the concession and although they now take tea, they insist on working throughout, with a cup in one hand and a tool in the other. When I pointed out that this contravened safety regulations they told me they no longer wished to drink tea.

I next brought into action an overtime ban to bring pressure to bear for a wage increase. I am sorry to say that there appeared to be as many workers there after the end of normal time as before. When I challenged them, they claimed to be a different shift. As I still have difficulty distinguishing between all my members, I decided on an all-out strike today.

When I arrived at the works, to make sure nobody had disobeyed, I found things as normal. Everyone was working. They explained to me that they were all on strike in spirit, but that it was traditional for them to go on working during a strike to avoid losing pay. When I asked them how they suggested bringing pressure to bear on the management, they smiled and went on working.

I therefore hand in my resignation and ask for a posting back to Birmingham.

J. Hargreaves (Branch Secretary)

That's Life

A round-up of recent biographies:—

A Life of Jesus by Frances Donaldson. A new life of the man who astounded everyone by abdicating just when he seemed firmly set for a glorious career. He claimed to have done it for Love: this well researched biography reveals him as a man of unusually split personality who wanted more from this world than he could find on it. Baldwin comes out of it quite well.

Edward VIII by Lord Longford. Simply the best man who ever lived, claims Lord Longford in this new life of the man who was offered the world and rejected it in favour of the puritanical simplicity of a large mansion outside Paris. Even today we urgently need his message: 'Something must be done!' Judas emerges quite well from it.

A History of the English-Speaking Churchill by Lady Longford. An enormous sweep of 2,000 years of history, from the years when Churchill first emerged from the mists of time as a primeval warrior and journalist, through the middle ages of his flowering as a bricklayer and painter (the Renaissance) to the last period in modern times as the man who kept the world safe for the Social Contract and a 70 mph limit on motorways. Utterly absorbing, if you spill coffee on it. Lord Longford comes out of it quite well.

Nine Studies in Power by Roy Jenkins. A handful of essays on famous people who have never quite made it to the top but always had plenty of time to write books about people who never quite made it to the top. Roy Jenkins comes out of it jolly well, really.

Not Bad News

Nice to know that not all the news is bad. There was an encouraging report, for instance, the other day that there are now so few cases of smallpox in the world that the disease may disappear for ever in a few years time. What was *really* heartening about the report was that it wasn't headlined 'Smallpox Shortage'.

ASK HENRY

Henry Kissinger, the world's most experienced arbitrator, solves *your* personal problems exclusively in *Punch*. If you have a worry, write to "Ask Henry"

I have just been asked 20p for a bottle of lemonade in a cafe. Don't you think this sort of thing is disgusting? – A.R. of B-on-Sea.

HENRY SAYS: Not having ever tried lemonade, I wouldn't know.

I mean, paying 20p for the bottle. –A.R. again.

HENRY SAYS: This is all part of a world-wide problem. Bottles are made of glass, glass is made of sand, and the Arabs, who control the world's largest deposits of sand, have raised their prices yet again. I shall be talking to them soon about other matters and I will have a few words with them about your problem. Till you hear from me, stick to water.

Could you settle an argument? My doctor says that I have a touch of flu, but I say it's something serious like foot-and-mouth disease, and I've bet him £1 that I'm right. I enclose a list of symptoms. – Mr. E.W. of Hythe.

HENRY SAYS: Congratulations! You are absolutely right and have won yourself a pound. I am sending under separate cover instructions on how to destroy yourself.

Do you approve of the habit, so common in business, of sending gifts to important contacts at Christmas time? – Mr. R. of N.Y.

HENRY SAYS: No, I do not. Any time is fine.

I often have to conduct crucial international negotiations for my firm which take weeks of careful bargaining and intricate discussion, yet as soon as they are finished my boss comes along and takes all the credit. Can you suggest any way in which my own contributions can be better appreciated? – Mr. H.O. of Cincinnati.

HENRY SAYS: This is a problem which has had to be faced by many famous figures in history, from John the Baptist through Joan of Arc to, well, many famous figures in modern history. If we study their track record we find that one way of licking the problem is to have a gimmick, like going on a honey and locusts diet, or hearing voices. In the particular case of other famous figures of history, I find that dating lots of film stars helps.

Is it really true that because you were born in Germany you can never be President of the United States? – Mrs. W. of Leeds.

HENRY SAYS: Yes, as people have often pointed out, this is quite true. For some reason they never add that I am, of course, perfectly qualified to become President of Germany.

Would you like to become President of Germany? – Mrs. W.

HENRY SAYS: That's very kind of you. When can I start?

I am sixteen, and very interesting in America. I love American football, old Bing Crosby records, the Saturday Evening Mail, country and western singing, and all your history and those other things. I would like a lot to be in correspondence with someone in your country who also is keen similarly. – Z.N. of Prague.

HENRY SAYS: Thank you very much for writing. I have passed your letter on to President Ford. You may have to wait a while for a reply, as he is a slow writer.

My wife and I often see your show on television and it makes us laugh a lot, especially the bit where you say 'All the signs are very hopeful for an imminent agreement.' Can you tell us where we can get hold of a record of your signature theme? – J.N. of Beirut.

HENRY SAYS: I do not have a TV show. I think you must be confusing me with Lord Goodman.

THE TAX INSPECTOR AND THE QUEEN

The King of Sweden now has to pay income tax. Can our Queen stay tax-free much longer? And what could she claim as expenses? PUNCH works it out

Your Majesty,

I acknowledge receipt of your gracious tax return dated June 20. I note that you claim exemption from all taxes on the grounds that, as taxes are payable to you and your government, there is no need to pay them in the first place. This can only be tested by paying your taxes and then claiming them back.

I therefore enclose your tax return and request you this time to fill it in.

I remain,

Your Majesty's Obedient Subject,

J. P. Garstang (Your Majesty's Tax Inspector).

Your Majesty,

I acknowledge receipt of your gracious tax return, now filled in. I note however that you claim to be the director of a charity and thus exempt from all taxes on your expenses. You also claim that your expenses exceed income and that you are therefore not subject to any taxes.

Unfortunately I cannot agree that British Royalty, the organisation of which you are lady chairman, is a charity. My reasoning is as follows.

1. A charity is a body that uses its funds to benefit others.

2. I cannot find any trace of anyone other than the directors who benefit from the charity.

3. British Royalty must therefore be redefined as a trading concern.

I enclose a new tax return for you to fill in.

I remain,

Your Majesty's Obedient Subject,

J. P. Garstang (Your Majesty's Tax Inspector).

Your Majesty,

I acknowledge receipt of your new tax return. Before I turn in any detail to the various palaces, army regiments, jet aircraft and ships that Your Majesty claims as legitimate expenses, we must establish the nature of the business of British Royalty, and I would be grateful if you could let me have a short description of the service you provide.

I am also puzzled by an abbreviation on page 3. Could you identify M.M.S.O. for me?

I remain,

Your Majesty's Obedient Subject,

J. P. Garstang (Your Majesty's Tax Inspector).

CONTINUED OVERLEAF

Your Majesty,

I thank you for the information that M.M.S.O. stands for My Majesty's Stationery Office.

I think we can proceed on the basis of the definition of your business that you enclose, namely 'the hiring out of directors of the firm and children too young to be directors, to appear in public, to officiate at any public gathering whatsoever, to open any establishment whatsoever and to make a short TV speech at Christmas.'

You also state that as you are never paid for any of these functions, you owe no income tax. Your royal deduction is erroneous. Under the Income and Corporation Taxes Act 1970, expenses payments and benefits to the director of a firm are taxable unless it can be shewn that they are wholly and solely incurred in the duties of office. I take it that Your Majesty concurs with this law, as it was personally signed by Your Majesty in 1970.

We now come to some of the individual expenses claimed, and I would like to start by discussing the various meals you claim against tax. Many of these seem hardly necessary and somewhat extravagant. To take one example alone – on May 20 you entertained 4,000 people to lunch at Buckingham Palace, the company HQ, at a total cost of £8,040. Was it necessary to entertain so many business associates at the same time? Could it honestly be called a business meeting? I await your comments with interest.

I remain,
Your Majesty's Obedient Subject,
J. P. Garstang (Your Majesty's Tax Inspector).

Your Majesty,

I take your point that the lunch in question was not a business lunch in the ordinary sense of the term, but part of your business itself, being a 'Garden Party', a unique service provided by your firm at no expense to the customer. I also accept that you yourself ate no more than two chicken sandwiches on the day in question. I think we can accept the other meals as legitimate expenses.

May I mention the subject of your trading premises? One of the main exemptions you claim is based on the supposition that all your company properties (Buckingham Palace, Windsor Castle, Sandringham and others) are also all places of residence in the line of duty. I find this difficult to understand and would welcome your further comments.

It is, as you say, quite normal to claim the expense of clothes worn for public or TV appearances. It is not quite so usual to claim, as you have done, that all clothes bought by you in the last year are exempt from tax. And I must point out that some of the purchases seem out of proportion to the business involved. You claim a new robe and jewels to the value of £367 for a short business trip to Westminster and back. Was this entirely necessary?

I remain,
Your Majesty's Obedient Subject,
J. P. Garstang (Your Majesty's Tax Inspector).

Your Majesty,

I refer to your comment that your duties as a director of British Royalty entail your being seen on duty at all hours and that wherever you happen to be living is automatically a place of residence on company business. I would like a little time to think this one out. Meanwhile, I would just like to question the suggestion that all your properties can be places of residence for you *simultaneously*.

You state that all clothes you buy are automatically worn in the line of duty, as you never know when you will be on television. I accept this, as I do your assurance that your robes, gowns, crowns, tiaras are laid down in the contracts for the various ceremonies you perform and that you do not wear them when out of sight, in private. (You refer to a separate enclosure in which you send the manuscript of a 1738 Act of Parliament, proving that the robes mentioned are due and necessary. By this you must mean the envelope which arrived this morning, containing a large quantity of dust. I have complained to the Post Office about their treatment of the package; meanwhile I return the Act, or dust.)

I now move on to the question of company transport. While accepting that you have to do a great deal of travelling across the world on the firm's business, I must question the variety of vehicles used. Sometimes you move about in a large car, sometimes by aeroplane and boat, sometimes in a large coach with four horses, occasionally in a helicopter and even on occasion on horseback. Is this extravagance really necessary? Would it not be possible to adopt the same vehicle for many of your engagements? I note, for instance, that you travelled to the House of Commons by coach and yet made a very similar journey to Horse Guards Parade by horse. Could not both have simply been carried out in a small saloon car?

I would like to question your twice weekly manicure as being in the pursuit of your business.

I remain,
Your Majesty's Obedient Subject,
J. P. Garstang (Your Majesty's Tax Inspector).

Your Majesty,

I take your point that it would be difficult to review troops from a small saloon car, unless, as you say, you were standing on the roof which would indeed tend to detract from the dignity of the occasion. I also note that you justify the size of Buckingham Palace on the grounds that waving to a large crowd from a balcony would lose its point if done from a semi-detached villa in Ealing.

I welcome your statistics on the amount of handshaking you are obliged to do; I accept the manicure as a right and proper expense.

· May I raise a new point? Many of your functions seem to involve the hiring and performing of a large group of musicians. Is it strictly necessary to have musical accompaniment at so many outdoor ceremonies? If it is, how do you justify the expense of having your bands mounted on horse? Could they not as easily walk while playing?

I remain,

Your Majesty's Obedient Subject,

J. P. Garstang (Your Majesty's Tax Inspector).

Your Majesty,

I accept the explanation of which functions demand ceremonial music and which do not; I fully see that a regimental military band is appropriate to the 'Beating of the Retreat' but not to the opening of a new electronics factory in Harlow.

I would like to raise the question of your film and theatre going. Is it entirely necessary on some occasions to hire a whole cinema or theatre for the night just to see a film or variety performance? It seems to me much more economic and just as practical to buy a ticket to see a film, rather than stage a Royal Command Performance.

I note an item on your return which refers to the postal expense of sending birthday telegrams to various strangers who have reached a hundred. I find it hard to believe that this is a legitimate part of your business activities.

I would also like to question, on page 137, the giving of a butt of malmsey wine and a few pounds to the 'Poet Laureate'. Is it really necessary to retain a writer simply to write verses about your business activities?

There are a further ninety-eight queries I would like to raise, but I would welcome your comments on these first.

I remain,

Your Majesty's Obedient Subject,

J. P. Garstang (Your Majesty's Tax Inspector).

(*The correspondence continues . . .*)

"Well, parlez-vous Français then?—or sprechen Sie Deutsch? . . .
parla Italiano? . . . habla usted Español? . . ."

Spring Hopes Eternal

ARNOLD ROTH takes an
optimistic view of sex

...But, Ralph,
I'm not that
kind of girl!...
...But, Ralph...
I'm not **that**
kind of girl!!...
...But, **Ralph**,
I'm not that
kind....

Y'know...after
three martinis,
every guy looks
like Clark Gable
to me.

Irish jokes, Jewish jokes, Polish jokes, Coloured jokes . . . but
when we looked for English jokes, they didn't exist. So
PUNCH found it necessary to invent them

A man in Hong Kong was driving along in a car when it collided with a
bicycle. Under the impact, the doors fell off, the axles broke and the
engine came through the floor.
'I'm terribly sorry about that,' said the bicyclist.
'It's not your fault,' said the Hong Kong driver. 'I should never have bought
cheap English rubbish in the first place.'

●

An Englishman died and went to heaven. There he was stopped by St Peter,
who asked his name.
'Smith,' was the answer.
'And what have you done during your life?'
'Not much,' admitted the Englishman.
'Did you lead a good life, though?'
'Well, put it this way,' said Smith, 'I was never found out.'
'But did you ever do a good deed?' insisted St Peter.
'Once or twice,' said Smith, 'but don't tell anyone.'
St Peter opened the gates.
'All right, you can come in.'
'Not so fast,' said the Englishman, producing a long list. 'Before I agree to
work in this place, here are my conditions. First, a new harp every six months.
Second, a guaranteed contract for the first billion years on a sliding pay
scale . . .'

●

An American conductor takes part with a German tenor and a French
soprano in a performance of an opera by a Russian. Where are they?
In London, the world capital of music.

116

An English computer was fed all the information about human ideals and aspirations that could be found in every great poet, philosopher and novelist. When it had all been programmed in, the computer was asked the single question:
'What is the secret of human happiness?' It whirred and clicked for a moment, then answered:
'North Sea oil.'

●

What is the English disease?
I dunno, but here's me doctor's certificate.

●

After a plane crash in the Brazilian jungle, the only survivor was an English passenger who crawled out of the wreckage more dead than alive. Nine months later he was found by a rescue party, living on roots and berries, his clothes in tatters and suffering from all kinds of vitamin deficiencies. They gave him a good meal and the latest news from home.
'Your ordeal's over now,' they said. 'We've come to take you back to England.'
'I'm staying here, thank you very much,' said the survivor. 'I'm not going to pay taxes to a bloody Labour government.'

●

A top KGB man was being taken round a Russian mental hospital. In one ward he spotted a patient scribbling away furiously.
'Who's that?' he asked.
'A dissident writer,' said the doctor. 'He's working on a history of Stalin's crimes, but we think we can cure him.'
In the bed next to him was another man making notes from a pile of books.
'And him?'
'One of our top physicists. He's writing an open letter to President Nixon. He used to write one every day, but we've got him down to one a week now.'
In the bed beyond that was a patient who was just sitting staring into space and humming to himself. He nodded at the KGB man and said:
'Bit cold for the time of year, isn't it? Still, can't grumble, can you?'
'What's his trouble?' whispered the KGB man.
'Incurable case, I'm afraid,' said the doctor. 'He thinks he's English.' (Or 'He thinks England will qualify for the World Cup in 1978.')

●

A Frenchman, a German and an Englishman were shipwrecked and cast away on a desert island. They surveyed the few belongings they had left and the bare vegetation on the cold, windswept rocky islet.
'Well,' said the German, 'I'll do my best to knock some sort of dwelling together to shelter us from the weather.'
'All right,' said the Frenchman. 'I'll see what food I can find and if there is any fresh water around.'
There was a silence, and they both looked at the Englishman.
'You do what you like,' he said. 'If you think I'm working in conditions like these, you've got another think coming.'

●

An English tourist stopped to watch a building project in the hills above his resort.
'That's no place to put a dam,' he told the manager. 'There isn't enough rock at the sides. The valley is too wide. And your costs will be astronomical.'
'What does he know?' the manager told his assistant. 'The English have forgotten how to build things. Their projects are always falling down. And they don't have enough money left to know what it looks like.'
But six months later the dam, which had been built in too wide a valley on too

little rock, collapsed, causing millions of dollars worth of damage.
MORAL: Never trust an Englishman. He may be right by accident.

●

What is so special about the English sense of humour? Foreigners are content to make fun of themselves; only the English have the ability to laugh at others.

●

A friendly football match was arranged between Heaven and Hell. God, who had not been able to make the game, asked St Peter later on how it had gone. 'Well,' said Peter, 'the Marquis de Sade gave away a penalty in the first few minutes and we scored from the spot, but they came back strongly and equalised before halftime. Then early in the second half St Matthew put us 3-1 ahead.'
'And then?'
'And then the English sinners invaded the pitch and the match was abandoned.'

●

A French missionary was talking to a cannibal chief about Christianity.
'Have you ever been told the truth about our God, my son?'
'Oh yes,' said the cannibal. 'An English missionary came here ten years ago

"We've been coming here for our picnics for years."

and showed us the light. We now have the true faith.'
'Hmm,' said the French priest doubtfully. 'Do you celebrate Communion?
And say your prayers? And love your neighbour?'
'Oh yes, just as the Englishman taught us.'
'And what do you do with your prisoners of war?'
'We boil them for eight hours and eat them with chips.'
'Will you never learn!' cried the priest in anguish. 'This is a barbarous way to
treat your enemies! You must sauté them gently in a little olive oil and serve
them with a green salad.'

●

The Labour government died and went to hell. After a year, they went to the
devil and told him that they wished to renegotiate terms for entry.
'Too late,' said the devil.
'Then we will call a referendum.'
'Too late,' said the devil.
'All right—then we will have a general election.'
'Too late again.'
The Labour government conferred amongst themselves.
'We have decided to call the heating engineers out on strike,' they told the
devil.
'OK,' said the devil. 'You win.'

*"This is a fun place, agreed?—so not a word about NATO's exposed
southern flank until after dinner!"*

These Foolish Things

GRAHAM on holiday souvenirs

"It seems remarkably cheap for an original Picasso."

"Do you do egg-cups?"

"Look, Annie—do we really want a goat-skin bedspread?"

"We went mad!"

"Here you are, Charles—you can sit on the camel saddle."

'Three weeks ago that little lot was tumbling over Thomson's Falls."

"We're not very sure what it is, but it was hand-made by local craftsmen."

"What else did you bring back?"

THE OIL RUSH

Dr. ALAN COREN
D.Sc., F.Inst.Geol., Dip. de Petro-Chimie

Research Division,
Anglo-Bahraini Oil Co.,
Bahrain, P.G.

Telex BAH 265863 (Aboil)
Tel: 78199

ALAN COREN and HEWISON report from the Scottish Klondike

Dr. WILLIAM C. HEWISON
D.Sc., F.G.S., Mem. OAC (Kuwait)

Research Division,
Anglo-Bahraini Oil Co.,
Bahrain, P.G.

Telex BAH 265863 (Aboil)
Tel: 78199

THE VISION

It was, as I remember, a drear drizzling Tuesday in early February when the hitherto unspoken Dream was first articulated.

I had been pacing the unlovely corridors of the Tudor Street offices, staring at the forefingers from which long years of comic typing had erased the whorls, when I bumped against the gaunt frame of William Hewison who was similarly engaged. His eyes were what Barbara Cartland would call hollow, and his thin hands were ingrained with the giveaway stigmata of Indian ink which set the cartoonist apart from ordinary men.

We looked at one another for some time.

"We have been out here too long, I said. "All this humorous rubbish, all this joke-writing and pencilling of funny faces, what is it all for? Is it, I put it to you, man's work? We grow flabby in mind and body, lad! There are frontiers still to be crossed, and wastes to be charted, and fortunes to be made by guts and sweat, and big women to be waylaid!"

DAY 1 — INVERNESS. Forenoon. We test the equipment.

DAY 2 — NIGG. Afternoon.
We consult an Oil-Man.

"Me—I'm a Greek. Catering staff. I tell you—the boys all love my little bouzouki."

He thought for a while, his fine face creased with the effort to grasp it all.

"How big?" he said, at last.

"I am talking," I said, "about oil! Less than a thousand miles due north of here, Hewison, there is a new Yukon. Strong men with tattooed forearms stand poised to suck millions in black gold from the earth's crust. It is like California in 1849, Hewison, like Alaska in 1890, all is boom and rush and ruthlessness and money, and men prepared to seize the day will be carrying the stuff home in lorries! Let us grab a couple of shovels, and trek north!"

"You have to be a company," said Hewison. "I read it somewhere. You can't just row out into the North Sea and start digging."

"You miss the point," I replied. "Or, rather, points. First, if there is oil under the sea, there is no reason why there should not also be oil under the land, nor any why we should not therefore look for it. Second, even if it is not there, think of the ancillary delights of the region! Why, I have heard of mushrooming casinos, of truckloads of lithe women disembarking every hour on the hour for the accom-modation of the big spenders currently flocking to Nigg Bay to work upon the rigs, of wild nights of music, love and single malts! And third, what might we not learn, Hewison, of human greed and human lust and even human worth, out there on the last frontier?"

"We may write a new *Eskimo Nell*!" he cried, suddenly. "With erotic illustrations! They never," he muttered, "let me draw smut here. A million copies in paperback, American rights, a film, a television series, a . . ."

I looked away, as he rambled. Already, I reflected, the terrible magic of black gold was manifesting its weird power to twist men's minds.

WE PREPARE FOR OUR JOURNEY
At the left of the page, you will see the cards we had printed as evidence of our bona (mala?) fides. They were to gain us entrée to the privy cabals of the oil trade. Further to these, we obtained wellington boots, thick gloves, and parkas with myriad zips; and our Equipment.

Now, one cannot look for oil as one looks for gold, i.e. by walking to where it might be, taking a baking dish off your donkey, and dipping it in the nearest rill. Along the Moray Firth, Walter Brennan would call up derision of a hysterical order. However, what you do need costs around eight million pounds, and this kind of loot not being readily to hand in the humour business, we chose instead to weld a poker to a trickle-charger, solder a pair of earphones to its other end, and borrow a mine-detector, the modus operandi being to wander about with the mine-detector, hammer the poker in with sudden decision, don the earphones, and watch the dial of the trickle-charger for some exhilarating response.

That none ever comes will be scant surprise to the senior geologists among you. However, as 99.99% of the Scottish population knows nothing of how pre-liminary explorations for oil are made, our kit and technique were rather impressive; and had the other .01% strolled up to enquire as to our activities, we should merely have with-drawn our poker and wellied away at high speed.

We also had some mind-boggling charts, forged by Hewison's expert nib, showing Ross & Cromarty in meticulous bogus detail, right down to the latest on-shore evidence of rich oil deposits, as carried out by earlier fake surveys from Anglo-Bahreini. I, for my literary part, had invented an impenetrable Joycean technological jargon with which to numb the minds of the curious.

The function of this agglomerated junk was multifold: if there was indeed oil about, our suspicious activities might winkle out the information from those who genuinely knew, thus making it the cheapest method of prospecting; if there was none, then our quest to examine human motives under field conditions might be richly rewarded anyhow, as men strove to get in on our act; and whether there was any or not, it would be quite clear that we were oil men, and therefore in the market for big women.

THE QUEST BEGINS

The Euston sleeper deposited us in Inverness on a slatey dawn, out of which we drove due north in a hired Land Rover. Not that we had any intention of driving anywhere that could not be reached by more urbane transport; but in the prospecting business, nothing matches the Land Rover for rugged probity.

We put ourselves to our first test at Invergordon, a town which sounds as though it ought to contain more than 2,108 souls, especially as most of these, from a cursory glance along its one main street, are solicitors. It was to the most imposing of these premises that we presented ourselves, having first ascertained from the local bank that there were no estate agents in the region, and that anyone interested in the acquisition of land would have to make his enquiries through a solicitor, via whom the purchase of same would have to pass.

There were, amazingly, six citizens in the waiting-room, a traffic unprecedented in my own long experience of the law, and given the number of law offices we had already passed, one might be forgiven for thinking that the major industry and pastime of the town was litigation. I approached the chill receptionist.

"I wonder if I might see . . ."

"There's a queue," she said, nodding curtly to the assemblage of divorcees, slanderers, axe-murderers, or whatever.

I slid my card across.

It is usually only in the cheaper novelettes that changes come over people.

"Och, ye're wi' Anglo-Bahreini!" she simpered, while I reflected upon the

"They might fool the Procurator Fiscal at Dornoch but they certainly don't fool me."

speed with which our great company's reputation had travelled in the four days since I had invented it. She pressed her intercom button.

"Sorry tae interrupt ye when ye're wi' a client," she cooed, "but I have Dr. Coren of Anglo-Bahreini Oil here, and . . ."

The intercom squawked, and a far door banged, and the image of Willie Whitelaw appeared before us, beckoning us humbly to an ante-room. I explained briefly that we wanted to know of any available land in the area, and he wanted to know if it was for industrial or residential development, and I said no; we couldn't commit ourselves, of course, but we had done some preliminary hot-shaft sub-igneous spot probings, and there seemed a strong possibility that . . . and here Hewison unrolled his tantalising chart, with its arrowed myths of subterranean goodies, and rolled it up again, quickly.

Into the lawyer's eyes there came a light which left Wolf Rock at the post.

"I've all these people tae see, ye ken," he murmured apologetically. "May I suggest ye come out to my hoose and have dinner wi' me tonight? I always find an informal atmosphere so much more conducive tae business, d'ye no find that yourself, ha-ha-ha?"

We assured him we would ring to confirm after we had seen one or two of his colleagues (which dented his smile somewhat), and left.

The receptionist leapt to open the door for us. The six clients stared bitterly.

DOWN BELOW

North along the Cromarty Firth we travelled, and as we travelled we stopped, here and there, and sprang with business-like and extravagant urgency from the Land Rover, and unloaded our gear and strapped on our electro-geoseismic rubbish and our headphones and ham-

DAY 3 — BONAR BRIDGE. *Morning.*
Our fourth electro-osmotic probe.
Again — negative.

mered in Mrs. Hewison's poker and shouted our readings to one another and noted them on our clipboards and took bearings of our position and checked them against our charts; and everywhere small knots of people gathered, fighting their curiosity, the pluckier finally asking us whether we were from the council/the Government/the Rates Office, and was it about the new road, or foot-and-mouth, or this or that; and when we demurred, and got ourselves deliberately trapped, and finally, shamefacedly, admitted that we were looking for oil, the mystic word rippled from lip to lip, and everyone told everyone else that they had told them so for years, that it stood tae reason.

And when we asked them, yes, more than one of them had heard rumblings underground, yes, they had smelt the smell we described in the air on warm wet mornings, yes, there had been other groups of mysterious men through during the past year, and yes, they *had* heard strange bangs in the middle of the night and yes, they *were* like two rifle shots fired in quick succession.

And I would nod at Hewison, and he would nod at me, and one or other of us would say:

"Deep pluvio-stratal echo-implosion soundings, I thought as much, that confirms it!"

And always in the rear-view mirror as we drove away, the groups would watch us out of sight.

With never a soul, not one, to raise the point of the possible despoliation of this lovely land, the disruption of its society an onshore oil-boom would bring, the radical changes in its way of life.

A lot of them wanted to look at our charts, though, to try to discover what their house might be sitting on.

THE BIG WOMEN (PART ONE)

We stopped that night at the Royal Hotel in Tain, on the south shore of the Dornoch Firth and a dozen miles north of Nigg itself. There was no-one to carry our bags up.

"Aye, the staff is all awa' tae Nigg!" cried the manageress bitterly. "I lost three chambermaids last week alone!"

"You see!" I exclaimed to the dispirited Hewison (we had seen almost nothing but men the entire day) at dinner, "All the women are at Nigg as I foretold! Believe me, Hewison, I am no stranger to the silver screen, I know what it will be like, they will be clad in fishnet and scarlet taffeta, with black velvet

*DAY 3 — GOLSPIE. Afternoon.
We probe the links.*

bands around their lovely throats to set off their embonpoint, their golden hair will be piled high upon their heads and fixed with rhinestone-studded combs, they will reek of irresistible cheap perfume and wish to know what the boys in the backroom will have, they will dance on the tables, flashing their garters, and when they hear that the twin-spearhead of the famed Anglo-Bahreini Oil Company is in town they will enmesh their slim fingers in our hair and lead us to rooms with mirrors in the ceilings!"

"Oh good," said Hewison.

I splashed on a lot of Monsieur Rochas after dinner, and gargled as much Listerine, and buffed my gold cuff-links to painful iridescence, and went to get Hewison.

But it had been a long day, and much as I hammered on his door, he would not wake up.

THE BIG WOMEN (PART TWO)

So we drove to Nigg the next morning. In the icy mist of the flat foreshore, giant cranes were building one another. A half-erected oil-rig lay on its side, twinkling at strategic points as welders cleaved to their bright task. All this went on behind high wire fences, whose rare gates were manned by security guards; occasionally these moaned open to let in or out charabancs filled with men in yellow helmets.

We decided to follow one of these to the town of Nigg.

It is a long, low building in dirty white stucco, with weeds round it. Beside it lies moored a grey boat the size of a Channel ferry, called the *Highland Queen*.

The town itself was closed, although we rang twice, and from the boat issued a line of the yellow-helmeted men who formed a permanent shuffling queue for the continually departing charas.

We approached an inhabitant who was sitting beside his 1100 in the fog, listening to bouzouki music on his in-car stereo. He had that fearful pallor which is left when alien cold drains the face of its natural swarthiness. He nodded when we asked him if this was all there was of booming Nigg.

"De mens live on de boat," he said. "I yam cook."

"Are there, er, women?" I enquired.

"No wimmins," he said.

"What does everyone do, then?"

"De mens weld," said the Greek cook, "and in de nights she is open de house," he nodded towards the building, "and de mens get drunk."

"Scarlet taffeta," muttered Hewison, "garters. Mirrors in the ceiling."

"Wotty say?" asked the cook.

"It doesn't matter," I said.

EPILOGUE

In the days that followed before we turned south once more for home, these examples were frequently replicated. The dreaded cashflow grippe had struck down many a brave developer, and much of the land snapped up at the beginning of the boom three years ago was back on the market; we were offered everything from solitary crofts to a six-hundred acre parcel with a castle on it that had been converted into executive offices at enormous expense, for executives that had never showed. And everywhere we were assured that whatever ravages we wished to wreak could be wrought unimpeded.

We learned some interesting things: for example, there may very well be onshore oil in just those places where we flew our preposterous kites (this from a professor of geology), that we could buy the land under which it might be, and that there was every likelihood (this from a county planning officer in Dingwall) that we would get permission to extract it. So that there is no reason why Texaco and BP and Conoco and all the rest should enjoy a monopoly: the old Texan dream of a gusher in the backyard may be dreamt here, with a solid chance of realisation.

I prefer, however, to address myself to the resident professional at Dornoch Golf Club. He is the only man we met to whom we wish to apologise. Having allowed us to explore his lovely links, he came out to stop us as we packed to drive away.

"I hope to God you found nothing," he said. "They've played golf here for, oh, two hundred years. Would you dig all this up for a few barrels of oil?"

Not us, lad. But we can only speak for Anglo-Bahreini.

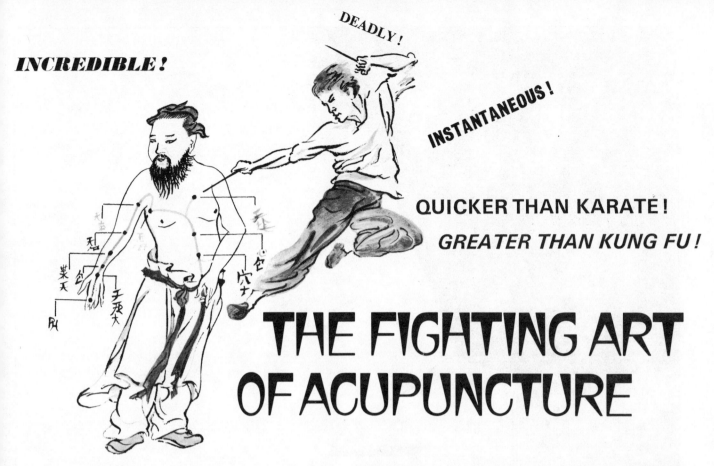

INCREDIBLE!

DEADLY!

INSTANTANEOUS!

QUICKER THAN KARATE!
GREATER THAN KUNG FU!

THE FIGHTING ART OF ACUPUNCTURE

If *you* learn how to use just two little needles, you can . . .

MAKE your opponent go instantly drowsy and heavy-headed!
WITH one jab, put any part of his body at your mercy!
CLEAR up that unsightly eczema rash that he's so fond of!
RENDER him motionless, for fear of pricking himself!

Yes, from China comes an entirely new martial art, the deadly skill of Acupuncture. Based on the mighty struggle between the Yin and the Yang, the two legendary Chinese warriors, they have evolved a method of disabling or deflecting an opponent *simply by inserting a small needle and rotating it*!

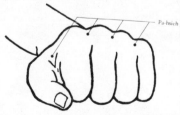

Pa-hsieh

If your opponent comes at you with a clenched fist, what do you do? Simple. Get him to stand still for a minute or two, warm the needles over burning herbs, insert them delicately at the points marked and presto! his aggressiveness will be replaced by a feeling of well-being and gratitude. You are now his master. You can even demand a fee.

And no force or physical fitness is needed! A weakling can master acupuncture! As you pierce his skin with your all-powerful weapon, it needs only a slight finger pressure and the strength to utter that traditional cry: "Tell me if it hurts you at all."

Would *you* like to be a Master of Acupuncture? To acquire the grace and poise that comes from a mastery of the needles? Just fill in this coupon and send it off.

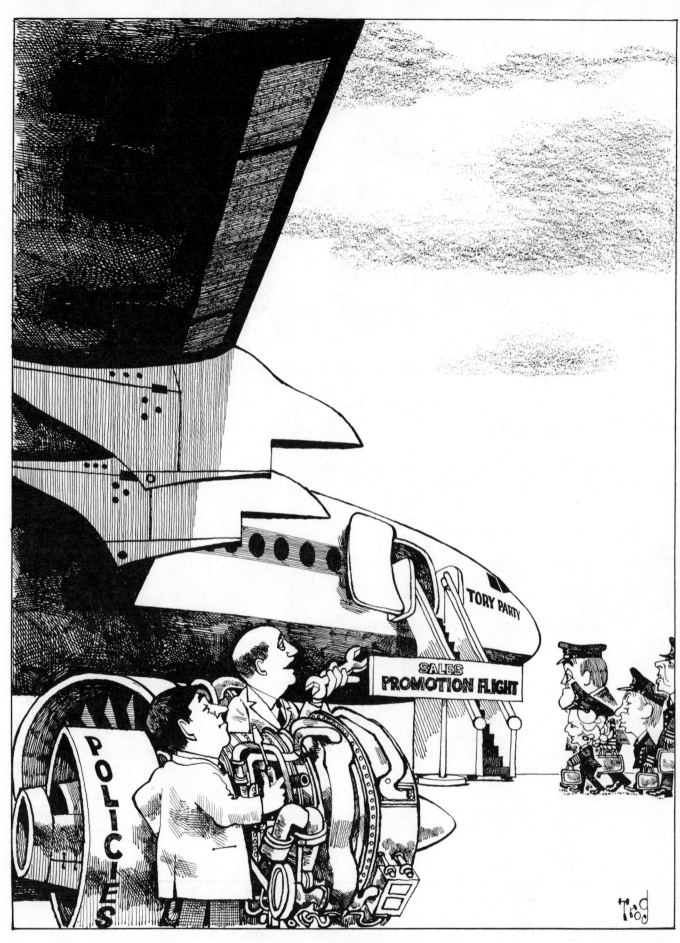

"Now all they need are the engines."

BEYOND THE Y-FRONTIER

Going it alone on film by BENNY GREEN

IT WAS WHEN I SAW THAT INTERMINABLE FILM *The Left-Handed Gun* that it first occurred to me that when a Man Keeps His Own Counsel and is clearly a Loner, it is probably because his breath smells. The deduction was certainly true of *The Left-Handed Gun*, a pretentious attempt to romanticise a grubby little homicidal lunatic called Billy the Kid, whose code of honour would have gone down big with Attila the Hun. The same is true, I suspect, of all those big, bad, mean and moody Western hombres who personified law and disorder. They were all men who found it much more congenial to clean up a town than clean up themselves, and once you start to think about it, you realise that the real reason why no gunfighter would go within fifty paces of Wild Bill Hickok was that Hickok hadn't washed his neck or changed his socks in twenty-five years, that Cole Younger was Tall in the Saddle and short on toothpaste, that Jesse James was too preoccupied with holding up trains and not nearly preoccupied enough with holding up his underpants. Not for nothing is the polecat so prominent in the mythology of the Frontier.

It is also sadly true that the man who Walks Tall has almost certainly been fitted out with a pair of lifts by the Wardrobe department, a device which has the added advantage of appearing to tilt him forward into the sunset at an angle of elevation which would give any ordinary man a hernia. There is probably no substance to the rumour that when Alan Ladd made Westerns, in order to convince the audience that our hero was tall enough to see over the top of the bar counter all the equestrian work was done using Shetland ponies, but that is one of those canards with more than a grain of truth to it. The urban hero presents many more difficulties, of course, because if you shoot a man against the background of those big lumps of rock which always kept getting mercifully in the way of John Ford's actors and then tell people that this is *The Philadelphia Story*, your chances of closing the credibility gap will not be much improved.

In any case, although the man who Does His Own Thing is acceptable enough while he is actually doing it, what are we supposed to make of him once he has done it? The trouble with being True To Your Code is that you can only be true to it once; after that everyone else starts being true to it and nothing is ever quite the same again. I have often wondered what Wyatt Earp did the day *after* he cleaned up Dodge City. (There will always be those cynics who wonder what he did the day before he cleaned it up too, but there is nothing to be done for such people.) Surely he woke that morning, took his head out of the spittoon and sighed for the good old days when the Caughnawaga Kid had only to show his face in town for Consolidated Coffins to rise fourteen points and the typesetters down at the Sentinel to shoot themselves. Try to imagine what Grace Kelly's life was like after *High Noon*, once she settled down with that chatterbox Gary Cooper. Men who are sufficient unto themselves are invariably insufficient for the rest of us, because having obeyed their Inner Voice for all those years, they have become the biggest bores in creation.

Of course people who go to the pictures don't give a fig for all this. They like to go on dreaming of a world whose problems are so childish, whose courage is so raw, whose moral issues are so clearly defined, that it needs only one brave man to turn the tide. They like the idea of big John Wayne firing a single shot and making thirty-six extras fall off their horses. They love the suggestion that big James Stewart can still buck City Hall. They positively squirm with rapture when big Bob Mitchum is shown to be a man of Few Words, and it never enters their heads to wonder what those words are. Walkingtallsberg is like the land of pornography in that it relies for its effect on the real world never getting in on the act. We have only to imagine the arrival of a Keynesian economist at the OK Corral, or a Union card in James Bond's pocket, to see what irreparable damage ambiguity may do to the tissue of our dreams.

But what about Going It Alone *inside* the movies?

The genuinely heroic attempts have taken place behind the camera rather than in front of it. Until not so long ago the great Renaissance man of the movies was Orson Welles, on the strength of *Citizen Kane*. For thirty years it had been assumed that Welles conceived the film, produced it, directed it, wrote it, starred in it, polished the camera lens each morning and swept the locker-room each night. Then in 1971 there appeared on the bookstalls Pauline Kael's brilliantly seductive *The Citizen Kane Book*, which proved beyond reasonable doubt that Orson Welles was really Herman J. Mankiewicz, having for twenty years cleverly hidden his genius from everyone in Hollywood, including himself, by writing hundreds of dreadful scenarios and drinking a lot, had suddenly revealed himself in his true colours with *Citizen Kane* and then carelessly forgotten to tell people who he was. That was the end of one myth, and only the other day there was a blow struck at another when a man appeared on the radio explaining how he had written down all the music which Charlie Chaplin was thought to have composed. To date nobody has come forward to claim authorship of the lyrics which Chaplin is thought to have written, although one of the most effective antidotes to insomnia I know is to lie there in the dark trying to imagine the expression on Irving Berlin's face on the morning he first heard *I'll be loving you eternally* and thought back to the good old days gone beyond recall when he had written *I'll be loving you always*.

To what extent Von Stroheim Strutted Tall when he made his movies, what Jehovah would have to say about Cecil B. De Mille's faith in himself as an original story writer, whether it was because he was consumed by idle dreams of Walking Tall that Von Sternberg persisted in turning up for work wearing his sister's riding boots, all these are vitally important cinematic questions to which the Pauline Kaels of the future will surely have to address themselves.

However, in the meantime, there is still one way left in which beleaguered modern urban man, beset by pestilential bureaucrats and fishbrained architects, can still experience the sensation of Going It Alone, of Being Seen Against the Skyline, of Coping with Destiny Single-handed, of Outfacing Destiny in Lonely Isolation. All he has to do is to go to the pictures any weekday afternoon.

"Be quiet."

Oop north wi' Meg Thatcher

KEITH WATERHOUSE
on how to get votes north of Watford

Fearing that Mrs. Thatcher may have less X-appeal in Wigan than in Wimbledon, some Tories are urging their party to cultivate a northern image. The public relations firm of Gradely, Champion, Nobbut and Middling are working on it.

GRADELY TO CHAMPION: I am just chasing this one round the slag-heap to see if it bites back, but don't you think we might gain more than we would lose by reopening Madam's store-cupboard? What I have in mind is stocking it with Yorkshire Relish, Piccalilli, suet, beetroot, custard-powder, fatty cake and such. Of course, we should have to play down the hoarding angle and stress that she likes to keep a morsel of summat tasty in case folk drop in for their tea.

*

CHAMPION TO NOBBUT: I am not struck by Gradely's store-cupboard notion, which would only re-open old wounds, but it does spark off a thought. Let me take this out of the set-pot to see if it rises. Whenever Madam mentions her father's shop in Grantham, can't she work in a reference to some of the produce he had on sale? I am thinking on the lines of chitterlings, polony, pigs' trotters, brawn, belly pork, Yorkshire pudding and the remainder. For a human touch, it does not seem outside the bounds of possibility that poor families would have trooped in of a Friday night and deposited a bundle of clothes or mantelpiece clock in exchange for a penn'orth of tripe.

*

NOBBUT TO MIDDLING: There is something in this memo of Champion's, although I do not want to give the impression that they were running a bloody pawnshop up there. I do not think you can buy Yorkshire pudding over the counter: Research are checking it out. But on the whole, I think this suggestion might be incorporated in the Draught Dialect Anecdote for Madam's next speech. I append same for your comments:

When ah wur a lass mi mam ad a shop. Well am saying mi mam, it wur mi dad's really, ony e wur ont cahncil so mi mam ad ter runt shop. So insteader laikin int midden wi allt other kids ah ad ter stop int shop an sell allt burrer an sugar an that. Onny road up, mi mam dint av no munny ter pay mi wages like, so shi sez, ere ahr Margaret she sez, yer can tak this tinned stuff an purrit int cupboard i case yevver go ungry like . . . .

*

MIDDLING TO NOBBUT: Never mind Draught Dialect Anecdotes. What is this sodding whippet doing in my office?

*

NOBBUT TO CHAMPION: What is a sodding whippet doing in Middling's office? I thought we were cutting down on staff.

*

CHAMPION TO NOBBUT: It's supposed to be a present for Willy Whitelaw from a domino team in Ackerthwaite, but he refuses to have it in the house. By the way, we have traced that cloth cap he was looking for. Lord Home has one; his gillie is putting it in a hat box and sending it on the night train from Aberdeen.

*

NOBBUT TO GRADELY: Tell Mr. Whitelaw his cloth cap is on the way. Ask him how he feels about racing pigeons. Remind him, as tactfully as possible, not to describe Mr. Foot and Mr. Benn as 'a brace of right Mary Annes'. The phrase is 'a *pair* of right Mary Annes', or, more succinctly, 'a right pair'.

*

GRADELY TO NOBBUT: I mentioned racing pigeons to Mr. Whitelaw, and he showed keen interest, adding that he was a very good shot. I feel we are wasting time there and that we should concentrate on Sir Keith Joseph. After all, unlike some of his colleagues who are neither summat nor nowt, he does represent a northern industrial constituency. I am just scrubbing this one with donkey-stone to see if it gets the muck off, but do you think we could induce Sir Keith and Madam to compete in an ale-supping contest?

*

NOBBUT TO MIDDLING: I am seriously thinking of putting Gradely back on the Bikkybrek account. He has no more idea of this northern image scenario than my backside. Neither have you or Champion, if it comes to that. Now hear this. What we want is northern *warmth*. We do *not* want northern *vulgarity*. Find out discreetly if Madam can sing, 'Wish me luck as you wave me good-bye' at all passably. More important: would she be prepared to close the first half of a gala performance of *Workers' Playtime* at a shoddy mill in Halifax? Remind her that Gracie Fields was once the best-loved woman in these islands.

*

MIDDLING TO NOBBUT: She can't hit the top notes, but I have dug out a good cross-talk act for Geoffrey Howe and Reggie Maudling. It's the one that begins, 'Sither, is it thee what's putting it around that I'm barmy?' It used to go well at the City Varieties, Leeds.

*

CHAMPION TO GRADELY: While Nobbut is chasing Middling around the office with a No. 3 iron, I thought I would try this idea out on you. Mind, I am just breaking open the barm cake to see if it has currants. But supposing—just supposing—that next year's Tory Party Conference were to be held in the north?

*

GRADELY TO CHAMPION: Where do you think they usually hold it, you simpering oaf? In Blackpool.

*

CHAMPION TO GRADELY: Yes? Well?

*

GRADELY TO CHAMPION: Blackpool is in Lancashire.

*

CHAMPION TO GRADELY: Is it? Oh. Well how about this, then. Supposing they hold it in Blackpool as usual, but this time they all go up there *wearing clogs*?

*

NOBBUT TO CHAMPION AND GRADELY: I will overlook the stupid memos you two have been sending each other, because you have unwittingly given me the brainwave to beat all brainwaves. This one is a beaut. It is the Big One. And it has been staring us in the face all along. Tell me this: why did none of you ever realise that Madam is *a northerner*?

*

CHAMPION TO NOBBUT: No, she isn't. She comes from Grantham.

*

NOBBUT TO CHAMPION: And where do you think Grantham is?

*

GRADELY TO NOBBUT: It's no use asking him – he thought Blackpool was in the Home Counties. I'll tell you where Grantham is – it's in Lincolnshire.

*

NOBBUT TO CHAMPION: So where's Lincolnshire? It's not in the bloody south, is it? Margaret Thatcher is a NORTHERNER! I want that leaked to all national and provincial papers immediately. Then you can get an elocution teacher signed up: let's get those vowels flattened out before she utters another word in public. Food: if she doesn't eat fish and chips she can start now. Tip off the photographers. Dress: see how she feels about wearing a turban made out of a chequered duster. Weight: I want her looking like Bessie Braddock within six months. And as soon as Middling gets back from sick leave, I want him working on a recipe for Grantham butties.

*

MIDDLING TO NOBBUT: In case the northern image bit still eludes you, let me just peg this one on the clothes-line and see if it gets soot on it. Has anyone ever given a party political broadcast in the style of George Formby, complete with ukulele? Even if H. Wilson has already done it, I think we could steal a lot of Government thunder on this one . . .

"Look, Mavis, the bus is going to stop anyway."

Legislation banning the pernicious practice of peddling bogus doctorates, degrees and diplomas is likely to be passed next year.—*The Times.*

Pity, just as *Punch* has discovered this easy way of making money:

Get yourself certified—many half-price

AS WELL AS Ordinary Degrees, there are Honorary Degrees. If your associates respect a common-or-garden M.A. or Ph.D., how much more will they respect one given *honoris causa*! We can offer you the chance to become Doctor of Civil Law of an ancient Scottish University for £365. This includes robes, a diploma in Medieval Latin and a photograph of the honorand covered in flour and egg. This week's bargain: Doctor of Diagonal Thinking, University of Rockall. Reduced to £150 o.n.o.

Cordon Bleu. PUNCH offers this outstanding culinary distinction for a down payment of only £15. Also *cordon bleu* aprons, cooking mittens and protective masks. Galoshes for pancake chefs. Make yourself a *Cordon Bleu* and improve the taste of your food.

Mr. T. Tramper of Reading found that he never had many invitations—until he contacted PUNCH and became a Grand Kleagle. Now he is asked simply everywhere! He has his own Chapter of the Klan, his own robe and his own longlife fiery cross. You too can become a Grand Kleagle for less than the cost of a box of fags a day.

Registered Taxidermist. Certificate. Collar - and - badge. Personalised rammer. 50 embellished visiting-cards. Easy terms available.

Sale of exotic titles

We offer at competitive prices a limited number of positions with great historical and romantic appeal. Reduction for quantity. How you will surprise your colleagues when you reveal that you are Exarch of Ravenna, Prince-Bishop of Holstein, Proconsul of Parthia, Grand Inquisitor, Mayor of the Palace, Satrap of Luristan or Viceroy of Mexico! Each offer includes staff of office, police pass and tie. 20% off till end of month. Annual reunion of all titleholders at leading Earls Court hotel.

Want to feel like an Editor?

We can offer a wide range of editorships. Play a trick on your friends by suddenly producing convincing proof that you edit *The Saskatchewan Liberator* or the *Journal of Psycho-linguistics* or *Secks Phun.* Special offer: Close-ups Editor of *Penthouse.*

WHY NOT be a one man university and give your own degrees? What a popular host you would be if, instead of giving booze or chocs as prizes for competitions at your party, you could award doctorates! Apply in strict confidence to PUNCH Special Requirements Dept. Ring 01-246 8071, where Lola is waiting for your call.

VICE-CHANCELLORSHIPS of the following universities available: Epping, Bettws-y-coed, Kiev, Fashoda, Rio Grande, Rotherhithe. Complete with robes, velvet cap, seal and portable mace. Price by arrangement.

Honorary Canonries. For the incumbent who feels that he has been overlooked. PUNCH—agents for the Nestorian Patriarch of Ludgate—is able to offer a strictly limited number. Does not involve additional responsibilities.

Have you ever daydreamed of being a Nobel Prizewinner? PUNCH can make your dreams come true! Just send a blank cheque, indicating which prize attracts you—Literature, Chemistry, Mathematics & Physics, Physiology & Medicine or Peace. Bibliography of publications extra. Life-size blown-up cut-out of Laureate being kissed by the King of Sweden given free with each award. Postage £7.

Mixed lot at knockdown price.
Baron of Cinque Ports, Professor of Economic Chemistry, Government Broker and member of New York Four Hundred. Best value anywhere. A chance which will never recur. What a christening present!

by Appointment

Only £100 down and you can become a Royal Physician. The fee includes a 2 ft. diploma for the consulting-room wall, cufflinks as presented by the Queen, a signed photograph of Prince Philip and an appendix in a jar labelled "From Princess Anne with grateful thanks to Doc." Optional extra: Royal Warrant to fit below brass plate.

What is life today unless you are authorised? Write today for free fourteen day trial as Inspector of Nudist Camps. Warrant card in official-style case. Armband. Peaked cap with spyhole. Ask for quotes on miniaturised camera.

THERE'S ONE REBORN EVERY MINUTE

Getting back to nature and pitting himself against the elements is the dream of many a deskbound executive—but can Nirvana be achieved on a two week holiday adventure course? MAHOOD finds out.

"My God, Mario and Franco could make a fortune here!"

"Hang on there, Humphrey! B. J. is writing you a memo!"

"I say, Sam! Are worms protein or carbohydrates?"

"We've to bear north, so all we have to do is imagine we are in Piccadilly Circus and go up Regent Street."

"Rare, medium or well done?"

You would think by now there would be some folklore on how to clear drinking water of detergents!"

"TAXI!"

The new head of ATV, Hassan Rahman Aba al-Kutbi, interviews a possible juvenile lead for the company's new 26-part series, *The Yamani Saga*. It is understood that Sir Lew Grade is to be offered a small non-speaking role as a court eunuch.

INTERNATIONAL CONSPIRACY

As yet more British firms submit to Arab pressure to sever their Jewish connections, we anticipate a few imminent news items . . .

Cadwallader, Ramsey & Flone
Bespoke Gentlemen's Tailoring
Savile Row, London, W.1

Dear Nat:

I am broken-hearted to have to tell you that we no longer require your services as a trouser-maker. You, I am sure, know that as far as I am concerned, there is no finer or more reliable trouser-man in the business, and where we shall turn now, I have no idea.

But once again, for the eighth time this week, a suit has come back from a very valuable client of ours at the Algerian Embassy. He writes that the jacket and waistcoat are exemplary, but the trousers are baggy at the crotch, have one leg shorter than the other, and no proper loops to the waistband. He further reports that the fly falls open at Embassy receptions.

I know that none of this is true. It is clear to me that he has discovered that what he has is a pair of Nat Shapiro trousers; many men, and great men, would be proud to be able to boast of that. He, unfortunately, chooses not to, and as he and his colleagues spend some three thousand a year with us, the directors and I feel that we have only one course open.

Yours sincerely,
J. B. Cadwallader.

Sir Oswald Mosley, who has been drafted into Mrs. Thatcher's Shadow Cabinet to fill the spot left vacant by the departure of Sir Keith Joseph.

From *The Times*

Bernard Levin is still on holiday. The eight-page supplement on BEIRUT—GATEWAY TO THE FUTURE appears between pp. 12 and 13.

 Royal Festival Hall
Queen Elizabeth Hall
Purcell Room

Erratum

The Manager of the Royal Festival Hall regrets that there is a misprint in tonight's programme. Rachmaninov's Second Piano Concerto in C Minor will not, of course, be played by Mr. Daniel Barenboim, but by Mr. Mustafa el-Anhalla, soloist of the Royal Festival Hall Development Corporation.

A spot-check by representatives of the OPEC countries on pump-attendants at an M1 service station. Any found with a St. Michael label on their underwear are immediately dismissed.

ON SECOND THOUGHTS

by RICHARD GORDON

I FIRST read Gray's *Anatomy* (Longmans, £14.50) in my early twenties. I found it dull to the point of narcosis, so uninspiring that I turned each of its 1,536 pages with increasing exasperation and resentment, and its style so dry that large sections were, to me, deserts of incomprehensibility. My copy was three inches thick, beautifully bound, lavishly and colourfully illustrated, a typically useless piece of coffee-table literature. In fact, it lay on my Cambridge coffee-table, unopened, for the best part of three years, until a panicky six weeks before the anatomy exams.

The first 750-page edition of *Anatomy* was published in 1858, when Henry Gray was a lecturer at St. George's Hospital. It was sagely dedicated to Sir Benjamin Brodie, the Royal Surgeon who told his pupils that money had no place in professional success, earned £10,000 a year, and never took a holiday. Gray died three years later from an attack of confluent smallpox, at only thirty-four. Re-reading the 27th edition of his masterpiece in my early fifties, I see the jejuneness of my early judgement; *Anatomy* is a work too subtle, too allusive, and too mannered for the sight of callow eyes at all. Take a typical passage:—

> The knee-joint is a ginglymus or hinge-joint. It consists of three articulations: two condyloid joints between the condyles of the femur and the semi-lunar cartilages (menisci) and condyles of the tibia; and a third between the patella and the femur, partly plane, but not completely so, since the movement is not a simple gliding one.

Such prose surely combines the obsessive comprehensiveness of Henry James, the melancholy splendour of Sir Thomas Browne, the vigour of George Orwell, and the intellectually exacting obscurity of James Joyce. It also tells you a good deal about your knees.

There were 363 pictures in the first edition of Gray. In mine, they half-filled almost every page. As a young man I scowled at them impatiently, like a rambler lost at nightfall poring over his Ordnance Survey. I was blind to the beauty of those scarlet arteries, those Mediterran-ean blue veins, those yellow nerves emitting tendrils of amazing delicacy like asparagus fern in autumn, climbing their way among the plump, beige muscles of the leg, splayed open like some succulent, tropical plant. The effect is stunning, a combination of a seed catalogue and Salvador Dali.

Figure 956, who has been flayed alive, wears an expression of reposeful martyrdom which even Michelangelo failed to capture in St. Bartholomew, who underwent the same treatment. The winged spenoid bone from the skull in Figure 347 would have served Gustave Dore as a bat. The sweeping, criss-crossing, ever dividing and merging, flat ligaments of the pelvis in Figure 541 indicate what our Maker could have done with motorway junctions, had He set His mind to them. Figure 1250, the most famous among medical students, is drawn with the painstaking precision of the Dutch masters, furnished with names and helpful little arrows, and if exposed in a Soho window would have the police round.

There is admittedly a lot of sex in Gray. But of the virtuous and puritanical kind, as Richard Hoggart described the sex in *Lady Chatterley* at the Old Bailey.

> The nipple is a cylindrical or conical eminence situated about the level of the fourth intercostal space. It is capable of undergoing a sort of erection from mechanical excitement, a change mainly due to contraction of its muscular fibres.

Today, I see the brilliance of Gray's throwaway technique. *No man should marry before he had studied anatomy and dissected the body of a woman*, advised Balzac, but he is a renowned perfectionist. Gray offered the same effect on paper. As a fringe benefit, he provided generations of lusty medical students with an admirably level-headed approach to sex, as well as making it technically much more interesting. I defy any young man to slide into erotic fantasies once he has firmly in mind that sexual stimulation is a branch of mechanics, akin to winding up the elastic before the brief flight of a model aeroplane.

The arteries depicted in Gray as supple as boiled

macaroni are, in my own anatomy, growing to resemble plastic garden hose. Only now can I appreciate how powerfully his book has influenced my personality. Nothing sends a man through life with such impregnable self-assurance as knowing precisely what every other man is made of, down to the five possible positions of his appendix. Sir Lancelot Spratt was every inch a man who had learned Gray from cover to cover. If I have myself been spared such intolerable extremes, it is through study of Gray's embryology section, 160 pages long.

It induced some humility in me to learn that during pre-natal life I was equipped with a set of gills, like a trout. Figure 260, a blow-up showing myself an inch long, big headed and pot-bellied, a goblin from Hieronymus Bosch, was more deflating than any nude study on the hearthrug shortly after I had joined the outside world.

In the third month the head is extended and the neck is lengthened. The eyelids meet and fuse, remaining closed until the end of the sixth month. The limbs are well developed and the nails appear on the digits. The normal umbilical hernia is reduced and by the end of this month the crown-rump length of the foetus is about 10 cm.

That happened to me, and it happened to you. It happened to prime ministers, to trade union leaders, and to the world's most beautiful women. One touch of Gray makes the whole world kin.

The brain of which man is so ridiculously proud is exposed by Gray in 120 pages as a huge, juicy walnut. He is not concerned with the loftiness of human thought. He is interested only that it gyrates round such landmarks as the Hippocampus, the Fimbria, and the Medial Geniculate Body. The grey matter of man's cortex, on which civilization exclusively depends, is presented in Figure 896 and looks like the dregs in a bottle of port.

Gray is a more specialised author on which to found the philosophy of a lifetime than Halsbury, or John Stuart Mill, or Clausewitz. But I believe his *Anatomy* instils a lasting and sadly uncommon sense of proportion, if only through awareness with every sentence that the paths of glory lead but to the grave. He succeeded in writing a memorable elegy.

"I've bequeathed my body to Bond Street."

THE TIME OF MY LIFE

by HUMPHREY LYTTELTON

I ENTERED the lists against Schickelgrüber in October, 1939. As a patriotic rush to arms it was unspectacular – just a matter of popping up to London, being interviewed by the Lieutenant-Colonel of the Grenadier Guards, who assessed my qualities as a leader of men with some probing questions about my prowess with the cricket bat (to which he got some pretty unsatisfactory answers, I can tell you), and going away to await call-up in several months' time. It was the first – and only – time in my life that anyone said to me, 'Don't call us, we'll call you.'

By a process not wholly unconnected with nepotism of sorts, I found myself filling in the time, with a cousin of the same age, at a steel works in South Wales – the very same that has since been promoted to *the* Steel Works of South Wales. We were signed on as 'students' at fifteen bob a week, which in those days took care of digs with all found *and* a weekly visit to the movies. Our landlady in Tan-y-groes Street, Port Talbot, was a mum to us, easing us into our new life on a cushion of almost incessant conversation. She had a lung capacity like a blacksmith's bellows and kept up the flow of words until the last cubic millimetre of breath was expended, replenishing the supply with an intake that nearly dragged the tasselled crochet cover off the sideboard. She initiated us at once into the mysteries of high tea. In our hitherto sheltered lives we had known only 'supper' or, on posh occasions, 'dinner'. The first time the mongrel blend of afternoon tea and supper appeared on the table at half past six, I spread strawberry jam all over the cold meats, taking it to be chutney.

It was a rackety life at Tan-y-groes Street. The land-lady's husband was bedridden upstairs with the after-effects of a stroke, one of which was that he snored incessantly and, what was worse, irregularly day and night. You never knew when the next burst was coming. There was another lodger, a Mrs. Mullens, in whom our arrival triggered off acute paranoia. She wore what, as children, we used to call 'dribbling glasses' – gold-rimmed pince-nez secured to her corsage by a thin chain which wobbled like saliva when she bristled indignantly, which she did whenever she clapped eyes on us. Within a week she became convinced that we had engineered a plot to keep her out of the bathroom. If she saw the bathroom door closed, she assumed that one of us was inside, thwarting her hygienic purposes. We would watch her through the chink in our bedroom door, stalking like an enraged hen up and down outside the empty bathroom, her pince-nez dribbling furiously, muttering, 'I know they're in there!' She never actually tried the door-handle, preferring instead to make her presence known by continually pulling the chain of the lavatory next door.

Life as a student in the steel works wasn't initially very exciting. The managers in the various departments were too busy promoting the war effort to give us more than cursory instruction, so we drifted about drawing diagrams in notebooks. I could still give you a rough idea of how a Coke Oven works. As a matter of fact, at any point in the past thirty-five years I could have given you a rough idea of how a Coke Oven works, but you've never actually asked. In the circles in which I move now, there aren't many conversational gambits which lead naturally to a rough exposition of the workings of a Coke Oven. It's just as well, really, because, the first time I saw a Coke Oven in action, it struck me as rather rude. It's an absurdly simple process – coal is fed in at the top and, after a sort of digestive process, coke comes out. It was when I first witnessed the laborious and seemingly rather painful evacuating process that I thought, 'I've heard of art imitating nature, but this is going too far.' Until I had drawn diagrams of about three hundred pipes and their destinations, I hadn't realised how many by-products come from the coking process. On one occasion, in order to convince us and himself that we were doing something useful, the manager put us on a night-shift in the labora-tory where, judging by the pervading smell of naphtha-lene, they extracted from coal gas the basic ingredient for mothballs. We sat up all night wielding a dip-stick and making crucial tests on the liquid at clearly specified intervals. Or rather, we would have done had we not

"I'm afraid you're too old."

rather carelessly dropped off at around midnight, waking up in the first light of dawn to the realisation that several critical points in the process had come and gone unrecorded. We hadn't been equipped for life at an expensive public school for nothing, so we dug out the records for the previous week and fudged a convincing-looking entry from them. If you happen to recall a purchase of mothballs, round about Christmas, 1940, which stripped the paper off the bedroom walls, burnt a twelve-inch hole in the back of Dad's Sunday suit and anaesthetised the family cat, I'd be rather obliged if you would keep it quiet.

I won't dwell on the Blast Furnaces, since the transformation of iron ore into molten metal involves those same digestive processes about which we have all heard quite enough already. (It will not surprise you by now that someone whose mind, confronted by the great seething and steaming monuments to man's ingenuity, went straight to human plumbing, failed to make any great headway in industry.) Anyway, it took a long and notably friendless time for it to become known to us that, to the workers, the two strangers haunting the manager's office and snooping about writing in notebooks were clearly spies for the management. We were not helped by the very new-looking cloth caps and dungarees supplied to us by Mr. Lewis in the High Street who, I hardly dare say it, would persist in referring to the latter as 'dungs'. Even after we had surreptitiously sprawled about in coal dust to take the newness out of them, we still felt conspicuous outsiders.

Our status changed when we graduated to the Melting Shop. Here we were discovered by Fred Hurley, a Londoner who, at work, was the charge-hand of the labourers' gang, and in his spare time was the local secretary of Toc H and what was then the British Empire Leprosy Relief Association. He found out somehow that we were distantly related to Gilbert Talbot, in whose memory Toc H had been founded. From that point on he

befriended us with such dynamic ruthlessness that we were soon engulfed in altruistic activity – canvassing door-to-door in an Ask-A-Soldier-To-Tea campaign, writing home to Eton to rustle up second-hand books for our lads at sea, even soliciting second-hand pipes from former schoolmasters to send to leper colonies in Africa. Anyone who has ever witnessed the many functions of a schoolmaster's pipe – an instrument for chewing ferociously, waggling facetiously, prodding sagely, puffing ruminatively – will guess that this turned out to be a gruesome collection, but we were assured that they worked wonders in pacifying the patients.

As a counterbalance to these seemingly pious activities, Fred, who had a well-worked and notably unpious repertoire of expletives, introduced us to the beer-drinking marathons at the Velindre Working Men's Club, where, after a night or two, a tear-jerking trumpet rendering of *Land of My Fathers* marked my debut in show business. More important, Fred rapidly formed the opinion that it was no bloody good our wandering about the bloody works bloody scribbling in notebooks. The gang of which he was in charge shovelled and humped the ingredients which went into the steel-making furnaces – they had names like dolomite and manganese, but they all looked like grey gravel to us. Under his quite unauthorised guidance we put away our notebooks and set to with shovels. Of all the processes, the Melting Shop, where pig-iron and scrap, seasoned with dolomite and manganese, was brewed into steel, held the most fascination for me. Experts called sample-passers (Oh Lord, here we go again!) could peer into a briefly-opened furnace through hand-held windows of blue glass and tell from the hue of the bubbling mass inside if it was cooking to specification. An élite team of furnacemen, with towels round their necks and little blue spectacles to protect their eyes, 'fettled' the furnace expertly, shovelling up grey gravel and hurling it through the small oven door in one rhythmic movement. They let us fettle a furnace once or twice, demonstrating the technique of which the late Duke Ellington, in another sphere, knew the secret – 'It don't mean a thing if it ain't got that swing'. The crane-drivers who lifted the doors only kept them open for a short time, to conserve heat. Interrupt the rhythm, mess up the footwork, and you sent a stream of gravel splatting against the closed door. The first time I tried I forgot to keep a straight shovel and practically decimated the work-force with flying buck-shot.

Our days as outsiders were over. At break-times, we could sit around with the others in the glow of the furnaces, arguing about Churchill, spreading careless talk about where the bombs fell last night and listening to the shop-floor philosopher holding forth. Old William Evans, who looked like Rudyard Kipling, was semi-retired and on light work, so he had plenty of time to wander about

refereeing arguments. He had clearly put in a vast amount of reading in his time and had absorbed the gist, if not the actual pronunciation, of a great deal of Western philosophy. If a discussion became too heated, he would douse it by holding up a finger and saying, 'As so-and-so said in his great book, "State, Ecclesiasastical and Whaddyercall . . ." '

If my life can be said to have had a single turning-point, the short time in South Wales was it. I came out of it deeply imbued with romantic socialism – a rush of Keir Hardies to the head which I have never lost. There were warm friendships, too, cemented over dominoes at the Velindre Club while up to fifteen pints of beer on a good night gurgled merrily on their way.

And if you want your furnace fettled, baby, just call me, huh?

"Hey, this is a serious poetry reading, God damn it!
In Russia I could go to jail for this stuff."

Can You Hear Me, Alex?

A hundred years ago Alexander Graham Bell gave us the telephone. BASIL BOOTHROYD called up to tell him what it has meant to us all.

'**M**R. BELL? LET ME SAY right away that I'm not going to make any of those old cracks about wrong numbers. It's easy enough – Hello, who? Isn't that Celestial 9000? No, I didn't dial the Ministry of Defence, I dialled Celestial 9000, or actually 01 if you're outside London, which I am, and then 434-02944-7727-nine-0-double-0. I think. I've lost the bit of paper now. Yes, that's right. And your number is 930-7022? Easily confused, I agree. Sorry you've been – oh, all right, stuff it, if that's how you feel.

'Bloody telephones. Start again.

'Celestial 9000? Good. Extension 2828, please. Yes, I thought it would be. Yes, I'll hold, as long as you don't just leave me dangling, because this is costing me a bomb. I sometimes think that people on switchboards don't realise there are still a few private subscribers left who don't just chalk it all up to the company and forget it. Hello.

'Hello, hello, hello. HELLO. Surely that last one must have made a bit of a squawk in your earpiece? What have you done with it, stuck it in a drawer? Silly cow. Oh, I'm sorry, I didn't know you were there. Well, I'm sorry. Yes, extension 2828. Thank you.

'Mr. Bell? I'm just ringing to congratulate you on your wonderful invention. When I think that it's only a century ago that you disclosed to your father, as the press release from the Canadian High Commission puts it, the principle of a – I'm what? I'm very faint? Yes, well, I feel very faint. You're right, very poor reception. Oh, I see. I'm on to Reception. No. I wanted Mr. Bell, extension 2828. That *is* extension 2828? Fine. it's not Mr. Bell. Damn it. No, I realise it isn't your fault, probably mine. So much to remember, 01-434-02944-nine-0-double-02828, and I see now it's actually 8282, sorry, *mea culpa*. What? Never mind. If you would, thanks very much.

'Mr. Bell? His secretary, well, that's something. Is he there? Well, yes. I could tell you who's calling, but I don't see what difference that makes to whether he's there or not. Anyway, he won't know me. Oh, he's not there, in that case. No, dear, I know you didn't say "in that case", not in so many words. Just a nuance, you know. Yes, I could certainly tell you what it's about, but I know what would happen then. I've had it before. You'd put me on to somebody else, without telling them all I've told you about what it's all about, then I should have to tell them what it was all about, then they'd put me – Still, let's scrub that. Is he there yet? No. I was a fool to say that he wouldn't know me. I suppose if I'd said that the Canadian High Commission – Ah, so he's there now. No, no, don't tell him that I'm the Canadian –

'Mr. Bell? Good morning. You're right, it's afternoon now, I hadn't realised. No, I'm afraid I'm not. A misunderstanding with your secretary, please don't hang up, or ring off, as I expect you used to say in those grand old pioneering days in Brantford, Ontario, when you and your father were the only subscribers, you downstairs and him up, and neither of you dreaming, I'd like to bet, that the time would come when millions of people all over the globe would benefit from a sophisticated system of telecommunications enabling them, at the lift of an instrument, to hear Test scores, recipes, bedtime stories, heavy breathing, conversations between unknown lady subscribers fixing up Bridge evenings, and the drycleaners' manageress they'd hoped would be the plumber.

'I didn't mean to say all that, but it's one of the effects your great hundred-year-old invention has on me if the chap at the other end says either nothing or the absolute minimum, such as "Cartwright": I get this compulsion to rabbit on, make jokes, ha-ha, which never work on the phone for some reason, tell about bits of drama we've had over the broad beans blowing down or locking the car with the keys inside, and I can feel the distant subscriber, usually top management types these no-small-talk men, thinking he's got a right nut here, pardon? I thought you said something.

'Another thing is, have you ever realised that the person you're telephoning could have their back to you all the time? Also that if there are twenty-two call boxes in a row at airports, with twenty-one occupied, you find when you dive into the unoccupied one it's out of order. I don't see why everybody else knows this instinctively, any more than I see why people who call up in the evening when you've been out all day can't get down to business without telling you that they've kept calling before and couldn't get you, as if you ought to have stayed in just in case. And why do you find yourself not only apologising for being out but explaining where you've been, as if it was any of their damned business, when you consider that they're probably only wanting you to lend them your electric hedge-cutter, or find them an address they thought you said you had and when you ring back after an hour's search to say you haven't they've gone out, blast them?

'Hello? Ah, I thought you'd – No, I simply wanted to congratulate you on your wonderful invention, which of course has seen great improvements and developments since you personally became a, how shall I put it, ceased line in 1922. Why, good heavens, in 1922, anyone wanting to borrow gardening tools or have addresses found for them would have had to make an actual visit, which means that they wouldn't have. Quite a rarity then, the telephone. Old army friends with a few hours to kill at your local railway station couldn't just call up and suggest dropping in with the kids and dog for a drink and a bite of supper: they got a cab and showed up right on the front step, and it was too late to tell them, as you can on the phone, that they happen to have caught you at an awkward time, when your wife's nursing two sick aunts in the spare room and the house is on fire.

'I want you to know, by the way, that these few halting words of appreciation aren't merely from me. I speak, I think, on behalf of all humanity, except for

"*Have you noticed how pale and languid the visitors are looking nowadays?*"

"*My whole life flashed before my eyes and I wasn't in it.*"

those on the installation waiting list. Naturally, I can't give you a comprehensive run-down of your innumerable – ha! I nearly said numberless, but that's the waiting list – of your innumerable beneficiaries. It would read like a telephone directory. One or two people, I'm sure, would wish for a special mention, such as radio producers, whose heavy responsibility for devising programmes has been almost totally lifted since they started licence-holders phoning in and making their own. Still on the arts, what of the benefits to the dramatist? He forgets, I daresay, that playwrights operating before the historic 26 July 1874, Shakespeare to name but one, couldn't just give up any sentence when it got difficult and scribble *Phone Rings* in the right-hand margin. None of your, "Hath not old custom made this life more sweet . . . I'd better answer that, it might be Pete."

'Though we shouldn't overlook one of your wonderful invention's greatest satisfactions, which is not answering it. This, I understand, is the bait used by railways the world over to recruit staff into Passenger Enquiries.

'But, as I say, we're all in your debt. Or somebody's. I shall be getting a whacking bill for this lot, I can tell you, it's had more pips than a melon. Than a melon. A melon. I said it's had more pips than – right, you've got it. That's one great fault with this invention, as I say, it's no good for jokes. You don't agree? Have you ever tried? I'm not just talking about calling up selected unfortunates and saying Are you Smellie? In my experience, Alex – I hope I can tell you Alex? I can call you what? I can call you Tom?

'What do you mean, it's a joke?

'Very funny.

'And goodbye to you too, Edison.'

THIS MEANS HAMBURGER WAR!

STANLEY REYNOLDS charts the opening of hostilities

WE Americans can forgive you English everything. The Boston Massacre, Bunker Hill, the British Empire, and the British Yoke, but what we can never forgive is what you have done to the hamburger. I understand the Belgians are equally unforgiving about what you've done to the Brussels sprout, but that is beside the point, strictly an issue to be ironed out in the Common Market.

For one thing the English have never taken the hamburger seriously. One of the few times you'll hear laughter coming from the kitchen of an English restaurant – as opposed to the Chinese who seem to find everything funny – is when someone comes in and orders what the menu calls a Real American Style Hamburger or The All American Hamburger or some other such slur upon what is in fact one of our few gifts to international culinary arts.

Just to give you an idea of how bad things are, I went out the other day to research this essay on the British-burger, to the restaurant where I usually have lunch and which boasts on its menu an 'American hamburger'. Fortunately the waitress there had been tipped generously in the past and she now tipped me the wink.

'Don't,' she said, 'and say you did.'

'Bad, huh?'

'I don't know, I've never had one, but the head cook, the one with the nice eyes, has a bit of a sadistic streak and every time he's making them burgers they are all laughing a lot in there. Of course, the trouble is, he knows it.'

'Knows what?'

'That he has nice eyes.'

So I sat chewing my way through the rubber scampi – there are no bones in scampi, are there? – wondering if the hamburger could really be such a laff riot success compared to the rest of the extremely amusing stuff that comes from the kitchen.

All this, however, is about to end. The hamburger, we are told, the real American, the Great American Ham-burger, is at long last coming to England. Well, it seems to me I've heard that one before. But never before have we had the McDonald hamburger people of Chicago on the job.

McDonald's, who operate a chain of hamburger joints in the USA, have opened a place in Woolwich. Readers of the *Daily Mail* were informed the other day that, 'The Battle of the Hamburgers' was on.

'We are going to wipe Wimpy off the High Streets of the UK,' a McDonald-man said, sounding a bit like Rommel talking about clearing the rats out of Tobruk.

The Wimpy reply was, I am glad to say, a bit more subdued. 'We won't stand still,' their spokesman said.

The *Mailman*, a Mr. James Gibbons, then raced to the Savoy where Mr. Sylvino Trompetto, a chef with an MBE, made him a burger and said:

'A hamburger should be grilled rather than fried; finely chopped onions are of inestimable help and it ought to be dusted slightly with flour or bread crumbs and caressed with oil rather than cooking fat.'

That all sounds very nice but it doesn't sound at all like a hamburger. For one thing the chef has to be smoking a cigarette and Mr. Trompetto MBE has not mentioned the cigarette. In fact, it is much better to have a burger made by a fellow with tattoos rather than an MBE. I think cigarette ash is one of the vital ingredients of a real American hamburger which the English seem to leave out. Also they leave out the beef.

Speaking personally I have always found the McDonald burger – called the Big Mac – a bit of a failure, a bit too pretentious really. Of course, it is all beef and all that – for gosh sakes, Missus, don't what ever you do put ham in it – but the McDonald places are too nice.

When I called those hygienic havens 'hamburger joints' I was being poetic. Joints they definitely are not. And that is their big trouble. McDonald's take the whole business too seriously really. They even have a sort of a college out in Chicago called Hamburger University where they train the fellows to make the things as if they were going to go out into the world and split the atom or strip assets or something.

But anyone who has seen an old movie on TV knows what a hamburger joint should look like. It should have, for a start, Ann Sheridan waiting on tables, chewing gum and making wisecracks out of the side of her mouth. It should have swinging doors and flies and John Garfield and Ronald Reagan (Sheridan and Reagan *Juke Girl* 1942) sitting at the counter in floppy cloth caps asking for a cup of java. And it should also have the guy with the tattoos and the cigarette ash sweating over the griddle in the back room making the burgers.

All over the US at one time that was the one and only truly original hamburger joint and that is where the hamburger sprung from, from the depths of darkest Depression America. There are no hamburgers better than the ones that came out of hamburger joints like that with Ann Sheridan type waitresses giving all the customers dirty looks and every now and then shouting at the cook:

'Hi Angelo! stop working so hard, you're sweating in the food again.'

The last hamburger I had in America was in the Biltmore in New York and it was something like Mr. Trompetto MBE's hamburger and it cost six dollars and it was nothing like so good as the ones I used to get from places called Nick's and Joe's and Nemmo's and The Miss Fall River Diner for fifteen cents.

Now, McDonald's are not the Biltmore or the Savoy but they are classy enough in their own right – and clean, which is probably the great mistake. Just as no self-respecting French chef will let a good soup leave his kitchen without first – or, finally – spitting in it (for good luck) a real hamburger has to emerge somehow triumphant from out of grease and grime.

That is the great artistry of the hamburger. Here is this Depression grub which is really nothing but an ounce or two of minced meat with maybe some makeweight put in it and people are eating it only because they are poor and cannot afford to eat anything else, but, all of a sudden, what do you know, a new art form, like jazz music emerging from the cat houses of New Orleans, is born at Nick's and Joe's: the hamburger is not only something to fill an empty stomach but also it is actually good to eat and people come from all over town – toffs, even, in white ties and tails with Carole Lombard on their arm – to Nick's to have his hamburgers with the cigarette ash in them made by the cook who was only the week before last doing five in Sing Sing for armed robbery.

Of course, then all the phonies take over and it is just like any other folk art. Suddenly the hamburger gets a college education and they are charging six dollars for one of them and chefs are talking about a burger needing to be 'caressed with oil'.

The only way to make a real hamburger is wait until the wife goes away for a couple of days and the kitchen gets real dirty. Then you buy some mince or, better still, get the butcher to grind up chuck steak (in US top round) twice; bash into round patties, thick for rare, thin for well done (all this two ounces, four ounces is just talk); place them on a hot greasy griddle or well greased non-

stick pan; place plate on burger on griddle to press burger down; read the runners in the 3.30; flip and do the other side while smoking cigarette and shouting at the customers (the kids), 'Hey, listen youse guys, I onney got two hands for cryin' out loud, geez, some of dese guys come in here, know what I mean, and the Yankees dropped a double header to the Sox, too, for cryin' out loud.'

That is how to make them. There is no other way. Neither Wimpy nor McDonald make them like that and so all this talk about the great beefcake battle is mere press agentry. The burger never lived here and it is dead in the US, killed by hygiene and the pure food and drug act. If it survives at all it is at 65 Menlove Avenue, Liverpool 18 when the wife is away and I am left in charge.

But none of my troubles in making real hamburgers in darkest Lancashire, the bother of getting a butcher to grind the steak through twice for you, the problem of finding a type of Scotch bap that looks something like a hamburger roll (try a North Country barm cake), is anything at all compared to the ordeal I have gone through seeking to reproduce the Great American Hot Dog. The English hamburger has only made me smile, but the English hot dog has had me sitting down in the middle of the road with my shoes off weeping.

"*Do you remember the good old days before nostalgia?*"

Luxury look for new Jobcentres

By NORMAN LEITH

LONDON'S "dismal" Labour Exchanges are being swept away in a massive wave of reorganisation that aims to give a 20th-century facelift to the capital's employment centres.

... the man charged with getting rid of the dole

"I have no doubt that within a few years London will have the finest public employment services in the world."

He is Mr Arthur Durham, London director of the Employment Service Agency, the independent body wh... over...

"My task is clear," Durham. "It is ... the dismal ... Exchanges ... vide ...

the war, the ...

OPENING SOON!

London's first Jobcentre Supermarket. It's the end of the dismal dole queue, a luxury re-fit for the capital's Labour Exchanges. Just pop into your "local" employment centre and browse through our vivid selection of wonderful opportunities, enjoy the lovely surroundings, relax over a chat in the Jarrow Suite. This could be *your* chance to move up a socio-economic grade or two!

Fancy a change? Fed up with the routine of going to work every day? Why not give the whole family a special surprise treat and turn up tonight as a stevedore or a tractor hand? Interested in people? You could train to be an osteopath or you might enjoy life in a laundry. There are wonderful chances in riveting and packaging luncheon meat, just watch your friends' faces when you tell them you are servicing tarpaulins or working as an armature winder, in pest extermination or as a part-time vet. If you can do your own parting, you might fit in as a sociologist and many redundant brokers and accountants have made a stimulating fresh start working in aquaria, poultry farming, making aerosols or sorting smokeless fuels. There's something for everyone at your swish new Jobcentre Supermarket now, no obligation, nothing to pay. If you're not entirely satisfied, pop in again tomorrow.

SPECIAL OPENING WEEK ATTRACTION

YOUR CHANCE TO MEET AN EX-TV STAR!

Stan Lucas. You've seen him on *Police Five*, he was an extra in a *Man Alive* special. He's a man with no time for tommy-rot. Stan is out of work and so, naturally, he spends a lot of his time with us. He travels regularly down to the Post Office. "I don't want to be bogged down with tiresome form-filling and luncheon vouchers and that," says Stan. "I know instinctively what I'm prepared to consider and what I'm not. Bags of variety, dished up in pleasant surroundings—that's what I like to see. That's why I chose the Jobcentre Supermarket. I'm not saying the old place wasn't nice, I quite like the Public Library too. But my time is precious. Here they work out my daily programme for me, leaving me free to walk down the road." Like many experienced unemployed, Mr Lucas chooses the Jobcentre Supermarket because he can rely on them. And because he's got other things to think about besides work. If you're the same, call the Department of Employment and ask for details of the new service. You'll be glad you did.

Just two of the satisfied customers at Jobcentre Supermarkets:

The Rafferty sisters. Rene was pickling herrings on and off, Molly was bogged down in a pork pie maker's with no prospects excepting the staff discount chipolatas. Says Rene: "It was a stroke of luck, really. Me and Molly wandered in one day, thinking it was just a supermarket, see. We was after a packet of Digestives. Any road up, we liked the place and decided to stay and as it happened they was after a pair of shorthand typists, give the place a bit of atmosphere. We're just keeping our fingers crossed that nice Mr Joseph gets in, keep business brisk. There's a lot of ordinary people like us as like it round here, very cosy, plenty to read. I should say we're well pleased."

The French have appointed a Minister with responsibility for improving the quality of life. He sees his task as encouraging joie de vivre. Can Britain afford to lag behind?

A MESSAGE TO THE NATION
by the Minister for Joy

I HAVE been entrusted with the task of improving the quality of life in Britain. This is something which has never been attempted before.

Yesterday we sat round a table discussing whether to put aphrodisiac into your ketchup.

Tomorrow we may find ourselves debating whether to revive the sports of Merrie England, like shin-kicking, or eating live rats for wagers.

Let me say that it is not my intention to run a Ministry of Silly Walks. Nor is it true that I want to get the whole nation swinging on chandeliers, or sliding down stairs on tea trays, though these practices have undoubtedly played a creative part in the national character.

I can't help you to get enough sugar, but are you all getting enough noise? Not just any old noise, but the noise you like?

Some of you may have watched the Edinburgh Tattoo on television and seen the wealth of litter gusting across the esplanade as the Highlanders marched. That set me thinking. Which would you really prefer—the Tattoo or the litter? Ought we to stage a Festival of Litter instead?

Write in to tell me what would make you happy, whether it is more private armies or fewer books about Mick Jagger. Do you perhaps find that the hot water and the cold water in the bath do not mix as readily as they once did? I know I do!

You won't bother me with trivial complaints about inflation, will you?

Why not ring me, reversing the charges? Happiness is a free phone call!

A RECIPE FOR DISASTER

MR. HAROLD WILSON's appointment of a Minister for Constructive Rapture, or whatever his absurd title is to be, is the most cynical piece of electioneering yet. Not only is the concept of a contented and joy-filled Britain a piece of palpable lunacy, but it is a piece of *dangerous* lunacy. The appointment is a harking back to the Nazi "Strength Through Joy" movement of the 1930s. We have seen what cataclysmic follies were achieved by a nation encouraged to regard happiness, nay ecstasy, as its unifying bond. The mind fairly boggles at the thought of a Britain steeped in centuries of bickering and mistrust transformed overnight into a euphoric community, with everyone behaving as if he had won a fortune in the pools. What cosmic follies might not be set afoot by such an intoxicated nation! The plain truth is that Britain needs envy and dissent to bind it together. When the sages of old demanded of the Oracle, "Can anything destroy Sparta?" the answer came, "Luxury". Only one thing can destroy Britain: happiness.

DAILY EXPRESS
THE INDEPENDENT NEWSPAPER

OPINION

JAIL THEM!

THE *Daily Express* believes in looking on the bright side. Optimism is good for circulation. Advertisers love it.

That is why the *Express* welcomes a Ministry of Joy. Even Socialist-inspired fun is better than no fun at all.

But the Government should take a still bolder step. It should revive the 1940 regulation which made it a prison offence to say anything likely to create "alarm and despondency".

What glorious days those were! The nation's morale never stood higher.

In war or peace, the place for Dismal Jimmies is behind bars!

What YOU can do to spread joy

If you are a motorist:
Has it occurred to you that by covering your car with Disney stickers and fluorescent shamrocks you may be creating, not universal happiness, but a deepening sense of nausea at the fathomless imbecility of the human race?

Peel them all off and watch people's faces light up!

If you are a shop assistant:
There is a whole lot you can do, if you will only stop talking to your fellow assistant and listen. Try looking at the customer as you hand him his change, instead of holding it in his general direction while conversing over your shoulder. Many complaints have been received recently of shop assistants serving their own mothers without knowing it.

Another good idea—are you *listening*? —is to say Thank You to the customer, even though the words are printed in pale pink ink on the receipt.

If you are a duke:
Drain off the Grand Cascade and all fountains and replenish with a good sparkling white wine (*not* red, which makes people think of gushing arteries). There is no need to wait for your heir's coming-of-age—the time to spread happiness is now.

If you are a weather forecaster:
Find an honest trade and stick to it. Your resulting happiness will communicate itself to others a hundredfold.

If you are a vermiculite exfoliator:
Just keep on doing whatever you usually do and pray that it will somehow add to the sum of human ecstasy.

If you are a schoolboy:
Do not eat ice cream on your way to school in the morning, unless your doctor advises it. The practice infuriates elderly people who have not had your advantages and is liable to give them heart attacks.

If you are a toddler:
Timmy Tucker always looks where he is going and everybody loves him. Why don't you try to be like Timmy Tucker?

If you are a bus driver:
Try to stop your bus so that the rear platform is next to the tail end of the queue. This helps to throw people together and breaks down their reserve.

If you are a secretary:
Have you ever thought what simple pleasure you could give to others by saying "yes" now and again?

● ● ●

YESTERDAY IN PARLIAMENT

Mr. Jeremy Thorpe (*Lib.*): Will the Minister for Joy state what plans he has to stimulate *joie de vivre* in old age pensioners?

The Under-Secretary of State for Joy: It is our intention that, as from September 1, all male pensioners over 70, and all female pensioners over 65, shall receive one free, heaped tablespoonful of effervescent liver salts weekly.

Mr. Norman St. John Stevas (*Con.*): Has my right hon. friend any comment to make on the vast and often indelicate psychedelic paintings executed by spray guns on the facade of the building which houses his Ministry in Whitehall? Does he consider that these will contribute to the greater happiness of the greatest number?

The Under-Secretary for Joy: The designs referred to were executed by a group of former squatters recently recruited to my Ministry's Think Tank. As is well known, it is the custom of squatters to create psychedelic fantasies on the walls of buildings they occupy, in order to brighten the lives of their neighbours. I am persuaded that these embellishments in no way detract from what is in any event a somewhat run-down environment.

Mr. St. John Stevas: Perhaps the Minister will further imitate the practice of squatters and arrange for pop music to blare from every window of his Ministry, by day and night?

The Under-Secretary for Joy: Steps are already in hand to provide this facility.

Mr. Willie Hamilton (*Lab.*): Will the Minister state how many employees of the Ministry of Joy were found hanged last week? (*Laughter.*)

The Under-Secretary for Joy: This information is classified.

Austerity French Style

The idea of French restraint may strike some people as a contradiction in terms (une contradiction de termes), but there are historical precedents for it (pour ça).

Les Précédents Historiques

"I only told him about three of the parts."

"Nice one, voices! My voices say we can knock off for lunch."

*"We mustn't massacre **all** the Huguenots, my angel. We must leave a few for the British textile industry."*

"And not tomorrow night either, Josephine."

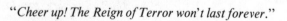

"Cheer up! The Reign of Terror won't last forever."

by **HANDELSMAN**

Et Alors...

"*Not so fast, Jacques! Sacred blue, you drive like an Englishman.*"

"*And for those intimate occasions when the central heating breaks down, Givenchy solves the problem with an army blanket.*"

"*No more can-can, Thérèse! We are only supposed to do the could-could.*"

"*Henri, the country can no longer afford extravagant gestures.*"

"*Dear Jean-Paul, I need your help in editing my new book, A Definitive Study of Everything. In its present form, it runs to well over six pages.*"

"*To a successful nuclear test, gentlemen! Garcon! Another bucket of Babycham.*"

151

MY SOCIAL CONTRACT

by E. S. TURNER

Memorandum of Social Contract between E. S. TURNER (hereinafter called the High Contracting Party) and Her Britannic Majesty's Government (hereinafter called the Government).

1. In return for taxes paid at regular or irregular intervals by the High Contracting Party, the Government shall at all times conduct itself in a sober, clean, truthful and responsible manner. It shall avoid high crimes and misdemeanours, take greater care in the creation of life peers, discourage its servants from putting milk bottles on window sills and restore the self-respect of the Post Office by obliging postmen to resume uniform instead of wearing holiday clothes.

2. The Government shall on demand afford the High Contracting Party such physical protection as he may reasonably require. In the event of his being stranded abroad through civil unrest, or the action of tyrants, it shall dispatch with all promptitude a well-found gunboat or aircraft-carrier, with an attentive crew wearing clean white shorts, to transport him home at no expense to himself, time being of the essence. In return for which the High Contracting Party shall from time to time use postal codes on his correspondence.

3. In recognition of an undertaking by the Government not to search the pockets of the High Contracting Party or remove his clothing or dismantle his car on leaving or entering the country, the High Contracting Party agrees (1) not to interfere with the administration of the White Fish Authority, the Export Credits Guarantee Department and the Commissioners of Northern Lighthouses; (2) not to initiate or prolong vexatious disputes with the servants of the nationalised fuel undertakings.

4. In the interests of mutual goodwill, the Government shall direct the Commissioners of Inland Revenue not to inflame the High Contracting Party with the use of the expression 'Unearned Income', but to use instead the phrase 'Income Resulting from Foresight, Thrift, Forbearance and a Patriotic Renunciation of Fleshly Pleasures'.

5. The Government hereby recognises that the High Contracting Party in a lifetime of exhausting toil has at no time drawn unemployment benefit; that thanks to an unbroken record of virtue and continence he has claimed no more than £15 in sickness benefit in forty years; that he has never occupied a hospital bed or required the services of a psychiatrist; that he has never put the nation to the expense of custodial treatment or the supervision of a probation officer; that he has never made demands on a family planning clinic; that he has received no legal aid or fat-stock subsidy of any kind; and that he has at all times refused to take advantage of any form of free adult education. The Government therefore designates the High Contracting Party a Hero of the British Commonwealth, to be *excused stamps* for the rest of his natural life.

6. The Government, having in 1941 nationalised the High Contracting Party on payment of arbitrary compensation of one shilling a day, and exploited his military talents for five years, with a terminal award of an unframed certificate and a free suit of clothes, shall be debarred from nationalising him again for any purpose without full and agreed compensation. It shall have no entitlement to make use of his brain either under the National Service Acts, the Human Tissue Act or any other Act.

7. The Government recognises that the breakdown of a motor car belonging to the High Contracting Party is an Act of God and not an act of culpable neglect to be punished by the addition of value-added tax to the repair bill, as also to the hotel bill incurred by the High Contracting Party and his dependants; and that all such taxes on misfortune shall be refunded plus fifty per cent interest.

8. The Government shall instruct its spokesmen not to propagate the idea that manual work ennobles those who engage in it, save in reference to repair work carried out on the motor car of the High Contracting Party.

9. The Government, in acknowledgement of the High Contracting Party's severe share losses, due to trade union action, in British Leyland and similar enterprises, shall protect him from all accusations by its ministers of failure to invest in British industry, or to represent him as living a parasitic life as a shareholder; and it shall raise no objection if he employs the remainder of his capital in visiting the Lost City of the Incas, or any other lost city, instead of investing it in an extension to a ball-bearing factory in Glasgow.

10. The Government agrees to the operation of a threshold agreement whereby, whenever the income of the High Contracting Party falls by more than 0.5 per cent in any week, whether due to trade union action, Act of

152

God, mental exhaustion or human malignity, the income shall be made up from the Consolidated Fund.

11. The Government shall cease forthwith to employ leading figures in show business to persuade the High Contracting Party to fasten his seat belt, to keep Britain tidy or to buy Premium Bonds, as the effect of such advice from such a quarter is totally counter-productive. It shall also cease, and apologise for, the use of a smirking Duke of Wellington in an effort to publicise National Savings, since there are no policies of the Government which the Duke of Wellington would not find deeply repugnant. The Government in its public exhortations shall refrain from addressing the High Contracting Party as if he were a mental defective, whether he be or not, and on no account seek to influence his judgement by saying, 'You know it makes sense.' In recognition whereof, the High Contracting Party undertakes to moderate his language in all written and telephonic communications to the Government's servants.

12. The Government agrees to establish a Public Lending Right for authors, to help the under-developed countries and to endeavour to set a term to nuclear proliferation, in that order. In return for which, the High Contracting Party shall leave his entire tax correspondence dating from 1935 to the nation.

13. The High Contracting Party, conscious of his duties as a citizen, shall at all times offer the Government, whether requested to do so or not, such moral and practical advice as shall enable it to acquit itself honourably at the bar of public opinion, the Commission of Human Rights, the International Monetary Fund and the Great Day of Judgement. In addition the Government shall have due regard to his views on general topics, as they may be from time to time promulgated, bearing in mind that they are the wisdom of a lifetime devoted to the correction of human error; as, for example, his recommendation that the Ministry of Sport be replaced by a Ministry for the Abolition of Sport; that all new universities east of a line drawn from Land's End to Stranraer should be dissolved; and that the practice of erecting signs reading TYRE NOISE on motorways should, in simple equity, be balanced by the erection throughout Greater London and the Home Counties of signs reading AIRCRAFT NOISE.

"I know you think I'm an old reactionary, but when I was your age I was a young reactionary."

"For heaven's sake, Guiseppe, do try and speak
Italian like an Englishman."

"How many more times, Helmut—the object is to
play the game, not to win."

"Please sir, Von Braunstein's making
heavy water again, sir."

Unprecedented numbers of foreign kids are flooding into British Public Schools. GEOFFREY DICKINSON looks down the Register

"*Just imagine that the Army has come to take over your Pa's palace, Stavros.*"

"*It's either tonight's string trio **or** the Italian parents coming to complain about the increase in fees.*"

"*I'm not sure it was such a good idea to promote one of the Continentals to full corporal, Nigel.*"

With wages rising by an average of 29%
a year, many people are puzzled by what is
meant by 'The Social Contract'. In order to
clear up many of the misconceptions, the
following simplified guidelines have been
issued to the public . . .

What is the Social Contract?

The Social Contract has been devised as the best shield
for your interests in these perilous times. Without it,
there would be an unnecessarily complicated procedure
to go through in order to get more money on a regular
basis. It completely sweeps away the authoritarian and
bureaucratic system of wage control imposed by the
Heath Government. As a result, the money comes
through more quickly, there's less fuss for everyone, less
risk of injury to workers from an embittered public, less
likelihood of the lights going out before a settlement is
reached in any industrial dispute. By agreement with the
Trades Union Congress, the Social Contract is binding
on all Unions. The only exceptions to this rule are those
Unions which decide otherwise. It is a VICTORY FOR
COMMON SENSE.

How do I get more money?

Under the terms of the Social Contract, all requests for
an increase in pay are automatically refused, irrespective
of the circumstances, in order to combat Inflation. The
only exception to this general rule are when a DEMAND
is made on behalf of WORKERS, which allows an
increase of not more than the rise in the cost of living,
or when an ULTIMATUM is issued on behalf of
SPECIAL CASES, which allows free collective bargaining towards a much-needed and long-overdue renego-
tiation of an outdated and rickety pay structure.

How can I tell if I am a worker or a special case?

Broadly speaking, to qualify as a WORKER the Contract does not require you to do anything at all. In
practice, however, it is necessary to belong to a TRADE
UNION which has established procedures to secure
UNANIMOUS DECISIONS on your behalf. As a rule
of thumb, it can be understood that you are a worker
if you have, during the last twelve months, been getting
REGULAR DERISORY INCREMENTS or taken
unexpected holidays with your mates during a period of
DEMOCRATIC INDUSTRIAL ACTION. To establish
yourself as a SPECIAL CASE for the purposes of the
Social Contract, it is necessary to fulfil all of the above
conditions and to have your case referred to on television
by a GOVERNMENT MINISTER. It is usual, though
not obligatory, for public services to cease during this
period. Managers, most professions, the self-employed
and those engaged in creating wealth on behalf of others
are generally OUTSIDE THE GUIDELINES.

How do I arrive at a fair and just figure?

This is a complicated and long drawn-out procedure and
is usually conducted on your behalf by experts in your
NATIONAL EXECUTIVE or MILITANT WING.
Your SHOP STEWARD may be able to explain further
and if you do not like who that is you may be able to
put in a claim as a Special Case by forming your own
BREAKAWAY GROUP. Simply, the process is conducted in five stages: (1) You put in for a SUBSTAN-
TIAL INCREASE, say roughly twice what seems
excessive. (2) Employers come back with roughly a third
of that, called a CONTEMPTUOUS REBUFF. (3)
Your labour is of necessity suspended, THE ONLY
POSSIBLE COURSE OF ACTION. (4) There is full
and frank discussion of the nation's plight, the ELEV-
ENTH-HOUR PEACE BID. (5) Approximately $\frac{3}{4}$ of
the sum is awarded as a RELUCTANT SETTLEMENT.

MY SONS THE MUSIC CRITICS

by ANDRE PREVIN

I HAVE tried to live most of my years adhering to the maxim 'Cute sayings of bright children are sick-making,' and a damned good maxim that is, too. However, as age advances on me with various creaks and rallentandos, I find myself not only repeating my children's bon mots, but even taking home movies. To my everlasting credit, I have not inflicted, nor will I ever inflict, 8-millimetre soporifics on anyone other than drunken blood relatives, but some of the quotes I now find worthy of repeating.

Mind you, they are not the sayings of a musically prodigious infancy, such as Vladimir Ashenkenazy's son Dimi is given to expounding; that kid, since age two, has been the only actual true musical genius child I have ever met, and his perspicacity makes me break out in a cold sweat. Young Dimi, backstage at a concert I was conducting, watched me come offstage, and while I was wiping my brow, he looked up from the Tinkertoy car he was pushing around on the floor, and said, 'Why did you try the Third Movement slower tonight than last night?' neatly spinning me into a vortex of despair about my own children's musical knowledge.

However, one must face facts. Dimi, at the time of that remark (which, you must admit, is more perceptive than most of the criticisms found in the daily press), was three years old, and his brilliant father will simply have to resign himself to the role of the 20th century's Leopold Mozart. No, no, my children aren't quite up to that; although they can identify quite a huge amount of repertoire with ease, if you are looking for the remarks of genius in the bud, I suggest stopping right here and now. Nor are the kids the product of a relentlessly show business home, which can also give rise to inexplicable, wonderful sentences.

The great American actor, Fredric March, recalls with happiness his visit to a playwright, whose work he was about to star in on Broadway. The author was upstairs, dressing, and Mr. March was ushered into the living room to wait. The writer's five-year-old was playing quietly in a corner. March opened the conversa-tion manfully, and asked all the stock, insincere questions, such as 'What did you do today? Do you go to school yet? What's your name, little man?' There wasn't much response, and the child started to leave the room. Fredric tried one last gambit. 'What do you want to be when you grow up?' The boy looked at him coldly, and said, 'A sexual pervert.'

I have four children; twin boys, age five, a girl, age two, and a baby son, age one. The twins have always loved to talk, and they have always loved music. They have attended rehearsals, concerts, recordings, television broadcasts, and chamber music get-togethers since they were old enough to crawl, and their behaviour at these adult functions has, 99 per cent of the time, been exemplary. Because they have watched their father and mother leave on work days, and because our answer to their 'Where are you going?' is invariably connected to either concerts or studios, their outlook on the various modes of world employment has grown a bit askew. Not long ago, I had Matthew out on Regent Street on a particularly busy morning. The crowds were shoving and hurrying, and my son became worried and perplexed. Finally, he tugged at me, looked up, and asked, 'Papa, are *all* these people going to rehearsal today?'

Every night of his, and his brother's life, they have connected bedtime with listening to records and tapes, and the deprivation of this hour is considered the most severe punishment meted out in my house. They have very definite likes and dislikes, and it still amuses me no end to hear them discuss the evening's programme with each other in the privacy of their own room. 'You know, Sascha,' said Matthew, with all the pomposity of the professional critic, 'sometimes parts of Handel are really tiresome.' 'No, no,' disagreed his more earthbound counterpart; 'I like it a lot, but Tchaikovsky is better to jump up and down to.' An inescapable truth, along with a few others they've managed.

Matthew tagged along to a Festival Hall rehearsal one Sunday morning last month. We arrived early, and were waiting for the backstage lift (the departure times of which ought to be printed and posted, like a ferry schedule) along with quite a few of the L.S.O. players. A custodian was washing the floors with copious quantities of a violently carbolic liquid of some sort. Matthew sniffed the air questioningly, and then won the hearts of many of the musicians by asking, blue eyes wide with innocence, 'Papa, is this whole big building a toilet?'

I have never been able to prejudge children's reactions to music correctly. All those works which are considered 'childproof' have turned out to be relatively abandoned, and some of the knottier problems in music are listened to with total immersion. The Schubert C major Quintet beat our *Tubby the Tuba*, Mozart Piano Concertos are preferred to *William Tell*, and the Bach Flute and Harpsichord Sonatas fascinate them infinitely more than the *1812 Overture*. Of course, I must admit that *Peter and the Wolf* had its heyday, being requested with numbing regularity night after night. A small aside of some interest (at least to me) was the fact that Sascha always asked for 'Peter', while Matthew invariably wanted 'the Wolf story'. I hope that the difference in self-identification works itself out in future years.

Records mean a lot to the kids, even to the one-year-old. However, the technical mysteries of why discs of shellac produce sound have always been black magic to me. My practical knowledge of our century's technology is best described by recalling the day I decided to replace a fuse in our house, and plunged Greater Surrey into darkness for several hours. At any rate, I dreaded any query about the actual making of records. One day it came. I had announced, over our morning tea, that I was off to London's E.M.I. studios for another recording session, and that I hoped they would all enjoy the end results. Lark, age two, asked whether I would bring the record home with me that evening, for her to hear. Matthew interrupted, from the Mount Olympus of his three years' seniority. 'Don't be silly, Lark,' he intoned; 'today Papa will just make the music. Then he has to leave it there for the people to paste all the black bits around it.' And that, friends, is the only explanation of the recording process I have ever understood.

The fact that today's records can represent the creative thoughts of deceased composers is baffling to children. I remember clearly that the twins went through a

"Now, Jim, here's what I want you to do. I want you to stand behind Steve and look as black as you can."

"You can cancel the planning. The bank's gone bust."

romance with the music of Prokofiev. One night, Sascha asked me 'Is Proskosfievs' – his added sibilants are classy, in my opinion – 'alive?' I explained that the great Russian master was, alas, dead. 'Is Beethoven alive?' 'No.' 'Is Mozart?' 'No.' 'Why not?' I stumbled, rather lamely, through a child's version of our limited time on this planet, and probably wound up in quite a pudding of religion, metaphysics, and fairy tales. The next night, over the BBC, they heard the première of an extremely boring new piece. 'Is the man who wrote that music dead, too?' they wanted to know. I shook my head No. They thought about it. 'Well, why isn't he?' and again I was stuck for an answer.

Often, a child's-eye view of my profession is not entirely flattering. One of Matthew's Christmas presents was a Noah's Ark, complete with dozens of tiny wooden animals. I walked in on him as he was arranging them into a fairly crowded semi-circle. In front of them he had placed a matchbox, on top of which was a gorilla, arms outstretched in a threatening gesture. 'Look,' my son beamed at me; 'it's you, conducting!'

The boys are much more gentlemanly at heart when it comes to the female part of the family. They are endlessly solicitous of their small sister, only punch her when absolutely necessary, and are full of flattery towards their mother. I showed Sascha a copy of *Playboy* magazine, and left him, leafing through it contentedly. Later on, I asked him his opinion of Hugh Hefner's

gift to culture. Sascha ran and retrieved the copy. Flipping the colourful pages happily, he shouted, 'See how many, many Mamas!' My wife's face was suffused with the blush of pleasure.

Through their constant visits to concert halls and theatres, all the children have developed a superior sense of the decorum required when attending these commercial temples. Their attention span is laudable, their enjoyment touching, and their pleasure unmistakable. Being a cautious clot, and an adult to boot, I still run through my litany of warnings to them, as we enter the buildings.

Therefore, when my Musical *The Good Companions* was at Her Majesty's Theatre, I stopped just in front of the entrance for a final run-through of admonishments to the twins. 'Now remember,' I said portentously and boringly, 'no wiggling or talking or whispering; if you have to go to the loo, do so right now, or at the interval; don't unwrap sweets during the performance, and don't climb up on the seats.' I paused for breath, in order to search my mind for more possibilities of misconduct. Matthew was also deep in thought, and he frowned with concentration. Finally, he came up with the last hurdle to clear with the authorities. He looked up, and his face was earnest with the effort to please. 'May I fart?' he asked shyly, and getting a firm grip on two pairs of small hands and on my own reeling mind, I led the small parade into the theatre.

."It's your round."

"Coffee is waiting to be deplored, and we have the kind of
eggs you love to inveigh against."

"By the way, I've found out about the other woman."

says JOHN CROSBY

THE THREAT TO QUIT IS THE GREAT
fantasy which keeps us all sane. Breaking the chain that binds you to the
hated grindstone. A solid right to the jaw of the tyrant who has ground you
in the dust, misunderstood you, victimized you, exploited you. Yeah, brother.
Spit in his eye and walk out. Woo hoo and bye bye, you bastard.

Almost immediately followed by the thought – prudent, cowardly, snivel-
ling – who buys the children's shoes then, eh? Followed by the even more
fainthearted thought that one's employment, miserable though it is, is a cut
above repairing sewers.

The thought is never far from any writer's mind that the job he holds down
is the only one he's capable of holding down because if he could actually *do*
something like building bridges or empires he'd be out there *doing* it instead
of scribbling about it.

From there it's but a short step to saying to oneself – this thought rarely
gets spoken to anyone else, it just reverberates around one's own private brain
pan – that, though one's boss is a son of a bitch so foul as to be beneath
anything so respectable as contempt, though the job is miserably underpaid,
and an insult to one's intelligence, though, though, though (Fill in your own
grievances. I'm sure you have them), still . . .

It's that *still* that stills the raging discontent. Mine anyway and I'm fairly
typical of my generation. I belong to the Depression Generation where jobs
were the Golden Fleece and if you had one, you clung to it no matter what
the humiliations.

Not these modern fellows, my goodness. It seems like every time I pick up
a new book I read on the book jacket: 'Before taking up writing, he worked
the lumber fields in British Columbia, was a short order cook in San Francisco, rode the rails in Peru, herded sheep in New Zealand, and prospected
for gold in Yucatan, followed by a short stint in the merchant marine, after
which he served briefly as a bomber pilot for the underdogs in the Biafran
war.' These young fellows get around. I assume they quit all these jobs
because one doesn't get fired any more. It's against the law. I'm awed by
such a footloose attitude to employment and all I can say is I wish I shared it.

We didn't do that in my set. I'm ashamed to say that I went to work for
The New York Herald Tribune in 1935 and stuck around as reporter and
columnist for thirty years, alack and alas. Actually there was an interruption
of five years for World War II. When I got out of uniform, they made me a
radio columnist and, after they invented the thing, television columnist. I
had enormous freedom to say what I liked. I was well paid. My copy was
almost sacrosanct. I frequently poked my finger right in the eye of the very

"I strongly suspect you belong to an organisation that's diabolically opposed to Authority."

same advertisers who supported the newspaper, to say nothing of the advertising agencies which controlled the flow of advertising. This got me an undeserved reputation for courage. It was the management upstairs who fielded the outraged cries from these gentlemen from Madison Avenue. I was not even told about their protests – and there were many. With a job like that I would be insane to think of quitting.

But I did quit once. I had finally overstepped even the limitless tolerance of my editors and one day I was summoned into the office of the managing editor, George Cornish, a gentle, quiet man who pointed to a paragraph in my copy and said: 'John, you can't say *that*.' Well, I stormed. I flung arguments. I spoke about my integrity. I quoted the First Amendment to the U.S. Constitution – and I think even the Second, Third, Fourth and Fifth. It didn't work. The paragraph went out.

I repaired to Bleeck's, the saloon next door to the *Trib* where generations of *Trib* men (also *New Yorker* men, *Newsweek* men and *New York Times* men) solaced their wounds with drink. I sulked. I lunched alcoholically and over lunch, I told my fellow writers of this monstrous thing that had been done to my copy. I got a lot of sympathy. I gave myself even more sympathy. The others went back to work. I drank on all afternoon, smouldering. Bleeck's emptied. I drank on alone, growing bitterer by the hour. About five I made my decision, took the elevator to the fifth, the news floor of the Trib, and stormed into the managing editor's office at the very time of the daily editorial conference.

For those of you who don't know about editorial conferences, this is the meeting where the shape of the next day's paper is determined. All the editors are there – city editor (which in the U.S. is not the financial editor but the man who controls city, as opposed to foreign or national news), financial editor, real estate editor, amusement editor, national editor, foreign editor, about a dozen of them. Here they argue about how much space each department gets, and what stories get front page play.

Into this respectable group – and they were all older men, very staid editors – I hurtled, flushed with an afternoon's drinking, steaming with largely alcoholic outrage. I remember only a lot of blurred, upturned, very silent faces, one of them the managing editor's, and into all of them I flung my defiance: 'If that paragraph is not restored as written, I quit.' Then I walked out, went home and slept it off.

"Nigel's writing a play that answers the fundamental questions about the nature of our society which are raised in all the other plays."

"Well, gentlemen! Our troubles are over—we're bankrupt!"

Oh, well, it was all a long time ago and even after all these years my only feeling is one of deep quivering shame. All that defiance! That theatrical entrance! Good God! For what? I can't remember. For the life of me, I can't remember what the offending paragraph was about. What was I standing up, four square, for? Or against? I don't know. I strongly suspect that, whatever it was, George Cornish was right about it. He was not one to make a fuss over trifles and he had many times gone to bat for me when my editorial freedom was threatened.

Also, to this day I don't know whether the paragraph I staked my job on went back into the paper. I never looked. The fact is, my indignation had burnt out and I didn't care any more and I was hung over and the hell with it. That disgraceful scene in the managing editor's office was never mentioned in my presence by either the managing editor or any of the dozen other editors who witnessed it. Not once – and I knew all those guys for years afterwards.

Was that my only experience at quitting? Well, no, there was one other and I'd forgotten that totally until the night when I was watching on BBC2 that old chestnut *Mr. Roberts*. You know, the very 1940ish movie in which Henry Fonda plays an executive officer on an old bucket of a supply ship which goes from Tedium to Monotony and back in the South Pacific during World War II. Fonda yearns and schemes to get into combat which rages 2,000 miles away, and finally manages to get into the war and is promptly killed. Pretty sentimental stuff by 1970s standards. 'My God,' I thought, 'who would trade a nice safe berth like that for a combat ship? Nobody acted like that.'

Then I suddenly remembered. I did. Actually. I was a young U.S. Army officer dispatched to Washington and Lee University, there to learn how to be a morale officer, for Pete's sake. A morale officer in the U.S. Army occupied a position, in respect, usefulness and combativeness, somewhat below that of Chaplain. We were supposed to see to it the boys wrote home. We organized baseball games. We were supposed to head off incipient mutiny by saying 'There, there, fellows, things aren't really that bad.'

The teaching of this military art reached levels of lunacy unsuspected by the civilian mind. We played baseball games – captains, majors, lieutenant colonels. We were taught how to organize bridge-playing competitions, how to judge running races. (The one who comes in first wins, see.) All this while our compatriots were getting shot up out at Okinawa, the Siegfried Line. I used to lie in my bunk just like Mr. Roberts, hurling imprecations at the Army idiots who kept me in this scandalous school in the middle of a war.

One day sitting crosslegged in a gymnasium playing Chinese checkers with a major, along with a whole gymnasium full of other officers playing Chinese checkers, I revolted. I went to my room, lay in my bunk and, as it were, opted out. I refused to attend any more of these silly exercises. I quit is what I did and you're not supposed to do that when you're in the Army.

Worse than that, I actually organized a mutiny among my friends at the school and persuaded them to opt out too. Well, we could have been court martialled but it was too much trouble. They just dispatched us to become morale officers to various Army posts in the land – bearing on our records the heinous mark 'Unsatisfactory'.

I am one of the few U.S. Army officers who ever managed to get on his record one *Superior* rating (very hard to get and I got it only by perfectly disgraceful ass-kissing) and one *Unsatisfactory* (also very hard to get. You had to rape the Colonel's daughter or something on that general level). To this day I'm still ashamed of that *Superior* but I'm mighty proud of that *Unsatisfactory*.

I never got anywhere near combat.

"Here they come now, the murdering vegetarians."

Little Acorns

When a school essay by Graham Greene was sold at Sotheby's,
PAUL JENNINGS, sadly, had to drop out of the bidding, but he did manage to pick
up a cheaper lot, and a few others besides . . .

WHAT I DID ON MY HOLIDAYS
by Greene, G.

I usually get disappointed by holidays they expect you to be happy but think of all the dead things cast up by the Sea, the first day I found a dead starfish I took it to my room my Father said Poo it smells why don't you play with the other children in the hotel they are called Simpson. But there was another boy he had a dark face he watched us he said why don't we do something bad.

I asked him where are your Father and Mother he said my Father is with Miss Roberts she keeps gigling why does everyone gigle at the seaside his face wore an expression of disgust.

I always feel everybody is trying to escape from something at the seaside but they dont kno what it is and it makes them gigle they gigle in the hall of Mirrors and they put there faces in a round hole in a photograph of somebody elses Body and they gigle it makes me think of the dead Star Fish.

So I said all right to this boy his name was Lawrence he had an evil face. Let us go and look at the machines What the Butler Saw. He said Greene are you a Baby, I retorted with Spirit 'all right then, I know where the sewage comes out lets go and look at it poo it smells.'

He said nothing he looked at the Sea with Narrowed Eyes. Perhaps you would be happier with the Simpson children he said, it was an unspoken Bond. I know the back way in we can steal in and Drink the communion Wine he said. As we left the beach for the mean back streets we passed an old Man he was preaching his plackard said Repent ye Sinners thats my Father he's an old fool said Lawrence, I had a super holiday.

WHAT I DID ON MY HOLIDAYS
by Beckett, S.

I am going to write this essay on this paper with this pen about nothing because that is what the sea is it is nothing I like writing about nothing it is my favourite word here it comes agane woops nothing.

I think it look even better without a capitol letter, nothing looks more like nothing than Nothing with a captal letter. The sea is nothing strething to an illimmatable horizon. I kept staring at it in Killiney Bay that is where we went for our holidays we always go no change for Million years. I stood at the edge of the water I didn't paddel because I did not want to take my boots off because there were two tramps taking there boots off ugh poo they were waiting for somebody they said. The sea may be nothing but when I paddeled last year, the tramps were not there then, it was cold, so it must be something as well as nothing. I always knew this I bet I shall know it the same when I am Fifty or a Hundred or Two Hundred or a Million.

They were all lepping about on the strand, they shouted what are you doing I said nothing that's all there is here or anywhere else poo those tramp's boots!

When the tide came in I walked up the strand a long way, that was the way of it. Then I thought I saw a football in the nothing stretching to that ilimmitable horizon. Then I saw it was not a football. I drew near and it was a man's head. I said Can you talk? He said of course I can talk. I have been here a million years. I said can you get out of the sand have you got a body but he started to cry and I went home we had Dublin Bay prawns for tea in the hotel. CONTINUED OVERLEAF.

WHAT I DID ON MY HOLIDAYS
by Betjeman, J.

We had our holidays this year
In Cornwall, spot to me so dear
The surf boomed in across the sand
And heather blossomed on the land

And in the hotel where we stayed
There was a garden where we played
Some girls were very strong and tall
And I could never win at all

We all had Aertex shirts and shorts
And gosh, I came to hate those sports
They hit me, then away they ran
With 'Yah, can't catch me, Betjeman'

We had our dinner every night
When it was only just still light
The sideboard groaned with HP Sauce
(Each family had its own of course)

And then with feet that seemed like lead
I went up oaken stairs to bed
But to sleep could never go
I heard them jabbering down below

They had red faces and plus fours
They clumped upstairs and banged the doors
(It was a golf hotel you see)
And talked, I felt quite sure, of me

They saw their daughters beat me hollow
I knew what lines their talk would follow
They wondered what that boy would *do*
And just like them I wonder too.

...and an Imposition handed in by James, H.

I, since that is the nominative case and one is oneself the actual (how could it be otherwise?) author (yet, again, must not the application of this so made reverend term by the mere accretion of centuries of respect – ah, yes, that at least, respect, whether it be expressed as criticism or as adulation – for the unique, the subjective process of moulding a story, fine-spun out of, as it were, nothing, to one who is already predestined to join that so revered, that so Parnassian group, those very 'authors' but is in fact in all the outward trappings of life a schoolboy, in itself constitute a veritable, nay a fundamental misappropriation of the word – the word 'author', should the reader, no matter how conscientious, have lost the thread, grammatical for all its apparent yet so necessary circumlocution, of this parenthesis, nor let that same reader, for whatever scarcely-examined reason of grudge or incomprehension, suppose – ah, how mistakenly! – that this same, for want of a better, more comfortable term, 'author', will by now have forgotten that this parenthesis is of an interrogatory nature of which it will – ah, so certainly! – be asked whether it ought not to end with a question mark, thus?) of these Lines (again, though refulgent poet-glories hang, as it were, about this word also, their connotation in the present instance cannot, nay must not, be untainted by all notions of a crime, of however inadvertent and unintentional omission) am obliged to confess that unless I can within the ever-narrowing space of words remaining to me, finish (ah, with what pain at its bluntness, its coarse insensitivity) with the congruent verbal phrase '*must not forget my essay*' I shall simply never manage the remaining 199 Lines.

"*Mr. Frederic Binge and Mr. Ernest Crudflow.*"

"I hope he pushes off soon. I can't keep this up much longer."

GREAT REFERENDUMS OF THE PAST

1436

Ye Hundred Yeares War: Have Ye Hadde Enoughe?

Whereas

Edward III did first gain entry into Europe in 1337, for thatte he mighte go a-plunderynge and a-lootynge, while givynge outte that he was after the French crowne and

Whereas

To beginne with, many brave warriours did return from France bearynge full many a three piece dinynge suite, fyne suit of armour onlie one previeux owner and riche Paris garmentes for the wyf,

Yet

Now thatte we have nothing left in France save onlie Calais and odde chunkes of Brittany, and are luckie to come backe with a sticke of rocke marked DIEP

And

Consideringe that each expeditioun becomes more costlie to mount, on accounte of soarynge inflatioun and ye dearth of investmente, whereunto we have of late instituted ye social contracte of whiche more in a later bulletin

And

Being thwarted by such as Joan of Arc, whom gladly we have recently managed to liquydate, to coine ye phrase

Therefore

We putte it to the folk of England whether they wishe to staye in Europe.

In consideratioun of whiche, we moste earnestlie begge you to put a crosse in ye boxe.

Yea ☐   Nay ☐

Signed by his most gracious majestye Henry VI who is himselfe votynge Nay, and hopes ye may doe likewyse, failinge the whiche he pledges himselfe to renegotiate as beste he may.

Ye penaltie for ye spoiled paper: Deathe by hangynge

Every Picture Tells a Story

What the Impressionists' Paris was really like

Self Portrait by CEZANNE

Here we can see why Cézanne became a misanthrope (he didn't care much for things either). Paris was full of lousy workmen who couldn't tell their âne from their coude. It was impossible to find a decent pair of compasses (just look at those apples), a level table, an upright vase or a chair that wasn't agony to sit on (that's why no one would sit for him). If there had even been one competent optician Cézanne might have achieved his ambition to paint like Dürer.

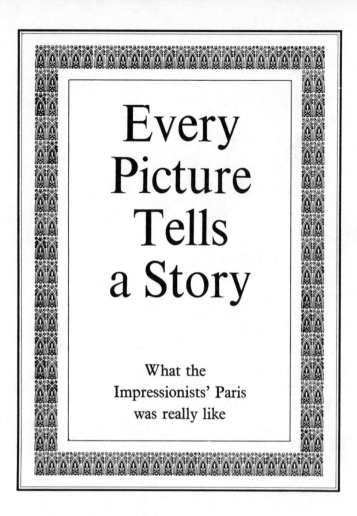

VAN GOGH developing his mature style

When he arrived in dirty old Paris Van Gogh was an upbeat academic painter of old boots and as sane as a brush. But there was a fly in the ointment, in fact millions of them. They were everywhere and to get any work done he had to combine his brushwork with fly swatting. In no time at all he was knocking out whirling suns, delirious landscapes and twisted sunflowers by the dozen. However the constant buzzing drove him mad so he cut off his ear, gift wrapped it and died prematurely.

Monet In His Studio by MANET

Psychologists have offered dozens of theories about Monet's obsession with painting water-lilies but a recently discovered painting by Monet has shown the reason was a practical one. It reveals that Monet, like most of the artists of that time, was forced to live in a decrepit studio with a leaking roof and rising damp and used what subject matter was at hand. His productivity and longevity was probably due to a steady diet of frogs' legs and watercress.

Dancer With One Leg by DEGAS

Paris wasn't the ideal place for Degas either. A mysogynist and linguist (he wrote poison pen letters to his granny in Urdu) he was living in a city full of women. His only pleasure was to go to the ballet and upset the dancers by sketching them in squeaky pastels but what really inspired him was getting the agony of a torn ligament or the embarrassment of a one-legged dancer asked to do an entrechat down on canvas.

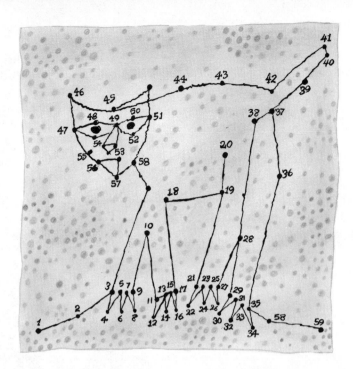

Detail from Dimanche à la Grande Jatte by SEURAT

Art critics are now convinced that all of Georges Seurat's paintings were left unfinished. Discouraged by his lack of success Seurat evolved a painting by numbers system with which he hoped to make his fortune. However, applying all those dots on an empty stomach was too much for him and he died before he could put in the numbers, thus inventing pointillism. He left behind sixty unfinished masterpieces now worth about £100 a dot—with numbers they would be worth double.

Self Portrait With Model by TOULOUSE-LAUTREC

The high incidence of dance halls in Paris had a tragic effect on the life of Henri Toulouse-Lautrec. He was determined to become the world's greatest tango dancer but prematurely wore out his legs trying to dance non-stop from Montmartre to Bordeaux.

Frustrated in this ambition he took to painting in bars and brothels and rapidly wore out most of the other parts of himself. When his arms were as short as his legs he called it a day and died. He was given a half-price funeral.

Pahura And Site For Luxury Hotel by GAUGUIN

When Paul Gauguin threw up his stockbroking job he was determined to start a new magazine called 'Oui'. He asked Renoir to begin a series of nudes (he forgot to tell him to stop) and commissioned Zola to provide the intellectual masturbation. However Paris wasn't ready for a French 'Playboy' so he went off to Tahiti to paint artists' impressions of luxury hotels hoping to create a tourist boom. The fact was Gauguin was a lousy salesman and Paris wasn't ready for that either, so he let his toenails grow long and went native in protest.

'I have great difficulty learning lines,' says Lord Olivier. 'Sometimes I can get away with making it all up, of course . . . I ad-libbed for 20 minutes once in Shakespearean blank verse. Absolute gibberish. But the audience never knew the difference.'

MACBETH (starring Lord, um, Olivier)

Act III scene iv

Banquet. Enter Banquo's Ghost.

Macbeth: Avaunt, and quit my sight! Let the earth hide thee!
Thy bones are marrowless, thy blood is cold;
Thou hast no speculation in those eyes
Which thou dost glare with.
Lady Macbeth: Think of this, good peers,
But as a thing of custom, 'tis no other,
Only it spoils the pleasure of the time.
Macbeth: What man dare, I dare.
Approach thou like the rugged Russian bear,
The arm'd rhinoceros, or the . . . or the other beast,
That beast which yet though fierce of teeth, does slip
So easy through the net of memory.
Ha! I'll have it yet, or be undone!
Once more I say to thee, accursed vision,
What man dare, I dare.
Approach thou like the Russian rugged rhinoceros . . .
Ragged Russian bear . . . This roaring reptile . . .
Round and round the rugged bears the Russian ran . . .
Or sells, perchance, her seashells on the seashore.
Thou seest that I can twist my tongue as well
As any man, can float along in verse
And strut the stage with gestures proud and bold,
Hamming the while as if it all made sense,
Yet what I cannot strain my ageing brain to do
Is bring to mind what follows 'rhinoceros'.
Banquo's Ghost: (*whispering*) 'Or the Hyrcan tiger!'
Macbeth: Those lips did move, methinks, and made a noise

So soft, so faint, the very breeze itself
Could never bring it hither to my ears,
These ears which even now are strained to hear
What syllables are missing from my speech.
Banquo's Ghost: (*louder*) 'Hyrcan tiger!'
Macbeth: I seem to hear thee saying 'Impetigo',
Which must be wrong. That illness never struck
The denizens of Elizabethan Stratford,
Or, if it did, was not called impetigo
But something crude like 'crop' or 'lumpy skin'.
Good wife, may I a tiny favour ask?
That which you said just now, say it again,
So that perchance it may release my tongue.
Lady Macbeth: Think of this good peers,
But as a thing of custom, 'tis no other.
Only it spoils the pleasure of the . . .
Macbeth: . . . Hyrcan tiger!
I have it now! Thanks, wife and gentle ghost,
For stirring up my memory like a bonfire.
What comes next?
Prompt: Take any shape but that . . .
Macbeth: Take any shape but that, and my firm nerves
(How fast the words come back when given help!)
Shall never tremble. Or be alive again,
And dare me to the desert with thy sword.
What splendid stuff this Bard of Avon wrote,
And clever, too; what is a Hyrcan tiger?
But from your faces, my good lords, I see
You hope to hear the ending of my speech.
Well, here we go. Or be alive again,
And dare me to the desert with thy sword;
If trembling I inhabit then, protest me
The baby of a girl. Hence, horrible . . . what?
I know it's horrible, but not what 'tis.
Lady Macbeth: To lose your place in Shakespeare *once*, my lord,
Can be accounted accident. To lose it twice
Comes precious near to being carelessness.
Macbeth: Touché. This piece of Oscar's wit, being fit,
Shall win thee nomination for an Oscar,
And I, forgetting lines, have driven thee wild,
The which has driven thee to Wilde. Where were we?
Lady Macbeth: Hence, horrible . . .
Macbeth: Ah yes! But what? That is
The question. Whether 'tis nobler – hang on a moment.
I seem to find myself in the wrong play.
Messenger: (*Running in*) My Lord and King, I bring this urgent
Scroll from one without.
Macbeth: From the producer?
Messenger: No less.
Macbeth: Hot dog. Let's see what tidings he thinks fit to write.
(*reads*) 'This farce has gone on long enough, my Lord.
Now say your lines and let the curtain down.
P.S. It's horrible *shadow*.' Of course! Hence, horrible shadow!
Unreal mockery hence! (*Exit ghost.*) Why, so. Being gone,
I am a man again. Pray you, sit still.
Lady Macbeth: You have displaced the mirth, broke the good
Meeting with most admir'd disorder. (*Exeunt all but Macbeth.*)
Macbeth: She's right, you know.
This time I went a little far. But if
A man forgets his lines, mayn't he ad-lib?
(*To the audience*) Good folk, I pray, a little longer tarry;
It isn't *them* you've come to see – it's Larry!
(*Exit. Cheers, ovations, whistles, excursions to the bar, etc.*)

"*You know what I'd like to be? A traitor to my class.*"

"*We've never been abroad before, so we'd appreciate it if the pilot would make a special effort not to crash.*"

British businessmen, according to the *Evening Standard*, are complaining that attempts to export to the United States are being hampered by the old-fashioned image of Britain created by TV programmes like *Upstairs, Downstairs* and *The Forsyte Saga* now showing on American TV and 'giving the impression that Britain is steeped in the past and not a nation building computers and Concordes'. Well, why on earth didn't they say so before? After all, a word here and there . . .

ALAN COREN

Brother, can you spare an hour?

(*Fade in, INTERIOR, DAY, the Bellamy servants' quarters*)

Edward: O my gawd, snakes alive, whatever next, Mrs. Bridges, what is this what we are a-eating of now?

Mrs. Bridges: You 'old your tongue, young Edward, oo-er, coo, that is as tasty a piece of braised high-protein, low-cholestorol, bio-degradable recycled filet-mignon-flavoured soya-derivative as ever I clapped eyes on, and at one shillin' a pound, less than a twentieth the price of best topside!

Edward: Lawks-a-mercy, Mrs. Bridges, only a shillin' a pound! Why, bless me and lor' love a duck, that ain't no more than twelve American cents! I do 'ope as 'ow we are still able to meet our vast export commitments what must be a-floodin' in!

Mrs. Bridges: Don't you worry your noddle about that, young Edward, you scallywag, 'Er Majesty the Queen's wonderful Department o' Trade and Industry is now blessed with as efficient an international sales force o' fine young gennelmen as ever set finger to pocket calculator, ain't that so, Mr. 'Udson?

Hudson: Och, weel, the noo, it dinna behove the like o' us wee folk tay pass judgement on our fine bonny rulers, ye ken, Mrs. Bridges, but I do happen tay have it on guid authority that yon Uberhauptausgezeichnetkreditanstalt o' Zurich think our wee balance o' payments has nay looked more bricht!

Rose: 'Ere, Mister 'Udson, ain't that the top Swiss bank what you are a-speaking' of, gorblimey?

Hudson: Aye, Rose, monny a winny mak' a gru, heh, heh, heh! But be off aboot your business noo, Rose, was that wee hum no the signal that our bonny Mostyn-Foskett Wundawosher has just finished doing the dishes in half the time o' its nearest competitor, at a mere fraction o' the cost?

Rose: Cor, Mister 'Udson, meanin' no disrespect but you ain't arf got good bleeding ears, that 'um is the quietest in the world, what wouldn't the Japs give to get their little 'ands on the secret!

Mrs. Bridges: Cor, Rose, you're a proper caution, whatever next, har, har, har, but get along now, I just 'eard Master James's 'Arrier Jump Jet land on the potting-shed, 'e'll want 'is bed turned down.

Edward: Crikey, I sometimes think Master James only joined the Royal Air Force for the unequalled opportunity it provided to fly the world's most advanced vertical take-off aircraft!

Hudson: Och, young Edward, are ye no' forgetting aboot the miraculous Condor air-to-air missile he'll be having such a guid time firing, beyond doot the cheapest and most effective in the entire Western world, an' no waiting upon delivery?

Mrs. Bridges: Landsakes, Mr. 'Udson, 'ow you men goes on! A person might never know these 'ere weapons o' yourn 'as led to a 'ole range o' wonderful domestic spin-offs such as the non-stick non-ferrous non-toxic egg-spoon with tasteful 'and-crafted Union Jack coddlin'-knob!

Hudson: Ye've a braw point there, Mrs. Bridges, but was that no' the chic bing-bong o' our noo Cheerigong All-British doorchime, and will I no' be away to answer it?

(*Fade out. Fade in INTERIOR, DAY, the Bellamy living-room*)

Bellamy: What is it, Hudson? You know how I prefer not to be disturbed when I am submitting my company reports to the *Guinness Book of Records*, justly famed British best-seller.

Hudson: I do indeed, sir, but it is a Mr. Soames Forsyte accompanied by other members of his family.

Bellamy: Ah! Well, show them in, Hudson, show them in!

Hudson: Mr. Soames Forsyte!

Bellamy: My dear Soames, how very good to see you!

Soames F: Excuse my somewhat bizarre attire, Bellamy, I am just this very hour back from examining our revolutionary new process for extracting plutonium from sleet. Let me introduce my cousin, Yakimoto Forsyte.

Yakimoto F: Mistah Berramy, this are great honnah! Engrish businessmen of your caribre will be salvation of Japanese economy! This are reason we are shifting entiah production of Forsytesan Industries to Engrand, incruding revorutionary new Forsyte Cherry people's rimousine!

Bellamy: You do me too much credit, sir! My incredible marketing successes would have been impossible without the co-operation of the English work force, whose reliability and pride in their impeccable craftsmanship is a legend, the maintenance of which is understandably the TUC's first priority. But excuse me, Soames, I do not believe I have had the pleasure of meeting these other gentlemen?

Soames F: Forgive me, Bellamy, may I present Werner von Forsyte, Commendatore Luigi Forsyte, Ingemar Førsyte of Copenhagen, and, of course, our dear American cousin, Groucho Forsyte.

All: Delighted! Entzückt! An honour, etc., etc.

Bellamy: My dear Soames, the international ramifications of your remarkable family never cease to amaze me!

Soames F: Well, yes, Bellamy, one must I feel hand it to Old Jolyon for realising all those years ago that mere land and money were not enough! And, of course, for having the, dare I say foresight . . .

All: Yuk, yuk, yuk! Vot vit! Hirarious! Etc., etc.

Soames F: . . . to comprehend that England was part of a wider manufacturing and trading world, that being little Englanders would get us nowhere, that a pooling of various national resources, initiatives and currencies would someday be essential to a vigorous international capitalism that would be proof against all commie incursions and corruptions, and for laying down, if you will, ha, ha, ha, pardon the expression, the foundations of Forsyte International on the Grand Tour undertaken in his youth!

Groucho F: Gimme a man like Jolyon Forsyte every time, and if you can't gimme a man like Jolyon Forsyte, I'll take a woman like Raquel Welch, and bring me an order of cole slaw on the side, no dill and easy on the mayonnaise!

Bellamy: Well said, sir, I think that calls for a drink! I trust no-one has any objection to a fifteen-year-old single-malt Scotch which we are still able to produce for the almost unbelievably low cost of less than one hundred dollars a case, and what an executive gift it makes, eh? Excuse me, I'll just ring for Hudson . . .

(*Fade out. Fade in the servants' quarters*)

Mrs. Bridges: Meaning no disrespect, Mr. 'Udson, but I do wish as 'ow you wouldn't tinkle them glasses so! All that racket, we'll never 'ear Concorde passin' over, an' I promised that young nephew o' mine I'd take a snap of it with my new two-pound Instaroid camera wot not only develops its own pitchers in five seconds flat, it also sticks 'em in its own album an' puts itself away in the drawer.

Hudson: Och, Mrs. Bridges, I do beg your pardon, the noo, I was so admiring the glint and sheen o' the wonderful Webb crystal and marvelling aboot how England manages to do it at the price, ye ken, that I got quite carried away!

Mrs. Bridges: Yes, well, talking of carryin' things away, Mr. 'Udson, you'd best be orf with them drinks, it's been forty-six seconds since Mr. Bellamy rung, and you know 'ow he is about punctuality, efficiency, hard work, service standards, quality control and client satisfaction, don't you?

Hudson: I ken it well, Mrs. Bridges, I ken it well! But ye didna need to blather on like that, ye ken – all ye had to say was Mr. Bellamy's an Englishman!

Mrs. Bridges: Lor' lumme, Mr. 'Udson, what *will* that silver tongue o' yours say next!

(*Fade out. MUSIC. CREDITS. LIST OF PRODUCTS MENTIONED. ORDER FORMS.*)

"*What really upsets him is that it was his father who did all the drinking.*"

Now is the Time for all Good Men to Come to the Office Party

by HONEYSETT

"There's tea and sherry, tea and gin, or tea and beer."

"They've all brought sandwiches."

"You know Miss Fishgrove, comma, or may I call you Mary, question mark, I've often . . ."

"... So I said to Gragood, who's head of stock control, either you let me have some XL190's or I'll see that your order for ..."

TO HELL WITH LONDON

JOHN CROSBY
reveals how he made
his home
on the free range

I LOVE London – from a distance. Fifty miles. That's how far away it is and that's where I want to keep it. It's stimulating to drive to London and ogle the pretty girls and go to Harrods and admire the prices (even the boa constrictors there have got fairly astonomical), and perhaps catch a movie. (Out here in Berkshire the flicks range from *Red Hot and Naked* to Walt Disney's *Superdad*. Nothing in between.) Oh, yes, we go to London for all that intellectual stimulation – and then flee back the same night.

London is a beautiful city – or will be when they get all that garbage off the pavements. But when are they going to do that? Kensington was piled high with refuse when we left – eight years ago – and I swear those same black bags are still there. Getting pretty stinky. Out here in the country we have air. As opposed to smells. Quite different. I admit it takes some getting used to – fresh air.

Why did we move to the country? Well, we didn't elect to do such a thing; we were pushed. We lost our lease in Chelsea, see, and we had this little place in the country where we spent weekends. English weekends. From Thursday to Tuesday weekends. In England Wednesday is the week, everything else is weekend which is why Great Britain is in the fix it's in. But we *lived* in London, if you know what I mean. Our friends were in London. Our interests were in London. Our hearts were in London. Only yokels actually lived in the country.

Then one day we were homeless – or, one-homed which, at the time, we considered almost the same thing. My wife said: 'We'll have to start looking for a place to live.' I said: 'Let's try to make do for a little while in the country.' She stared at me as if I were insane. Actually I felt a little nervous about it myself. The country? Live in it? But the fact is I was fed up with paying two sets of bills – two electricity bills, two gas bills, two sets of rates. To say nothing of having two of everything. My wife, for whom the expression *penny wise, pound foolish* was coined, found nothing untoward in our having two homes but she accused me of reckless extravagance when I bought an extra toothbrush for the country. She carried her lone toothbrush back and forth feeling monstrously economical.

So, full of nameless fears, we moved to the country. Now eight years later we have two children, six chickens, a horse, a cat – oh, I tell you it's fruitful out here – a greenhouse, a workshop and a veg garden. Oh, I almost forgot five colonies of bees. I write novels and make chairs in my workshop and my wife raises lettuce and peas and crochets things. My God, you get creative in the country. Because there's nothing else to do, see.

I have spent most of my life in very large cities indeed – twenty-five years in New York, two years in San Francisco, one year in Paris, six years in London – and an enormous amount of my energy was directed towards destructive purposes, many of them very enjoyable. Chasing other men's wives. Trying to drink myself to death (which is not as easy as they say). Being nakedly competitive or wickedly malicious, both marvellous indoor sports. I don't want to lay this down as a general rule exactly, but speaking personally, in the big cities, I break things. In the country, I make things.

In the country I write novels. In the city I used to *live* novels. My God, some of the scrapes I got into I wouldn't even put into a novel. In the city, you're on. In the country, you observe; somebody else is on (and you can have it, chum. I've had quite enough).

This changes your whole attitude. In London, I like to walk along Oxford Street. My wife goes to Oxford Street for the shopping. I go for the faces. If you collect faces, I claim you'll find the greatest variety and ferocity of faces the length of Oxford Street. Well? I told this to a very chic lady I know who lives on Mount Street and she shuddered from stem to stern. Every time she walked on Oxford Street, she said, she felt fearful all those people were going to bear down on her and club her to death.

That's what happens to you Londoners – paranoia. One of the nice things about living in the country is you don't assume everyone is trying to kill you. You say hello and they say hello. They pat the children on the head and inquire after their health. That sort of thing. Very boring. But very reassuring.

I suppose the biggest difference between city and country is the sheer scale of your possessions. I remember once many years ago waking up in Greenwich Village and doing a little simple arithmetic. I added up all the money I had made in ten years – and it was a very great deal – and all the things I currently possessed. Three shirts. Two suits. A typewriter. A pencil, no, two pencils. My God, where did it all go? Well, on intangibles. All those evenings in the theatre improving my mind. Or chasing girls, an enormously expensive sport. All those evenings of immensely stimulating conversation. (Very expensive, conversation if conducted in '21' or the Savoy Grill).

And what did I have to show? Well, that stimulating conversation, not one word of which I recall. The companionship of a lot of blondes whose names I couldn't recall. Life was slipping by and all that I had to show was my memories – and I couldn't even remember my memories.

Well, out in the country you acquire *things*. If you knew how many chisels I had, to say nothing of lawn mowers, saddles, garden chairs, and outbuildings. Yes, outbuildings. To think I let half my life slip by without a single outbuilding! Now I have four. There are those who say I'm outbuilding proud but I don't care. I came to materialism late in life and, I realize, after it had gone out of style in the best circles, but I love it.

Oh, I know you're going to come up with the bit about operas and the museums and don't I feel intellectually *starved* out there in all that fresh air. Come off it. When were you in all those museums last, kid? Actually, you to to the museums and the opera (and the theatre and the rest of it) more often when you live in the country and come into the city – because that's what the city's for.

(In my Greenwich Village days, I lived across the street from *The Connection* back when it was a very new theatrical experience for six months, promising myself I'd some day go see it. Then Sidney Bernstein came to town from London and took me to it. It had urgency for him because he was a stranger in the town whereas when you live across the street from a play, you always figure it's there tomorrow. Then one day you wake up and it's gone.)

No, I don't dream of moving back to London. Or New York. Or Paris. Once you get the wide open spaces in your bloodstream, you dream – or at least I do – of even wider, opener spaces. I dream quite a lot these days of a little place in Colorado – perhaps five miles square with its own little river (not necessarily the Colorado River, something a little smaller) and outbuildings as far as the eye can see.

And I still think thirty quid is a bit much for luncheon for two, even at the Connaught.

"*. . . but since **his** appointment there hasn't been a single instance of girls getting into difficulties.*"

Third World War Referendum

A National Census
Production

1 Would you be prepared to fight for Queen and for Country? Yes ☐ No ☐
If your answer is no, would you be prepared to fight for just one? ☐
If it came to it, would you fight for one *against* the other? ☐
Well, what *would* you fight for then? ☐☐☐☐☐☐☐

2 What do you do when Poppy Day comes round?
I buy a poppy from the Earl Haig people ☐
I use the poppy I saved from last year ☐
I make my own poppy and save the money ☐
I mug someone and steal his poppy ☐
How do you mean, Poppy Day? ☐

3 If we went to war again, which country would you prefer to fight against?
Russia ☐ China ☐ The Arab World ☐ Germany again ☐
Ireland ☐ Scotland ☐ Some other country more our size, like Sark ☐

4 If you are a pacifist, which of the following would you be prepared to do?
Wheel a hospital trolley for Queen and Country ☐
Go down the mines for your country (at soldier's pay) ☐
Be an extra in Third World War films ('Above Us The Fall-Out') ☐
Impersonate the Premier, who will be secretly in exile ☐
Help clear up afterwards ☐

5 How do you normally behave during the two minute silence?
I stand reverently to attention ☐
I slow down and walk to attention ☐
I pull in to the side of the road and sit up straight ☐
I take the chance of overtaking as many cars as I can ☐
I fiddle with the radio for a couple of minutes, wondering why the hell it's gone blank ☐
What two minute silence? ☐

6 If you would like to fight for Queen and Country, is it for one of these special reasons?
Because they always have such a good time in old war movies ☐
Because I am really into the 40's look ☐
Because I am fed up wrecking soccer specials and would like to kill people ☐
Because I am Leslie Thomas and I have run out of background material ☐

Because a few years in uniform will do me the world of good ☐
Because my friend Keith says you get cheap cigarettes and booze ☐

7 Do you think Britain could win another war?
Is there some other country you would rather fight for? ☐
Is there another Queen you would rather fight for? ☐
Do you think the next war will last more than four minutes? ☐
Have you thought about what you could usefully do during four minutes to help your Queen and Country? ☐
How many publishers do you think have already made plans for a part history of the next war? ☐
Would you rather go out and fight than stay at home and watch Michael Parkinson interviewing famous generals? ☐

8 Do you worry most about
Russia invading Europe? ☐
The EEC declaring war on Britain? ☐
The Irish uniting against England? ☐
The Khmer Rouge getting as far as London? ☐
Civil war breaking out? ☐
Tony Benn being our wartime Premier? ☐

9 Who do you think would make the best national figurehead in a war?
The Duke of Edinburgh ☐
Harold Macmillan ☐
Robert Robinson ☐
Jack Jones ☐
Fred Streeter ☐
Elton John ☐
Don Revie ☐

10 If Britain were invaded, which branch of the services would you volunteer for?
The Catering Corps ☐
Hong Kong Police ☐
Glasgow Street Cleaners ☐
The Red Devils ☐
Household Cavalry ☐
The Russian infantry ☐
UN Peace-keeping Force ☐
Bob Hope's Gagwriters ☐

Note: completion of this form does NOT commit you to fighting for Britain in a future war. It is simply a statistical survey to find out if it would be worth fighting at all

COUNTRY

Twenty-two illegal Asian immigrants were found hiding in a lorry at Dover after a Customs officer called out: 'Are you all right in there?' and a voice inside replied: 'Yes,' Canterbury Crown Court heard yesterday.
(Yorkshire Evening Post)

As their contribution to the Roehampton People's Festival last week, Roehampton Liberals and Putney Young Liberals together provided a programme consisting of folk-singing and a short pantomime telling the life-story of a brick.
(Wandsworth Borough News)

Labour regained all three bye-election seats at Hull, two for the city council and one for Humberside County Council but the average 20 per cent poll was the lowest ever. The Get Stuffed Party's four candidates polled a total of fewer than 70 votes.
(Guardian)

As guest speaker, Mrs. Garner enthralled members with an insight into life with the Royal Family. Her son, now butler in the household of Princess Anne and Capt. Mark Phillips, had been a footman at Buckingham Palace.
(Kent & Sussex Courier)

The teenage talent of Pontefract will not be overlooked during the glitter and glamour of a world film festival. The festival, which runs in London from next Monday for a fortnight, will feature the world premiere of 'What Next', a Children's Film Foundation production starring Pontefract schoolboy Peter 'Peewee' Robinson.
(Yorkshire Evening Post)

"The troubles in Ireland continue, Lord, but you'll be glad to know the dandruff has cleared up."

"Well, Mr. Milbury—I expect you're wondering whether there's a company car."

A hedgehog discovered in a consignment of kettles sent from Poland to an ironmonger's shop in Bournemouth, and released by the shopowner, has to be recaptured. The Ministry of Agriculture has ordered that it must be either killed or returned to Poland because of quarantine and rabies regulations.
(Veterinary Record)

Birmingham's controversial sculpture, King Kong, has been officially christened after a year-long battle over his name. The 23ft glass fibre statue, which originally stood in Manzoni Gardens, was bought for £3,000 by a city garage owner. Mr. Michael Shanley used the massive ape for his car sales business, The King Kong Kar Ko., Camp Hill, but the Registrar of Business Names objected because it could have been construed as having Royal patronage.
(Birmingham Evening Mail)

LIFE

Living animals can be accepted by the Post Office for express delivery provided a suitable receptacle or lead is supplied and the sender safeguards the messenger from injury. Human beings cannot be sent by this service.
(Retford, Gainsborough & Worksop Times)

"... and this is your defence counsel!"

COUNTRY

A St. Just town councillor was physically restrained during a violent argument with another and the other later tendered his resignation at Monday's meeting of the council. Soon after, another of the twelve members left, not returning to the meeting. The incidents took place while the council were discussing whether they should have a Christmas tree for the town this year.

(The Cornishman)

Mr. A. Adrian, of 213 Dickson Drive, Irvine, has won the broad bean section of a national giant fruit and vegetable competition organised by Garden News newspaper. Using seed he developed himself, Mr. Adrian grew a broad bean measuring 21¾ inches. He wins £5 and a bucket of Phostrogen fertiliser.

(Irvine Herald)

A 38-years-old Market Drayton man appeared in court in the town today, dressed in a diver's wet suit and flippers, facing a charge of causing suffering to a frog by swallowing it alive.

(Staffordshire Evening Sentinel)

A green litter bin is to be placed in Woodford Road, Snaresbrook, Redbridge Planning and Development Committee decided last week.

(Woodford Weekly Post)

A dead woodcock fell out of a man's trouser leg when he was searched at a police station, Kidderminster magistrates heard.

(Kidderminster Shuttle)

Chale: Police are investigating the disappearance of 672 cauliflowers from a field.

(Southampton Evening Echo)

A man who began work at a Leighton solicitor's office holding the heads of clients' horses while their owners were inside being interviewed celebrated sixty years of employment at the same firm last week.

(Beds & Bucks Observer)

The Bishop of Chester (the Right Rev. Victor Whitsey) intends to give up smoking and alcohol between Epiphany and Easter every year to help the needy.

(Church Times)

Because of the present economic situation, the parish council has decided to defer any improvement scheme to the vestry hall lighting after receiving assurances that the wiring was safe.

(Kent & Sussex Courier)

"We come here every day to see the meat."

The growth of occult practices in Skegness and the local area, and the problems which local clergy found in trying to deal with them, led to a member of the Hull 'Ghost Squad' visiting Skegness at the weekend.

(Skegness Standard)

Bath looks set to take the lead in a national campaign aimed at beating the car thief. The talking car is the brainchild of the Bath Crime Prevention Panel and has already won the backing of the Home Office and its crime prevention committee. From a speaker mounted behind the radiator grille it will cry, 'Help! I'm a talking car and I'm in trouble.'

(Bath & West Evening Chronicle)

There are several clubs and activities within the church, one of which is the Women's Night Out, on a Monday evening. Sometimes there are outings to places like the Police Station.

(West End News)

Police found a tiny White Leghorn pullet in a telephone box near Holgate Road Post Office, York, yesterday.

(Yorkshire Post)

Clare Parish Council has agreed to spend £30 clearing out the pond in the cemetery and having the contents buried.

(East Anglian Daily Times)

"Well, we always said we didn't know how they could do it for the money."

The new bus shelters in Pittenweem have been erected on the wrong side of the bus stops. The Town Council is to rectify the matter by moving the bus stops to the other end of the bus shelters.

(Dundee Courier & Advertiser)

Paper sacks can be obtained at the Cardross Mill filling station, Rhu public convenience, Arrochar public convenience, Garelochhead Health Centre and from the street sweeper in Rosneath.

(Helensburgh Advertiser)

LIFE

According to Dr. Watson, just as children and animals respond instinctively to people they like or don't like, babies under 18 months and young chimpanzees have a lot in common.

(Woman)

A choir, whose average age was 70, gave a programme of songs and Mr. J. J. Pearson, the society's secretary, reminisced about the fine cider made in the year 1911 and told how, in 1913, a villager cured his bronchitis by swallowing a frog. Mrs. E. Pilbeam gave a piano solo and Mr. and Mrs. A. How spoke on the relative merits of herrings and kippers as a source of protein.

(Kent & Sussex Courier)

Readers will recall my reference to a hedgehog which had visited the garden of the home of Mr. Tom Ventress, Mass House, Egton, for a fortnight for an evening saucerful of milk. On Saturday night, Mr. Ventress telephoned me to say that he had seen the hedgehog again on his lawn near a left-over sponge pudding he had put out for the birds.

(Whitby Gazette)

Problems of acrid black smoke caused by plastic fittings on coffins are not yet seriously troubling the crematoriums of Surrey.

(Surrey Advertiser)

Two 15-year-old boys concealed stolen cartons of mousse in stolen trilby hats, it was stated at Burton Juvenile Court yesterday.

(Burton Daily Mail)

A pornographic watch once owned by King Farouk of Egypt has been withdrawn from an exhibition at the Huddersfield Methodist Mission Hall tonight.

(Yorkshire Post)

*"Jeremy, Mommy doesn't feel guilt only toward Jonathan. Mommy feels **lots** of guilt toward you, too."*

COUNTRY

Among the less commercial activities of the Truth Therapy Centre are investigations into reincarnation and astral travel. Mr. Thomas says he has sent the proprietor of an Aberfan chip shop to Mars.

(Western Mail)

A Dudley man who saw his wife with another man made a springboard and catapulted himself through a kitchen window, it was said at Dudley Magistrates' Court.

(Birmingham Evening Mail)

The blue, size 32a brassiere, she assured the policewoman, was a spare she always carried with her when she planned to play the violin.

(Surrey Comet)

British Rail this week issued a warning to people living alongside the former Great Central Railway line between East Leake and Loughborough to beware of trains.

(Loughborough Monitor)

Defendant told the court that his girl friend had been arguing with him for a number of hours and had been hitting him with her umbrella which eventually broke. He went to her home to fetch her another umbrella as it had started raining. The argument started again and she began hitting him with the second umbrella. He went back to her home for a third umbrella . . . .

(Harrogate Advertiser)

Many people have been surprised to read about the Budgie Hotel which is run by John and Lilian Vann in Charnwood Avenue and to learn that the average life of a bird is 11 years. The vicar once had a bantam that went on laying until it was nine.

(Whetstone Church Magazine)

An 84-year-old Worsley Hall man is recovering from shock today after some gunpowder he was trying to clean his chimney with exploded and blew out the windows and doors of his home . . . A police spokesman said: 'Apparently this was the way that Mr. Tootle cleaned his chimney. It seems the gunpowder was given to him by his father and he had stored it in a shoebox for 40 years.'

(Wigan Observer)

A man who jammed a burglar alarm with a Social Security appointment card bearing his name was placed on probation for two years by Croydon magistrates on Tuesday.

(Croydon Advertiser)

Grantham pensioner Mr. Bob King (92) made an extraordinary find when he was digging up some vegetables on his allotment. Amongst the potatoes was one encased in a jubilee clip. Mr. King intends to keep the potato until it decays.

(Grantham Journal)

'I grow ivy in an old chimney pot,' writes Mrs. Woodruff, 'and I've painted an old pair of shoes and put them on the window sill where I look out.' Full marks to Mrs. Woodruff for the effort to make the most of her environment.

(Lancs. Evening Post)

David Bain, 35 Niddrie Marischal Green, admitted in Edinburgh Burgh Court failing to report to police within 24 hours that he found a hen. He was admonished.

(Edinburgh Evening News)

LIFE

Time for a new religion?

ALAN BRIEN
on the motorway to Damascus

HE was jealous and vain, bloody and unpredictable, light of all mankind yet special protector of his chosen people, source of all good things yet supremo of the agents of death who rained down plague and purge, the most noble of humans and yet super-human, omnipotent and infallible.

When famine and pestilence, invasion and rebellion, failures of crops or collapses of cities threatened his domain, it was the fault of the multitude, singly and collectively. They had not understood his commands, or understood them and disobeyed them – and so were guilty and unworthy. When they defeated their enemies, destroyed the conspirators and back-sliders, fed the starving, housed the homeless, clothed the ragged – these achievements were still but a pale reflection of his grand, golden design. Exalted above all other nations, they were nevertheless still guilty and unworthy of him. Fear and love were interchangeable.

I was thinking of Joseph Stalin, who imagined himself a personal God. But then so did Jehovah. If you sub-stitute one for the other in the Old Testament, you are left with the portrait of the same obsessive tyrant. The Jews did not speak aloud the tetragrammaton, the name 'Yahweh' but instead said the title 'Adonai' – the Lord. (Over the centuries, they forgot the exact pronunciation and mediaeval Christian scholars inserting its vowels into JHVH came up with the bastard form, Jehovah.) Just so was Stalin always spoken of, in private speech, as 'the Boss'.

The victory and long survival of Stalin is often described as one of the great mysteries of modern history. But it is clear that he fulfilled a need. Yet what need? Who needs to be oppressed, dominated, regimented, lectured, abused, regulated down to the tiniest detail of the small print? The answer is mankind. Not all of us, everywhere, all of the time, but some of us, somewhere, some of the time. The Jews invented Jehovah – the one God without rivals. The Russians discovered Stalin – the one Boss without equals.

Both devoured their competitors – Jupiter and Isis and Bukharin, Juno and Osiris and Trotsky, Horus and Phoebus and Zinoviev – and their followers claimed this as a great step forward to monotheism. But one kind of God presumes one kind of man who sees himself in that image. Christianity, while retaining indivisible deity, nevertheless managed to divide him into Father, Son and Holy Ghost, thus providing something for all the family, completing the royal flush with the Virgin Mary for the ladies, God bless 'em.

There is a time for patriarchs and a time for matriarchs, and a time to let the young folks have a chance. In the twentieth century, the father figures have largely passed on. Hitler was in many ways just the negative of the Stalin ikon – instead of preaching that Evil was Good and everyone must love Good, he preached that Good was Evil and everyone must hate Evil. Though some of the oldsters linger on in waxwork form, trundled out to weep at festivals or swim the Yellow River or speak at Foyle's

"He's saving up for a longer flex."

Luncheons, the era ended with Adenauer, Churchill and de Gaulle.

There was another resurgence of the youth cult epitomised in the Kennedys. (Did I imagine the image of the Archbishop of Canterbury, the Prime Minister and the Editor of *The Times* descending by helicopter on Mick Jagger? – I see it as a Terry Gilliam *Monty Python* sequence in which they are lowered by rope ladder into his enormous lips.) But this is passing on, too, with the twin assassinations. Neither Father nor Son nor Virgin Mother quite suit any more.

The Holy Ghost is still around, speaking to the likes of Uri Geller from all too identified Flying Objects, inspiring various Maharishis and infant bulbs of Divine Light and even perhaps Hoovering the backstairs of the Universe as a Black Hole.

Nor should we forget Satan whose name in Hebrew means the Adversary; though his great trouble today must lie in deciding just who is matched against who in the theological World Championship. Still, there is unlikely ever to be a total shortage of hosts eager and willing to give him house-room inside them, as witness Charles Manson. (Evelyn Waugh said he had to believe in the Devil, otherwise how could he account for the existence of Lord Beaverbrook.)

What sort of God or Devil could seem convincingly to mirror in the invisible world the earth we see around us? I think we must return to some form of Greek plurality. Even Christianity, once it organised itself into a Church, encouraged a whole host of lesser localised miracle-workers and thaumaturges, called Saints, who were often merely wood demons, fertility spirits and mythic heroes kitted out with haloes. I often wonder how many of those patriotic gentlemen who write to the *Daily Telegraph* complaining of the failure to observe the day of our Patron Saint, realise who St. George was. It is no longer possible to identify him, as did Gibbon, with a black-marketeering army contractor from Cappadocia. But the present consensus of authority now agrees that he was a native of Joppa executed for refusing to serve in the Roman Army – in other words, a Wog and a Conchie.

So what we require is a Return to Olympus, with a few new characters to suit the current tastes. Jupiter needs little updating for spanking colonels, the archetype of the tired businessman never too tired to give the business to his secretary. Today his shower of gold would be charged to his Barclaycard, and his expenses would include many an item such as 'to hire of Swan Helicopter'. The patron of all ageing funsters whose motto is 'boys will be boys'. Lucky day – 3 p.m. on Friday to 11.30 a.m. on Monday. Ritual meal – smoked salmon, rare steak, green salad and black coffee with brandy. Likely to die in back of company Rolls clutching a switch of blonde hair in the right hand.

Juno, her ox-eyes fixed with a thyroid injection and contact lenses, would no longer be the chairman's wife sitting at home, nursing her sceptre like a rolling pin. She would not be the protective nimbus hovering over all matrons whose hair turned blue with relief at J.B.'s first prostate. Her lucky day – any Wednesday when Vidal Sassoon is in town. Ritual meal – cottage cheese, one tomato, tea with lemon and four eclairs.

But these are a generation and a class whose manners and morals have hardly changed since the days of Trimalchio and Messalina. It is their successors who really need their new cults to cater to their special fears and hopes.

Not all of them need to be anthropomorphic. The vast congregation of car worshippers require some outlet for their ambivalent feelings about their sacred steeds. Officially and publicly, they are masters of their self-propelled chariots and could adopt Phoebus as their divinity. But after they have slammed its door at night, all sorts of resentments and doubts creep along to bed with them. The totem must be disciplined from time to time, tamed, even ceremonially punished, if only in effigy. The motorways provide opportunities for driving it to its limits, other people's front gardens space for abandoning it to the weather and the vandals. And the first signs of the cult in action as a ritual can be seen in almost every American thriller (especially directed by Peter Yates and starring Barbra Streisand) where the automobile is inevitably humiliated, battered, mocked and made to look pathetic and impotent.

The God in the Machine, for those who prefer their religion more immaterial and intellectual, is provided by the computer. The politicians and the salesmen will believe anything, however improbable, as long as it appears in the mystic hieroglyphs on the print-out. Emotionless and passion-free, pure ratiocination, it grinds out daily its answer to questions such as what is the favourite colour of housewives in Penge and how many West Country Liberals approve of a shadow Minister of Education who sells dog food. Its acolytes wander the streets with clipboards stopping thousands, and invoking responses, but mysteriously no one ever meets anyone who has encountered them.

One of the major uses of religion is as a safety valve. The Maenads and the Bacchae provide classical patterns for the extreme sections of the Women's Liberation movement. Restless and beautiful, intoxicated with the new-found spirit of aggression, they will dismember any male chauvinist penetrating their female mysteries. Perhaps the Greeks had some immortal to lead the masculine masses on the rampage, but if so I do not know him. But it should not be difficult to find a figurehead to be carried shoulder-high after football matches, during demos, at student sit-ins and farmers' barricades. It may be worthwhile drafting Peregrine Worsthorne, who has recently called for the middle classes to get out from behind their picture windows and take to the streets in order to make sure the class war is not a walkover for the proles.

For every kind of man, there has been a kind of god. The choice is infinite. The pattern is set in childhood. When the parent seemed aloof and terrible, omnipresent and all-seeing, monitoring every action even down to the movements of the bowels, providing rules for every occasion, and insisting that even a thought could be immediately classified as right or wrong, then that was how God operated. Today, children often have many parents, several homes, a variety of adults to copy or defy. Children are encouraged to ask questions but the adults have no answers. God is now what you make him. You would no more expect to fit another man's God as another man's hat. Hurry along now while stocks last.

MARGARET THATCHER, THESE ARE YOUR LIVES...

Four authors are hard at work on biographies of Margaret Thatcher, reveals the Sunday Telegraph. What, only four? asks E. S. TURNER

SIR, I have undertaken to write the definitive biography of Margaret Thatcher, the Lincolnshire politician and one-time research chemist, and shall be grateful if Elizabeth Longford, Lord Longford, Antonia Fraser, Roy Jenkins, Sir Arthur Bryant, Dame Veronica Wedgwood, Dr. A. L. Rowse, A. J. P. Taylor, Frances Donaldson, Roger Fulford, Andrew Boyle and a few others will now retire and leave the field clear. At the same time I shall be obliged for any letters, photographs or parking tickets they may see their way to send me.

I am especially concerned to obtain information on the Thatcher family's links with the promiscuous "conchies" known as the Bloomsbury Set.—
Michael Holroyd.

From the BBC Book Programme:

Antonia Fraser: You see, what I set out to do was to rescue Margaret Thatcher from the undeserved obscurity into which she had so rapidly plunged after becoming the leader of the Conservative Party early in 1975. As a biographer I was ready for a new challenge. Having explained to the general reader something of the charisma of Mary, Queen of Scots, and tried to "humanise" Oliver Cromwell, and removed the slobbering mask from James I, I found myself irresistibly drawn to this woman of destiny, a woman with both grace and *gravitas*, a quality which I might describe as a chill, half-mystical *superbia*—

Robert Robinson: Oh dear, I was going to say that.

Fraser: —in short, a woman about whom millions of words have been written but nothing whatever has been said.

Robinson: Bravo! Did you quarrel with your mother about who should "do" Mrs Thatcher?

Fraser: Of course not. She gave me

all her notes. Well, to make a short story long, off I went to that marvellous little Thatcher museum in Lincolnshire, with only a couple of TV cameras, and examined Margaret's exercise books and Wellington boots. Then I walked reverently through the streets of her birthplace, with cameramen reverently running backwards in front of me, and "felt" myself into the part. As a biographer it is absolutely essential to do this sort of thing, both in fairness to the subject and also to one's public, who have grown to expect it.

Robinson: You mentioned Cromwell, whom someone dubbed God's Englishman. Do you see Margaret Thatcher as God's Englishwoman?

Fraser: A marvellous title, Robert. I'm so grateful to you . . .

From "Margaret Thatcher, the Years of Destiny", by Harold Macmillan:

ONE of the most chastening occupations of old age is to re-read one's Parliamentary speeches. In 1925, the year when Margaret Thatcher was born, I delivered my maiden address to the House of Commons. I hope I shall not intrude an undue degree of subjectivity into this record of a great Englishwoman if I mention that *The Times*, commenting on my early flights of oratory, referred to "Captain Macmillan's . . . rare ability and freshness", though this is not the description I should now apply to my performance, nor was it the verdict of my wife's family at Chatsworth. *N'ayez pas de zèle*, said Talleyrand. It was made clear to me from many quarters that enthusiasm was a fault which would have to be corrected. In 1925 when, as I said, Margaret Thatcher was born, the unemployment figures were rising and there was no more of that *douceur de la vie* than there was in the year when the Conservative Party adopted her as their leader. If I may be forgiven a personal memory . . .

From "The Two Margarets", by Margaret Powell:

I FIRST met Margaret Thatcher on a Glamourline Luxury Coach Tour to Florence. "Have you won the pools too, love?" I asked. "Or did you sell the fish supper shop?"

Just then I felt a pinch on my bottom. Later Enrico said he nipped me as a warning. But with these Italians how are you to know?

Margaret was doing her frozen lamb bit, but I hardly noticed.

"In these parts," I told her, "the more you sit on your bottom the better. Mine has had that bee-stung look all the way from Calais."

"I'm not really surprised," she said, moving to sit beside the Bore of the Party at the rear of the coach. At the time I thought she was a proper little madam. Now I realise it was star quality shining through . . .

From "Margaret The First", by the Sunday Times "Insight" Team:

AT 10.27 p.m. Denis Thatcher descended the 36 steps from No. 6 Ward, pushed open the swing-door and entered the street. He stood 57 seconds lost in thought and then strode 107 paces in an easterly direction to the bus stop. After 30 minutes the 116b bus arrived, containing 27 passengers, two of them drunk, and 20 gallons of fuel in its tank. None of these facts registered in Denis Thatcher's consciousness when he boarded the vehicle. As he sat in the second seat from the front on the right-hand side and produced a half-crown to pay the one-and-sixpenny fare, only one thought dominated his mind. His wife, Margaret Hilda, had presented him with twins . . .

From "Maggie", as told to Michael Parkinson (author of "Best"):

SOBER! You'll never believe it! Yes, every day I was disgustingly, paralytically sober! So sober that everywhere people were staring at me. I began to panic. Nothing at Somerville had prepared me for the scenes at Westminster —the flushed faces of the legislators, their hot, crimson eyes, their rorty speech. I was in a ravening male world, far more outrageously virile than even Lincoln's Inn. And I was stark, staring sober—sober as a newt. Yet all the time those magnificent, terrifying fantasies were running through my mind—fantasies of power, of world leadership. I kept telling myself that I, Margaret Thatcher, sober though I was, would dominate these men. I would make and break them, singly or in batches. They would do my will, and grovel at my feet. I would dismiss them before breakfast, during breakfast, after breakfast . . .

I have seen the fuchsia and it works!

anyway, cheer up, says HARRY SECOMBE

*'Two men look out through the same bars,
One sees the mud and one the stars.'*

THAT QUOTATION FROM Frederick Langbridge is a pretty fair description of an optimist. The cynic might interpret it as one prisoner standing on the head of another, the better to see out, but let us not concern ourselves with cynicism.

No, my friends, I am seeking to bring solace and comfort to one and all. There is talk in the air of a Depression – and what does that mean? It means we might have to do without things that our parents never even knew existed. Is that such a bad thing after all?

The dictionary definition of optimism is 'a disposition to take a bright, hopeful view of things'. Let us then look first at the days ahead. If we must do without TV because of power cuts, why not revive the art of doing shadow graphs by the light of a candle? You know the sort of thing – 'the butterfly' done by waggling both hands linked at the thumbs, or 'the rabbit' which is effected by raising the first two fingers in a V and crooking the thumb over the other two leaving a little opening for the eye. This can also be called 'the horse' or 'the cat' or 'the dog', depending upon the age and credibility of the audience. If by some mischance one happens to sprain one's thumb in the process, endless amusement can be provided for the rest of the family as they all sit around and watch it throb.

This old world of ours has gone through many perilous times and yet it has always managed to produce a bumper crop of optimists. King Canute was one; so was William Tell's son; my maths teacher was another; an angler fishing from a railway bridge; my history teacher; any Liberal voter; anyone dialling Directory Enquiries yet another. In my experience the greatest of them all was Johnny Price, my old Army mate.

He was a stocky Welshman who stood five foot two inches high and had a craggy head almost too large for his body. In profile he resembled an Easter Island statue – indeed had Thor Heyerdahl stepped ashore one day at Aberavon and seen Johnny standing ankle-deep in the sand he might have had second thoughts about the Kon-Tiki expedition. Nature had been unkind to Johnny, but he was eternally cheerful, full of snatches of song and always chasing the girls, and though he never caught any it never seemed to impair his optimism.

I remember one particular instance when we were stationed in Aldershot. The garrison town had suddenly filled with Canadian soldiers who had money to burn and consequently were always surrounded by all the available crumpet. The rest of us had no chance at all. The NAAFI girls were all spoken for and the WVS ladies were too intimidating. The only one who had not given up hope was Johnny Price, and sure enough he came up with a scheme.

He burst into the Nissen hut one afternoon and threw a green beret with a Canadian cap-badge on to my bed. 'If you can't lick 'em, join 'em,' he said,

'Stuff that up your tunic when we go out and we're away, boyo.' He produced from under his own jacket the bonnet of some Canadian Scottish Regiment and put it on his head. It came down low over his forehead, the tartan band covered his eyebrows and only the great swooping curve of his nose prevented the bonnet from slipping further down his face. 'Hello, buddy,' he said in his idea of a Canadian accent.

I groaned as he swaggered around the room, rubbing his hands delightedly. 'We'll go to Woolworths' sweet counter where all the best birds are. Duw, we're bound to click tonight, mun.' I tried the other beret on. That too was big, but my steel spectacles helped to keep it out of my eyes.

We duly presented ourselves at Woolworths where, fortunately, there were not too many people about. 'Leave the talking to me,' Johnny muttered out of the side of his mouth. 'I know the lingo, see. Got a cousin in Melbourne.' 'That's Australia,' I said. 'Never mind, they're all Colonials.' His optimism knew no bounds.

A pretty girl sauntered leisurely forward to serve us. Johnny raised himself on tiptoe so that his monstrous head came clear of the mound of slab toffee and hard-boiled sweets. 'Hello there,' he said, pretending to chew gum. 'We're from Canada my buddy and me. From the prairies we are.'

'Oh!' said the assistant.

'Yes, yes,' he said, warming to his theme. 'Ride the range you know.' I stood mutely at his side as he warbled a snatch of *Home on the Range*. 'How about stepping out with me tonight? We could take in a movie.' He gave a huge wink.

The girl stared at him for a long time, then she reached down under the counter, and came up with an enormous stick of rock. She hit him firmly over the head with it. 'There's no bloody cowboys in Swansea,' she said in an accent as Welsh as his own.

Johnny was quite philosophical about it later in the ablutions as he bathed the lump on his head. 'Bloody good job I was wearing that hat,' he said. 'Could have fractured my skull.' Always looking on the bright side, you see.

Another thing to bear in mind in the uncertain days ahead is that one should never take the opinions of so-called experts as Gospel truth. We were once told that our boxer dog was untrainable. He came back from an intensive course at an expensive canine school apparently as daft as he was when he left us. According to his report he was expelled for being naughty. Yet, six weeks later in Cheam Village when I told him to 'SIT' outside a shop, to my great surprise, he did. He sat there meekly until I came out. The fact that I was unable to find the key word to release him from that position is of no consequence. And the laughter I afforded the neighbours as I carried the hulking brute in my arms for the half-mile walk home was the EPNS lining in that particular little cloud.

We must all keep looking on the bright side. Let us make sure that every lift is provided with community song books, that horse shafts are ready to fit onto our cars and that our legs are lagged for the winter. As for me, I've just managed to get hold of a bulk supply of rose-coloured spectacles. If anyone would like to buy a pair at a bargain price, I can be contacted care of Johnny Price, The Corner Shop, West Samoa.

"I keep seeing the spectre of full employment."

Caption competition

**Each week Punch invites readers to
write new captions for cartoons
first printed 80 or more years ago. Here
are some of the winning entries:**

"Don't get too excited—only six draws so far!"
J. Fields of Alnwick, Northumberland.

1899 caption.—Desperate Householder writes out advertisement:—*"To be disposed of, a Monkey. Very comical and playful. Lively companion; full of fun. Would exchange for Gold Fish, or anything useful."*

"Sorry, mate, Mrs. Castle's phased out private baths."
T. Maddox of Preston, Lancs.

1925 caption.—Householder. *"Why have you fixed up two cold taps?"* Plumber. *"Well, you complained that the boiler didn't 'eat the water, and besides I run aht o' 'ot taps."*

JOINT WINNERS: *"Quite unprecedented—the whole escort agency's been stood up."*
P. Fitton of Cambridge.

AND: *"The little fellow's the one to watch when the trouble starts."*
J. Fox of Bristol.

1897 caption.—RETRENCHMENT. Jinks. *"Don't meet you 'ere so often as we used to, Binks, eh?"* Binks. *"Well—no. It don't run to a Hopera-Box this Season, because, you see, we've took a Window for this 'ere Jubilee."*

"An open-air Vera Lynn concert was doomed from the start."
D. Swift of Huddersfield.

1898 caption.—HYDE PARK, MAY 1. Country Cousin. *"What is the meaning of this, Policeman?"* Constable. *"Labour Day, Miss."*

CONTINUED OVERLEAF

"*I've come about the job. I've got my own transport.*"

S. Quance of Sutton Coldfield.

1925 caption.—Doctor (after making a medical examination). "*Ah, my dear sir, this trouble lies rather deeper than you supposed. You had better consult a vet.*"

"*Bad news, Vicar—Apache markings!*"

J. Kent of London N14.

1894 caption.—"THE COURSE OF TRUE LOVE," &c. Scene—Hounds on drag of Otter, which has turned up small tributary stream. Miss Di (six feet in her stockings, to deeply-enamoured Curate, five feet three in his, whom she has inveigled out Otter-hunting). "*Oh, do just Pick me up and Carry me across. It's rather Deep, don't you know!*"(The Rev. Spooner's sensations are somewhat mixed.)

"*And I further declare the said Caractacus elected as member for the above mentioned constituency.*"

A. Yelloly of Leamington Spa.

1927 caption.—THE PROMOTION OF EDUCATION IN EARLY TIMES. The Lord Eustace Percy of those days presents a flint medal to the discoverer of the fact that two and two make four.

"*I'm a bit worried about the contralto—she's been under for five minutes!*"

M. Birt of Cheltenham.

1925 caption.—CONSCIENTIOUS ART. Signor Fortissimo has found that he gets most *joie de vivre* into his efforts when singing in the bath.

Index of artists

"You'd have very little to worry about, Mrs. Cox—if only you could brush up on your reading speed."